WAR UNDER THE RED ENSIGN 1914–1918

WAR UNDER THE RED ENSIGN 1914–1918

BERNARD EDWARDS

Pen & Sword
MARITIME

First published in Great Britain in 2010 by
PEN & SWORD MARITIME
an imprint of
Pen & Sword Books Limited
47 Church Street
Barnsley
S. Yorkshire S70 2AS

ISBN 978 1 84884 229 8

A CIP catalogue record for this book
is available from the British Library

Typeset in Ehrhardt by S L Menzies-Earl

Printed and bound in England
by CPI

Pen & Sword Books Ltd incorporates the imprints of
Pen & Sword Aviation, Pen & Sword Maritime,
Pen & Sword Military, Wharncliffe Local History, Pen & Sword Select,
Pen & Sword Military Classics, Leo Cooper, Remember When,
Seaforth Publishing and Frontline Publishing

For a complete list of Pen & Sword titles please contact:
PEN & SWORD BOOKS LIMITED
47 Church Street, Barnsley, South Yorkshire, S70 2AS, England.
E-mail: enquiries@pen-and-sword.co.uk
Website: www.pen-and-sword.co.uk

Contents

No cross marks the place where now we lie,
What happened is known but to us.
You asked, and we gave our lives to protect
Our land from the enemy curse.
No Flanders Field where poppies blow;
No Gleaming Crosses, row on row;
No Unnamed Tomb for all to see
And pause – and wonder who we might be,
The Sailors' Valhalla is where we lie
On the ocean bed, watching ships pass by,
Sailing in safety now thru' the waves,
Often right over our sea-locked graves.
We ask you just to remember us.

Author unknown

Dedication

This book is dedicated to the memory of Captain Charles Algernon Fryatt; an innocent victim of war, if ever there was one.

Author's Note

At the outbreak of war in the summer of 1914 Great Britain and her Dominions owned and operated forty-three per cent of the world's merchant shipping: 20 million tons gross, all sailing under the Red Ensign. This huge fleet dominated the oceans, bringing in the raw materials to feed the country's smoking factories, and in turn delivered her manufactured goods to the rest of the world. The same ships fed Britain's burgeoning population, carrying in grain from America, meat from the Argentine, sugar from the West Indies, tea and spices from the East. Britain lived and prospered by her sea trade, and to cut her umbilical cords, the endless cavalcades of deep-laden ships sailing in and out of her ports, would be to condemn the nation to wither and die. So reasoned the German High Command in 1914.

There were two main categories of ship in the British merchant fleet, tramps and cargo liners. The tramps were very basic ships, strongly built but little more than floating boxes designed to carry maximum cargo at minimum cost. They were invariably old, underpowered, and more often than not in need of a decent coat of paint. As the popular name implied, they followed no set itinerary, trading between ports of the world at the whim of the charter market. The cargo liners, on the other hand, were built along finer lines, with a good turn of speed, and were engaged exclusively on advertised sailings between specific ports. They considered themselves to be the elite of the British fleet, but they could not match the sheer moneymaking power of the tramps.

The men who manned both tramps and liners, many of them then not long out of sail, were tough, resourceful, and infinitely long-suffering. Of them, the maritime historian Edward Blackmore said at the turn of the century:

> To many of the softer minded people of the world, it is a wonder that any man would ever desire to be a sailor. They think of the forsaking of home and friends, the many hardships, the terrible

> risks, the being cut off from the many luxuries and comforts that the well-to-do enjoy on shore, and are astonished at the wilfulness which makes men endure the one and cast aside the other for the sake of a life at sea.

The truth was, and still is, that the sea was like an addictive drug to these men, offering them the freedom to roam the wide horizons and the ability to leave all the petty irritations of an increasingly demanding world far behind. The sea was in their blood, and they would have no other life.

No one, not even the Admiralty, seriously thought these easy-going sea wanderers would play more than a passive role in the great struggle for supremacy at sea that formed the all-important backdrop to World War 1. To his cost, the enemy underestimated their courage, resilience and sheer bloody-mindedness. All the might of Germany's Imperial Navy, with its shoals of silent-killer submarines, failed to subdue them. Britain's umbilical cords were not cut, and this eventually lost Germany the war.

Chapter One

Curtain Up

The sun rose majestically out of the Indian Ocean in the east, blood-red and swollen with the promise of another sweltering day to come. As the first golden rays fingered the guano-streaked peaks of Hallaniyah Island, three small boats entered the bay of Ghubatt Ar Rahib, the roar of their powerful outboard motors echoing back from the tall granite cliffs fringing the bay.

Anchors rattled down, the roar of the motors was stilled, and the first divers went over the side, leaving a silvery trail of bubbles as they sank into the depths. For Steve Dover and Peter Collinson, leaders of the expedition, this was a routine dive: clear water, sandy bottom – only the capacity of their air tanks would limit the horizons of their exploration. But for Chris Lees, who followed them down, the dive had a very special significance. At the bottom of the shotline, 28 metres deep, a rendezvous with the past awaited him.

The story goes back eighty-four years to the summer of 1914, when Europe had just embarked on a brutal war of attrition that was to last for four blood-soaked years.

On 6 August 1914 the British cargo liner *City of Winchester* was in the Gulf of Aden, having battled her way across the Arabian Sea, then in the grip of the raging South-West Monsoon. The 6601-ton steamer, under the command of Captain George Boyck, had sailed from Colombo six days earlier on the return leg of her maiden voyage. In her lower holds she carried jute from Calcutta, and her tween-decks were crammed tight with 30,000 chests of tea: the entire season's crop of Ceylon's best Broken Orange Pekoe. In the jargon of the sea, she was 'full deadweight and full cubic', down to her tropical marks with every cubic inch of her space below decks filled to overflowing with high-freight cargo. Her owners, Ellerman Lines of Glasgow, could not have asked more of her.

When, on 31 July, Captain Boyck took his ship out through the breakwaters of Colombo harbour and felt her lift sluggishly to the long swells coming in from the south-west, he left behind him an island buzzing with rumour and counter-rumour of impending war in Europe. The assassination of Archduke Ferdinand of Austria-Hungary by a half-crazed Serbian student some five weeks previously was threatening to set a politically tinder-dry Europe ablaze. There were those cocooned in this tropical island paradise who said it would never happen, but the main protagonists in Europe were reported to be already reaching for their guns. A power-hungry Germany, backed by Austria, seemed intent on taking on the combined might of Russia, France and Great Britain. The signs were ominous, but George Boyck did not hesitate to take his ship to sea. Like so many British seamen, who since the defeat of the French and Spanish fleets at Trafalgar in 1805, had sailed the high seas unmolested, he had no doubts about the invincibility of the Royal Navy. The Navy would make short work of any enemy who dared to interfere with British shipping.

In 1914, Great Britain and her Dominions overseas owned forty-three percent of the world's merchant shipping. She lived by these ships, which carried her goods to the far ends of the earth, and in turn brought back the raw materials for her smoking factories. The defence of this trade called for a fighting navy of massive proportions, and in 1914 the Royal Navy had afloat 50 dreadnought battleships, 41 pre-dreadnoughts, 58 heavy cruisers, 119 light cruisers, 17 aircraft carriers, 550 destroyers, 272 sloops, 39 monitors, 171 submarines, 109 motor-torpedo boats, and a host of other small craft. Her merchant ships need fear no enemy.

The first angry shots of what was to become known as the Great War were fired by the Austrians on 29 July 1914 when they attacked Belgrade in retaliation for the assassination of Archduke Ferdinand. Germany moved three days later, declaring war on Russia on 1 August, on France on the 3rd, and on Belgium on the 4th. Britain affirmed that she would stand by her allies, and at 10.30 pm on 4 August, her Government announced that a state of war existed between Great Britain and Germany.

War became reality on that August evening when the *City of Winchester* left the storms of the Arabian Sea behind and entered the Gulf of Aden. Her wireless operator, Alan Lees, grandfather of the diver Chris Lees, was on watch in his wireless cabin, listening in to that other world over the far horizon. The night was hot and sultry, the static caused by distant thunderstorms crackling loudly in Lees' headphones, sometimes completely blotting out the faint rattle of morse. What little news of the war Lees was able to glean was not earth-shattering. German troops had invaded Belgium, in response to which Britain, France and Russia had ordered general mobilisation; otherwise, there was no serious fighting.

The reports coming over the ether told Wireless Operator Lees nothing of the war at sea, which had been under way in earnest for several days. At 4 pm on 3 August, eighteen hours before the official declaration of war, the British oil tanker *San Wilfrido,* leaving Hamburg after discharging a full cargo of oil, struck a mine off Cuxhaven and sank. Fortunately none of her crew were lost, but they did become prisoners of war. There were also rumours that another British merchantman, named as the *Craigforth,* had struck a German mine in the Bosphorus, and was hard aground. These minings may have been largely unintentional, but they were a warning to a complacent British Government and a harbinger of things to come.

When the *City of Winchester* sailed from Colombo on what promised to be a routine passage, some 2,600 miles to the south-west the German light cruiser *Königsberg* was steaming out of the port of Dar-es-Salaam in German East Africa. SMS (*Seine Majestäts Schiffe* – His Majesty's Ship) *Königsberg,* first commissioned in 1907, had been extensively refitted in Kiel in 1913, and now mounted ten 105-mm guns, ten 37-mm quick-firing cannon, and two submerged torpedo tubes. Her twin screws, powered by two 3-cylinder triple-expansion steam engines, supplied by eleven boilers, gave her a top speed of 24 knots and a cruising range of 3,750 miles at 12 knots. She was a powerful fighting machine, designed to operate alone, but she was cursed with a voracious fuel consumption. When steaming at full speed, her eleven boilers, each fed by three furnaces, burned in excess of 100 tons of coal a day. The maximum capacity of her permanent bunkers was 400 tons, and even with coal piled high on deck, the absolute maximum fuel she was able to carry was just 820 tons. Her designers, perhaps envisaging her spending her days in the North Sea, had unintentionally bequeathed her a serious weakness that would one day be her undoing. In Indian Ocean waters, where distances were vast and most of the accessible ports were in

British hands, the *Königsberg* would always need a loaded collier in attendance.

The *Königsberg* was manned by a total complement of 321 men, and under the command of *Fregattenkapitän* Max Looff. Her original assignment had been to show the flag and promote German interests on the east coast of Africa, a far from onerous task naval ships of all nations were saddled with in peacetime. The light cruiser had sailed from Kiel on 25 April, and after a leisurely passage around the Cape, arrived in Dar-es-Salaam on 6 June. There she took over from the ageing sail and steam corvette *Geier,* the Imperial Navy's guard ship on the coast of East Africa. Soon after reaching Dar-es-Salaam, Loof received orders from Berlin to the effect that, in the event of war, he was to take the *Königsberg* to sea immediately, and lie off the coast awaiting further and more detailed orders. Reading between the lines of his secret orders, *Fregattenkapitän* Looff was under no illusions but that the *Königsberg*'s real role in the coming conflict would be that of a commerce raider creating havoc amongst British merchant shipping carrying cargoes to and from the Indian sub-continent and the Far East.

The *Königsberg* spent several lazy weeks in Dar-es-Salaam overhauling her engines and taking on fresh stores. Then, on the morning of 31 July, the German East Africa Line's steamer *Tabora* entered the port bearing the news that three British cruisers of the Cape Squadron were on their way up the coast. It was obvious to Looff that war was now imminent, and not wishing to be trapped in Dar-es-Salaam, he put to sea just as soon as sufficient steam could be raised on the cruiser's boilers.

The *Königsberg* sailed in the nick of time, for she was only ten miles out from Dar-es-Salaam when her masthead lookout reported the masts and funnels of three warships on the horizon. Soon the British ships were hull-up and identified as the cruisers HMS *Hyacinth, Pegasus* and *Astraea. Hyacinth* mounted eleven 6-inch guns, *Pegasus* eight 4-inch, and *Astraea* two 6-inch quick-firers and eight 4.7-inch quick-firers. On the face of it, they heavily outgunned the *Königsberg,* but in fact they were all well past their prime, *Pegasus* having been condemned for scrap in 1904 but kept in service as war threatened. Not one of the British ships could muster more than 20 knots.

The *Königsberg* had not yet worked up to full speed, so the British cruisers quickly overhauled her and took station around her. This put *Kapitän* Looff in a quandary. Officially, Britain and Germany were not yet at war, and he had no good cause to turn his guns on his uninvited escort. On the other hand, war was imminent, and the British ships were well positioned to blow him out of the water should hostilities suddenly commence.

Looff was rescued from this embarrassing situation when a heavy squall blew in from the south-west, the driving rain momentarily hiding the *Königsberg* from the British ships. He immediately reversed course, and steamed away to the south at full speed. *Hyacinth* saw him go, but she was unable to raise enough speed to give chase.

Having gone south for an hour, taking the *Königsberg* out of sight over the horizon, Looff then headed out to sea, steaming throughout the night at full speed. This successfully threw off his pursuers, but steaming at full speed for almost twelve hours made a great hole in the German cruiser's bunkers.

At daylight on 1 August, Looff reduced to a more economical speed, and headed north towards Cape Guardafui at the entrance to the Gulf of Aden. There he intended to position his ship in the main sea lane used by British merchantmen on their voyaging to and from India and the Far East.

Six days after sailing from Dar-es-Salaam, on 5 August, the *Königsberg* was off Cape Guardafui, wallowing in the heavy cross sea set up by the South-West Monsoon, which was then at its height. The German cruiser was now desperately short of coal, and it was almost with a sense of relief that early that morning Looff received a wireless message from Berlin. It contained just one group of four letters, EGIMA, this being the code word for war. As from midnight on the 4th, Germany had been at war with Britain, France and Russia.

Guardafui, the eastern extremity of the Horn of Africa, is for much of the monsoon obscured by a thick sand haze, as it was on this first morning of the war, and *Kapitän* Looff was proceeding with extreme caution as he rounded the cape on dead reckoning and crept into the Gulf of Aden. Now that the waiting and uncertainty was over, he was free to go hunting, but first he must have coal for his bunkers.

Before sailing from Dar-es-Salaam, Looff had been assured that the Hansa Line's *Reichenfels*, loaded with 6000 tons of good steaming coal, would always be on call for the *Königsberg*. However, a string of urgent wireless signals sent to the *Reichenfels* had gone unanswered. Unknown to Looff, the German collier was detained in Colombo, having been seized by the Royal Navy within minutes of the declaration of war.

Having heard nothing from the *Reichenfels* by midnight on the 5th, Loof broadcast a coded appeal to all German merchant ships in the area to contact him with a view to handing over any bunker coal they could spare to the *Königsberg.* This was a desperate measure, but it might just succeed.

Much to *Kapitän* Looff's surprise and delight, shortly after 11 am on the 6th, the North German Lloyd steamer *Zieten* was seen to be overhauling the *Königsberg,* which was then on reduced speed. Unfortunately, the *Zieten* could offer only moral support. Homeward bound from the Far East, and with the possibility of bunkering on the way uncertain, she had no coal to spare. Even so, Looff decided to keep the North German Lloyd ship with him.

Looff's hopes were again raised, when hard on the heels of the *Zieten* came Hansa Line's *Goldenfels,* also on her way into the Mediterranean. All would have been well, but *Kapitän* Diedrichsen of the *Goldenfels* mistook the *Königsberg* for a British cruiser, presented his stern and steamed away at full speed. This in turn led Looff to believe that the *Goldenfels* was a British merchantman, and he gave chase at 20 knots.

With the *Goldenfels* hard pressed to make 12 knots, the chase was not prolonged, but it cost the *Königsberg* dear, making great inroads into her already dwindling supply of coal. When the two ships realised that they were on the same side, they hove to alongside each other, and Looff informed *Kapitän* Diedrichsen that it was his duty to hand over as much of his supply of coal as he could spare without jeopardising his own ship. Grudgingly, Diedrichsen agreed, but he warned Looff that he had bunkered his ship in Bombay with local coal. Bombay coal, usually shunned by shipmasters, was just burnable in the unsophisticated boiler furnaces of a merchant ship, but was totally unsuited for a 24-knot warship. Notorious for the copious clouds of dirty black smoke it produced, the Indian coal would advertise the presence of the *Königsberg* for many miles around, and continued use would soon clog up her boiler smoke tubes. With darkness coming on, Looff reluctantly allowed the *Goldenfels* to go on her way. He would have to look elsewhere for fuel.

Looff continued his search, and at around eight o'clock that night he sighted and stopped another west-bound ship. Once again luck deserted him. She turned out to be a Japanese NYK passenger liner, and as Japan was still neutral, Looff decided not to interfere with her. Time was beginning to run out for the *Königsberg.*

It was now quite dark, but the moon was up and the visibility good. The lights of the Japanese passenger ship were just dropping below the horizon when the *Königsberg*'s masthead lookout reported a ship approaching from the east. Looff studied the dark silhouette through his night glasses, praying that this time his desperate search for bunker coal was at an end. The stranger had the distinctive look of a British cargo liner, tall funnel, accommodation amidships, long fore deck, and she was steaming without lights. Looff waited for her to pass, and then followed in her wake.

The *City of Winchester*'s wireless room was abaft the bridge, and on this hot and humid night Alan Lees had the after door wide open and hooked back in an attempt to get some air circulating in the cabin, which was becoming unbearably hot. At about 8.30 he gave up any pretence of listening to the chatter of morse, slipped off his clammy earphones, and swung round in his chair to gaze out into the night.

It had not been a comfortable crossing from Colombo, Lees reflected. Beam-on to the heavy swells of the South-West Monsoon, the *City of Winchester* had rolled incessantly, a long, ponderous roll that strained every rivet in her stout Geordie-built hull. Mercifully, now in the comparatively sheltered waters of the Gulf of Aden, that was all behind her. She rode easily and upright, with just the occasional rogue swell that had found its way into the Gulf giving her a gentle push now and again. Only the monotonous thump, thump of her engines disturbed the silence of the tropical night. Since rounding Cape Guardafui the sombre, rain-swollen clouds of the monsoon had cleared away to reveal a sky of black velvet, sprinkled with a myriad twinkling stars. The moon, which had risen as the sun went down, hung like a great yellow globe, in the ghostly light of which the *City of Winchester*'s wake stretched all the way back to the far horizon like a silver pathway to the East.

Captivated by the beauty of the night scene, Alan Lees leaned back in his chair, his eyelids drooping. Then, he saw a dark shape cutting across the frothing wake, and he was suddenly wide awake.

Lees heaved himself out of his seat, went to the after door, and stepped out on deck. By the light of the moon it was plain that the dark shape he had seen was no merchant ship. She had the distinctive outline of a warship, sleek, low in the water, and with three funnels that belched black smoke. The wireless operator went back into the cabin and lifted the bridge voice pipe from its bracket.

Captain Boyck, called to the bridge by the officer of the watch, entered the wheelhouse just in time to see the other ship's signal lamp flashing urgently. The terse message in morse code was: 'What ship? Where bound? What nationality.' The officer of the watch picked his signal lamp and replied, 'British ship *City of Winchester*, bound London.'

It was routine for merchant ships passing in these distant waters to exchange pleasantries by lamp, more to help kill the boredom of a long passage than anything else. But to George Boyck this challenge seemed suspicious. Merchant seamen did not attach a great deal of importance to a ship's flag, and would not normally inquire about nationality. Furthermore, whoever was on the other ship's lamp was certainly no merchant seaman. The morse was too fast, too precise for that of a hard-pressed ship's officer who used the lamp only occasionally. Then Boyck, like his wireless operator, became aware of the menacing outline of the overtaking ship, and his blood ran cold.

As the stranger, her creaming bow-wave now visible, drew closer, Boyck's worst fears were realised. She was unmistakeably a man-of-war, and her guns were trained on the *City of Winchester*. There was still a possibility that she might be a British naval ship making a routine challenge, but Boyck, his ship being completely unarmed, was not prepared to risk defiance. When the lamp flashed again, and he was ordered to heave to, he did so without argument.

It was all too easy for *Fregattenkapitän* Max Looff. Quite by chance, he had found his first enemy merchantman, and she was surrendering without fuss. Little did Looff realise that he was also making history by being the first German warship to take one of the enemy's ships in this war that was barely two days old.

Looff sent a boat across to the *City of Winchester*, now lying stopped with a boarding ladder over on her lee side, and with an officer on deck to receive the visitors. It was still not clear to Captain Boyck whether his challenger was friend or foe. He was enlightened when he found his bridge being taken over by armed German bluejackets, led by a decidedly unfriendly officer. Boyck was obliged to suffer the humiliation of surrendering his ship. Meanwhile, Alan Lees, threatened by a German bayonet, was forced to witness the wilful destruction of his precious wireless equipment.

With the *City of Winchester* completely under German control, Boyck was ordered to get under way again and follow in the wake of the *Königsberg.* Throughout what remained of the night the two ships steamed north-north-east, and as dawn broke anchored in the deserted bay of Mukalla, an indent in the coast of Arabia some 200 miles east of Aden. In the course of the morning, they were joined by the *Zeiten*, and the *Ostmark* of Hamburg –Amerika Line. Later in the day, all four ships left the bay, and headed north-east along the coast.

The odd collection of ships arrived off the Kuria Muria Islands on the morning of the 9th, and anchored in Hallaniyah's Ghubatt Ar Rahib bay. The *Zeiten* moored alongside the *City of Winchester*, and after Captain Boyck and his crew, with the exception of the second officer, third engineer and carpenter, were taken off, the Germans stripped the British ship of her bunker coal and provisions. Her charts, sextants, compasses and sailing directions were sent across to the *Königsberg.*

When everything that could possibly be of use had been taken out of the *City of Winchester,* her third engineer was taken below at gunpoint and ordered to open up the sea chest. This done, and with the sea pouring into the engine room, the British ship was abandoned completely. When everyone was clear, the *Königsberg* opened fire on the helpless merchantman with her 105-mm guns, pumping shell after shell into her hull and upperworks. The *City of Winchester,* her maiden voyage not yet completed, sank in Ghubatt Ar Rahib, where she lay undisturbed until Chris Lees, grandson of Wireless Operator Alan Lees, arrived with the British expedition eighty-four years later. Meanwhile, her unexplained disappearance with the bulk of Ceylon's tea crop caused panic on the London tea market.

Today, if you have a mind to navigate the shallows of the tortuous Rufiji River, which flows into the sea on the coast of old German East Africa, now called Tanzania, another page of history may be turned. On a bend of the Rufji, 12 miles upstream, if you hack away the mangroves on the near bank, you will find a weathered brass plaque which marks the graves of thirty-three German seamen, and reads: *Beim Untergang S.M.S. Königsberg am 11.7.15* (Here sank S.M.S. *Königsberg* on 11.7.15). Nearby, buried in the mud of the river bed is all that remains of the light cruiser.

After disposing of the *City of Winchester*, aware that ships of the Royal Navy would be soon hunting him, *Kapitän* Looff took the *Königsberg* to the south at full speed to find refuge in the empty wastes of the South Indian Ocean. Her boiler furnaces were being fed with coal taken from the *City of Winchester*, poor quality Bombay coal, and her progress had been slow. Fortunately for her, British warships were thinly stretched in this area, and she escaped detection. Then, ten days after leaving Hallaniyah, the *Königsberg* appeared off the British-held island of Zanzibar.

The German cruiser's appearance off Zanzibar proved most inopportune for one of her old adversaries, HMS *Pegasus.* The *Pegasus,* suffering similar boiler problems to those of the *Königsberg*, was lying at anchor in Zanzibar harbour, cleaning her boiler tubes, and with no steam up. Presumably, Captain Ingles had deemed it quite safe to immobilise his ship in the lee of Zanzibar.

The *Pegasus,* although armed with eight 4-inch quick-firers, was easy meat for the *Königsberg*'s *guns*, which pounded her to pieces as she lay helpless at anchor. In the bombardment that lasted just forty-five minutes, thirty-eight men were killed. The *Pegasus* sank later that day.

Kapitän Looff quickly began to regret his impetuous attack on the *Pegasus,* for within a few short hours all the world would know that the *Königsberg* had reappeared. He decided to head south for the Cape, his intention being to attempt the voyage back to Germany. But shortly after leaving Zanzibar astern, the *Königsberg* suffered a major engine breakdown involving a broken crosshead and serious steam leaks. It was not possible to carry out repairs at sea, so Loof was forced to abandon his escape plan and seek a safe refuge nearby.

The following appeared in the *New York Times* on 11 November, 1914:

> LONDON, Nov.10 – Here is the Admiralty announcement of the bottling up of the German cruiser *Koenigsberg* on the east coast of Africa.

> After the whereabouts of the *Koenigsberg* had been indicated by the attack on the *Pegasus* on the 19th of September, a concentration of fast cruisers was arranged by the Admiralty in East African waters and a thorough and prolonged search by these vessels in combination was made.
>
> This search resulted Oct. 30 in the *Koenigsberg* being discovered by HMS *Chatham*, Capt. Sidney R. Drury-Lowe, hiding in shoal water about six miles up the Rufiji River, opposite Mafia Island, German East Africa. Owing to a greater draught, the *Chatham* could not reach the *Koenigsberg*, which probably is aground except at high water.
>
> Part of the crew of the *Koenigsberg* has been landed and is intrenched on the banks of the river. Both these intrenchments and the *Koenigsberg* herself have been bombarded by the *Chatham*, but owing to the dense palm groves amid which the ship lies, it is not possible to estimate the damage done.
>
> Pending operations for her capture or destruction, effective steps have been taken to block the *Koenigsberg* by sinking colliers in the only navigable channel to the river, and she is now imprisoned and unable to do any further harm. The fast vessels which have been searching for her are thus released for other service.

With the *Königsberg* securely bottled up in Rufiji delta, HMS *Chatham* was joined by the 6-inch gun cruisers *Dartmouth* and *Weymouth*. The three warships then settled down to await developments. Looff, meanwhile, his engines stripped down for repairs, was digging in. The *Königsberg* was moored so that her 4-inch guns covered all the approaches to her hiding place, while her 2-inch quick-firers were taken ashore and placed behind earthwork defences manned by a garrison of gunners and observers.

The British cruisers, prevented by their deeper draughts from penetrating further inland, resorted to lobbing shells in the direction of the German cruiser, but the range was too great for the shots to do anything more than annoy the crocodiles sunning themselves down river. This was not a situation to the Admiralty's liking. They could not afford to keep three cruisers standing guard over the Rufiji, but to withdraw them would probably lead to the *Königsberg* breaking out again to threaten the British sea lanes. Eventually, a compromise was reached whereby the two shallow draught monitors, HMS *Mersey* and HMS *Severn,* then stationed in the Mediterranean, were sent for.

After a long voyage under tow from Malta, *Mersey* and *Severn* finally arrived off the Rufiji delta at the end of June, 1915. At first light on 6 July, supported by two spotter aircraft, the monitors moved upstream to within six miles of the *Königsberg*'s lair before opening fire with their 6-inch guns.

The German cruiser registered the first hit, damaging the *Mersey*'s guns, and putting her out of the fight for the day. The *Severn* carried on firing, and succeeded in inflicting minor damage on the *Königsberg*, before both monitors received orders to withdraw down river before darkness closed in. This first attack, during which 635 shells were fired and only six hits recorded, was in effect a dismal failure.

The British monitors ventured inland again on 11 July, when the *Severn* succeeded in approaching to within 11,000 yards of the *Königsberg.* This time the monitor's fire was much more accurate, and within ten minutes the German ship had suffered major damage, and was down to three guns. The end came at 12.52 pm, when a British shell went home in the *Königsberg*'s magazine, and she blew up, killing thirty-three of her crew and wounding many others, including *Fregattenkapitän* Max Looff.

Although in her brief wartime career the *Königsberg* sank only two British ships, the *City of Winchester* and the elderly cruiser *Pegasus,* the mere threat of her presence in the Indian Ocean paralysed shipping in those waters for over ten months. At the same time, twenty British warships were tied up searching for her. It is conceivable that she might have escaped retribution, had it not been for the *City of Winchester*'s dirty Bombay coal Looff had been obliged to confiscate and burn. It is quite possible that this contributed to the engine damage that forced the *Königsberg* to take refuge in the Rufuji River.

Chapter Two

The Silent Menace

In the opening months of the war, the German Imperial Navy's campaign against Allied merchant shipping was almost exclusively in the hands of its surface ships. Strategically placed mines claimed some victims, but the majority of the ships fell to the marauding light cruisers *Emden, Karlsruhe* and *Königsberg*, backed by the armed merchant cruisers *Kaiser Wilhelm der Grosse* and *Kronprinz Wilhelm.* Between them these surface raiders sank a total of forty ships between the outbreak of war and the end of October 1914. And this was all achieved when operating strictly in accordance with the Prize Rules.

The Prize Rules, drawn up at the Hague Conventions of 1899 and 1907, stated (a) that passenger ships must not be sunk, (b) the crews of merchant ships must be placed in safety before their ships were sunk (lifeboats were not considered to be a place of safety, unless close to land) and (c) only warships could be sunk without warning. The German Imperial Navy was fighting a gentlemanly war, a war in which, at this point, the submarine, the new and untried weapon, had no part.

The submarine was the brain child of David Bushnell of Middlesex County, Connecticut. Bushnell, an American engineer with a flair for bizarre inventions, not only discovered that he could make gunpowder explode under water, but also built a primitive submersible craft. With his 'submarine' Bushnell seriously embarrassed the powerful British fleet during the War of Independence of 1812. Unwittingly, perhaps, David Bushnell had pioneered a new and potentially deadly form of sea warfare.

In the century that followed, the submarine slowly progressed from Bushnell's Heath-Robinson-like submersible to a sophisticated maritime weapon with a formidable potential for destruction. When world war came in the summer of 1914, the Royal Navy's E-class ocean-going submarine, 181 feet long and displacing 660 tons, had a surface speed of 16 knots, and was armed with five 18-inch torpedo tubes and a 12-pounder deck gun. However, British naval thinking was still basking in the glory of Trafalgar, and it was confidently assumed that this new war would be fought at sea by lines of battleships pounding each other with 15-inch guns. Although fifty-six E-class had been built and were ready for action, they were regarded by the Admirals, and many politicians, as being unethical weapons. Rear Admiral A.K. Wilson described the submarine as 'underhand, unfair, and damned un-English'! Wilson went as far as to urge the Government to 'treat all submarines as pirates in wartime and hang their crews.' Initially, the German Naval Staff was of a similar mind, but its thinking would soon undergo a radical change.

In August 1914, the German U-boat arm had twenty-five submarines operational. Eight of these were considerably superior to anything the Royal Navy possessed, having more powerful diesel engines, larger torpedoes, and a cruising range that exceeded that of the British E-class by 1000 miles. However, the first war patrol mounted by the German boats proved to be a complete failure, giving credence to the opinion of submarine warfare held by senior naval officers on both sides.

Two days after war was declared, a flotilla of ten U-boats left Heligoland and ventured out into the North Sea. The flotilla's orders were to find the British Grand Fleet, and taking advantage of the surprise – for no one seriously believed that submarines would be used in earnest – sink as many of its ships as possible. The operation was doomed from the start. Soon after leaving Heligoland, the U-boats ran into dense fog and became hopelessly lost. One of their number, *U-9*, then experienced engine trouble, and was forced to turn back. The other boats ran clear of the fog, and continued to the north until they found the British fleet off the Orkney Islands two days later. *U-15* approached, and fired a torpedo at the battleship HMS *Monarch*. The torpedo missed, but its wake was spotted by an alert lookout on the *Monarch,* and *U-15*, once the attacker, became the attacked as destroyers raced towards her. She escaped only by crash-diving and going deep.

With the element of surprise lost, the U-boats conceded defeat, and headed for home. Once again they ran into a dense North Sea fog, and as they were feeling their way through the murk, the unfortunate *U-15*'s engines gave up the ghost, and she lay drifting on the surface. Inevitably, she was sighted by one of the many British ships patrolling the area. The commander of HMS *Birmingham* was quick to take advantage of the situation when he found the helpless submarine. He immediately rang for full speed and rammed *U-15*. She went down with all hands, thus earning for herself the dubious distinction of being the first U-boat to be sunk in the war. Later, when she was reported overdue, Berlin assumed she must have hit a mine.

The first major attempt at submarine warfare had proved to be a dismal failure, but the mere fact that it happened provided a wake-up call for Britain's hidebound admirals. In a move that bordered on panic, they withdrew the Grand Fleet from the North Sea to bases on the remote coast of Western Scotland, then set about making the main fleet anchorage at Scapa Flow submarine-proof. But while the stable door was being closed, the U-boats, undeterred by their early failure, began to hunt further afield.

On 5 September, *U-21*, commanded by *Oberleutnant-zur-See* Otto Hersing, was patrolling off the mouth of the Firth of Forth, when she sighted the ageing light cruiser HMS *Pathfinder.* This time the British ship's lookouts were found wanting, and Hersing was able to make a submerged approach, the choppy sea hiding his periscope. One well-aimed torpedo hit in the vicinity of *Pathfinder*'s main magazine, and she blew up with a spectacular display of flame and smoke. The cruiser, the first victim of modern submarine warfare, sank in four minutes, taking 259 men with her.

Seventeen days later, on the 22nd, the three elderly British cruisers *Aboukir*, *Crecy* and *Hogue* were on patrol off the Dutch coast, steaming in line abreast two miles apart. The cruisers had no destroyer screen, and apparently oblivious to the threat of submarine attack, were not zig-zagging, but keeping rigidly to set courses. They were completely unaware that they were under observation from below the surface by Otto Weddigen's *U-9*. Biding his time, Weddigen torpedoed the unsuspecting cruisers one after the other. This latest indication of the Admiralty's complacency cost the Royal Navy three ships and 1,460 men. Of the incident, Weddigen's First Watch Officer *Oberleutnant-zur-See* Johannes Spiess later wrote: 'In the periscope, a horrifying scene unfolded . . . We present in the conning tower tried to suppress the terrible impression of drowning men, fighting for their lives in the wreckage, clinging onto capsized lifeboats.' For the first time, the sheer horror of unrestricted submarine warfare was revealed for all to see.

Not unexpectedly, Otto Weddigen received a hero's welcome on his return to Kiel. He was awarded the Iron Cross First and Second Class, while every man of his crew received the Iron Cross Second Class. *U-9* was back at sea again in early October and patrolling in the eastern approaches to the Pentland Firth in company with *U-17*, under the command of *Oberleutnant-zur-See* Johannes Feldkirchner. Early on the morning of the 15 October, the two boats were at periscope depth off Aberdeen, when three British cruisers hove in sight. These ships were on their guard, steaming at full speed, and zig-zagging, but as the miracle of Asdic had not yet arrived, they were quite unaware that they were being watched.

Having passed directly over the submerged *U-9*, the heavy cruiser *Hawke,* obligingly stopped and lowered a boat to pass orders to the other two ships. Weddigen, scarcely able to believe his good fortune, took careful aim on the stationary cruiser, and fired both his bow tubes. The range was short, and Weddigen's torpedoes could not possibly miss. HMS *Hawke* blew up and sank in a few minutes. Of her complement of over 500, only 49 survived.

Johannes Feldkirchner in *U-17* was an astonished witness to Weddigen's spectacular destruction of the *Hawke*, and as soon as the smoke cleared he hurriedly manoeuvred into position to attack the other cruisers. He was too late, for by now the British ships were withdrawing from the area as fast as their pounding engines would take them. And as they fled a flotilla of British destroyers came racing in like a swarm of angry bees. The U-boats were forced to retire at speed, *U-9* returning home in triumph, Otto Weddigen being awarded the *Pour le Mérite* (the coveted Blue Max).

Feldkirchner, on the other hand, seemed fated to return from this patrol empty-handed.

When he steamed out of the Firth of Forth on a foggy October morning three days after the cruiser *Hawke* met her sudden end, Captain L.A. Johnston, master of the short-sea trader *Glitra,* was not over-concerned for the safety of his ship. The 832-ton *Glitra,* owned by Christian Salvesen of Leith, was on a legitimate commercial voyage, carrying a cargo of coal, coke, steel plates, and drums of oil from Grangemouth to Stavanger in neutral Norway. It seemed highly unlikely to Johnston that the enemy would spare a second glance at his 32-year-old ship and her mundane cargo.

Once clear of the Isle of May, Johnston brought the *Glitra* onto a north-westerly course for Stavanger. Deep-laden, with black smoke rolling back from her tall, spindly funnel as her sweating firemen hurled coal into her roaring boiler furnaces, she advertised her progress for all to see. Unusually for the time of the year, the wind was no more than a gentle breeze, and the sea was a flat calm. After consulting his barometer, Captain Johnston concluded that the weather would hold and that they were in for a good passage.

The *Glitra* and her seventeen-man crew had sailed these waters many times, summer and winter, and they had no fear of the weather. They were, however, despite Johnston's optimistic approach to the dangers of the war, slightly apprehensive of what lay ahead. Bad news travels at lightning speed at sea, and the loss of five British cruisers to the German U-boats in just over a month was the talk of the messroom and officers' saloon alike. Actually, the *Glitra*'s men should not have been unduly concerned. The German admirals, delighted though they were with the U-boats' victories over the Royal Navy, still had no plans to use this new weapon against unarmed merchant ships. Both the C-in-C of Germany's High Seas Fleet, Admiral Hugo von Ingehohl, and the Chief of Naval Staff, Admiral von Pohl, considered the use of the submarine against British commercial shipping as barbaric, and most probably an infringement of International Law. However, both these high-ranking officers were soon to change their minds.

Frustrated by his failure to come to grips with the British cruisers off Aberdeen, *Oberleutnant* Feldkirchner had taken *U-17* further to the north. For a long time he lay submerged off the Orkneys, waiting for a suitable target to show up in his periscope. He was not aware that the Royal Navy had temporarily withdrawn its ships from Scapa Flow, and his vigil went unrewarded. Running short of fuel and provisions, Feldkirchner decided to abort the patrol, and return to Kiel. Resurfacing, he set course to the east, intending to make a landfall off Stavanger before entering the Skaggerak. At the same time, some 150 miles to the south, the *Glitra,* having cleared the Firth of Forth, was also heading for Stavanger. U-boat and merchantman were unwittingly on converging courses.

Two days later, at noon on 21 October, the *Glitra* was 14 miles west-south-west of the entrance to Bokn Fjord and approaching the Stavanger pilot station at Skudesnaes. Journey's end was in sight, and, as always when approaching port, there was an air of relaxed anticipation aboard the British ship. There was a lot of hard work to be done, hoisting derricks and preparing the ship for berthing, but the prospect of a run ashore in neutral Norway was a powerful incentive. All hands turned to with a will.

As she approached Skudenaes, the *Glitra* hoisted the single code flag 'G', indicating that she required a pilot. This was acknowledged promptly, the pilot cutter putting out from the shore and heading for the *Glitra* with her bow-wave frothing. Captain Johnston reduced speed, then took the way off the ship altogether. A pilot ladder clattered over the side, but as the cutter drew near to the *Glitra,* she suddenly sheered away and headed back for the shore.

Puzzzled by the cutter's action, Johnston looked around the horizon, and it was only then that he became aware of the submarine. She was on the surface about three miles astern, and stealthily overtaking the *Glitra*. The Norwegian pilot cutter's sudden flight was explained.

Taking a closer look at the overtaking stranger through his telescope, Johnston, had no hesitation in identifying her as an enemy submarine. Although his ship was an unarmed merchantman trading to a neutral port, he feared that the U-boat's intentions were far from friendly. He rang for full speed and ordered the helmsman to come round onto a more northerly heading, intent on putting some distance between himself and the enemy. The U-boat followed the *Glitra* round and increased speed. The British ship, having been stopped, was gathering way very slowly, and the gap between the two vessels narrowed at an alarming rate.

A tense half-hour passed, with the *Glitra*'s engineers and firemen making a brave effort to work up to speed, but without much success. The U-boat, five knots faster than the British ship, came abreast of the *Glitra*'s bridge, and then pulled ahead, crossing her bows. The two-letter flag signal 'WZ' – *You should stop your vessel instantly* – flew from the short mast on her conning tower. The gun mounted abaft the tower was clearly manned, and aimed at the *Glitra.*

Johannes Feldkirchner had the unarmed *Glitra* at his mercy, but stopping a merchant ship was as yet unprecedented, and he was unsure of the procedure to follow. International law was quite clear on the subject. The Rules of Prize Warfare, laid down in the sailing ship era, still stood, and they clearly stated, it will be recalled, that, while it was permissible to sink an enemy warship without warning, a merchant ship must be first stopped, and her crew 'placed in safety' before she was sunk. Under the Rules, lifeboats were not considered to be a place of safety, unless they were so close to land as to be almost ashore. There being no room on board *U-17* for the *Glitra*'s 17-man crew, it would be up to Feldkirchner to tow her lifeboats to within a few hundred yards of Skudesnaes. This would involve venturing into neutral waters, and as he could see two Norwegian torpedo boats patrolling off Bokn Fjord, Feldkirchner dismissed the short tow as too risky. He had no wish to be involved in an international incident, which might well end with U-17 being interned by the Norwegians.

On the bridge of the *Glitra* Captain Johnston viewed with increasing trepidation the menace of the German submarine, which was now slowly circling his ship. He was contemplating making a run for the safety of Norwegian waters when *U-17*'s gun barked, and a spout of water was thrown up 50 yards off the *Glitra*'s bows. Clearly, for the 8-knot British ship, running away was no longer an option. Reluctantly, Johnston rang the engine room telegraph to stop, and the *Glitra* slowly drifted to a halt.

The submarine, the German ensign proudly flying at her stern, approached to within 100 yards of the *Glitra* and launched a collapsible boat. With oars dipping smartly, the boat crossed the intervening strip of water and came alongside the merchantman. Using the pilot ladder, which still hung over the ship's side, an armed boarding party, consisting of an officer and four men, reached the *Glitra*'s deck. Captain Johnston waited for them on the bridge. Although he was now aware that this was more than a routine examination of his ship's papers, he was somewhat taken aback when the German officer, ranking perhaps sub-lieutenant, or less, put a Luger pistol to his head, and rudely ordered him off his own bridge. As Johnston, his anger boiling up, started to descend the ladder to the main deck, the officer, who spoke good English, informed him that he would be allowed ten minutes, and no more, to get his crew into the lifeboats. After that, his ship would be sunk. The cocked Luger silenced any protestations Johnston had in mind.

The abandonment of the *Glitra* by her crew was not a dignified operation. Captain Johnston argued that his men be allowed to go below to collect a few articles of clothing, but permission was refused by their German captors. The lifeboats were launched at gunpoint, and before Johnston and his men boarded the boats, they were witness to their ship's faded Red Ensign being torn to shreds and contemptuously stamped on. It was an act of petty vandalism unworthy of the German Navy.

Johnston took his boats clear of the ship, and lay off to await events. The survivors were forced to watch while *U-17*'s prize crew stripped the *Glitra* of all useful gear, including her charts, sailing directions, chronometers and compasses. In his war diary, Johannes Feldkirchner noted that the *Glitra*'s charts were recently corrected and showed the Admiralty routes recommended for merchant ships in the North Sea, the latest positions of navigational buoys, and, the locations of new British minefields. In her dying hours the old *Glitra* had yielded valuable intelligence to the enemy.

Her engine room opened to the sea by her captors, the *Glitra* took more than two hours to sink, and when she went down, it was with the German ensign flying at her stern. Captain Johnston and his crew were silent witnesses to the loss of their ship.

When the *Glitra* finally went to her last resting-place, *U-17* moved in and passed a rope to the British ship's lifeboats. Feldkirchner then towed them to within less than a mile of Norwegian waters before casting off. The Skudesnaes pilot cutter, having watched from a safe distance as the unfamiliar drama was played out, then took up the tow, escorted by one of the Norwegian torpedo boats. Captain Johnston and his men were landed at Skudesnaes, and later taken to Stavanger by ferry. When a suitable ship was available the seventeen survivors, none the worse for their unexpected ordeal, were returned to the United Kingdom. After landing on British soil, Captain Johnston expressed his anger at the treatment he and his crew received at the hands of the new German U-boat Arm:

The submarine sent a boat aboard with five men. With revolvers

> in hand they ordered the British flag taken down, threatening to shoot me if I did not obey. Furthermore they notified me to make haste, and they allowed me not more than ten minutes to let down the lifeboats and take off the crew.
>
> I took down the flag, whereupon the German officer tore it out of my hands and trampled it underfoot. I was forced to take the ship's papers back when I attempted to take them off, and none of the crew was allowed to take any of his belongings.
>
> The crew went in two lifeboats, which the submarine quickly towed 500 yards from the *Glitra*. Three Germans remained on board for a few minutes, searched the ship thoroughly and rapidly, and one of them evidently opened the bottom valves, because the rear of the ship began to sink. Then in a short time the *Glitra* disappeared quietly beneath the waves.

In stopping and sinking the *Glitra* on that calm afternoon off the coast of Norway, *Oberleutnant-zur-See* Johannes Feldkircher had opened a new page in the history books. *U-17* became the first submarine ever to sink a merchant ship, thus heralding a new and terrible era in sea warfare. The apparent ease with which Feldkirchner had carried out the operation went a long way to persuading the German High Command that the U-boat might be the answer to Britain's hitherto unchallenged command of the high seas.

Unaware that he had achieved heroic status, *Oberleutnant* Feldkirchner returned home fully expecting to face a naval court martial for his unauthorised sinking of a British merchantman. Quite to the contrary, he found himself and his crew feted. As a result of his action both Admiral von Ingenhohl and Admiral von Pohl had changed their views on the conduct of the war at sea, and were now prepared to authorise all U-boats to capture and sink Allied merchant ships, providing that the Prize Rules were adhered to. Strange though it may seem today, the Norwegian owners of the cargo lost with the *Glitra* were so outraged that they attempted to sue the German Government for recompense. The following, solemnly recorded in the American Journal of International Law in October 1916, serves to illustrate that submarine warfare in its very early days had elements of farce:

The Glitra

Imperial Supreme Prize Court in Berlin

Decided September 17, 1915

In the name of the Empire: In the prize case of the English steamer *Glitra*, home port Leith, the Imperial Prize Court in Berlin, in its session of July 30, 1915. Rendered the following judgement:

The appeals of the claimants named under Nos 9 and 12 of the disputed judgement are rejected as unfounded. The costs of the appeal are to be borne by the claimants.

Reasons.

On October 20, 1914, the steamer *Glitra*, belonging to the firm of Salvesen & Co. of Leith, and bound with a cargo of piece goods from Leith to Stavanger, was captured by HM submarine *U17* in 50º 04' N 05º 14' E and sunk with her cargo, after the crew had left the ship.

In reply to the request of the Prize Court, according to Section 26 of the Prize Court rules, the 13 parties mentioned in the disputed judgement as possessing interests in the cargo, claimed compensation on account of the destruction of their property. The claimants are partners of Norwegian firms; Claimant No.2 is a Danish insurance company representing the rights of its Norwegian insurer.

Not unexpectedly, the 'gentlemen's war' was extremely short-lived, and the full horror of what Johannes Feldkirchner and *U-17* had initiated became clear six days later.

On 26 October 1914, the 4590-ton French passenger liner *Amiral Ganteaume* sailed from Ostend, bound for Le Havre. She had on board 2,500 French and Belgian refugees who were fleeing from the fierce battles raging around the Belgian cities. On her way down Channel, she made a brief call at Calais, and then continued on to Le Havre. She would have expected to be safely berthed behind the breakwaters of Le

Havre within two hours of leaving Calais, had it not been for the enterprising U-boat commander who decided to intervene. Another unsavoury page of history was about to be written.

One hour after sailing from Calais, the *Amiral Ganteaume* was rounding the forbidding headland of Cap Gris Nez, and running into a freshening westerly wind. She had another eight hours steaming ahead of her before she reached Le Havre, but there was no concern for her safety. This stretch of the English Channel was heavily patrolled, day and night, by British and French destroyers and armed trawlers, several of the latter being in sight from the bridge of the *Amiral Ganteaume*. Understandably, no one on that bridge was expecting a chance meeting with the enemy. Certainly, neither lookouts nor officers noticed the stick-like periscope projecting just above the surface on the liner's port bow.

Beneath the periscope was the sleek outline of *U-24*, on her first war patrol, and under the command of 32-year-old *Kapitänleutnant* Rudolf Schneider. A regular Navy officer, Schneider had been in the service since leaving school in 1901, but his time had been spent exclusively in surface ships. When he finally rose to command in August 1914, he was appointed to the newly commissioned *U-24*, then only few months out from the *Germaniawerft* yard in Kiel.

On that late October day in 1914, Schneider was lying in ambush off Cap Gris Nez at a point where a regular procession of troopships passed carrying reinforcements from British ports to France. When he saw the *Amiral Ganteaume* approaching at full speed, her decks crowded with men, Schneider immediately identified her as an enemy troopship, and prepared to attack.

The French ship may have looked to be trooper loaded with hundreds of fighting men, and a legitimate target for *U-24*, but, Schneider was still bound by the Prize Rules. He was obliged to bring his submarine to the surface, challenge the enemy ship, and then ensure that all her passengers and crew reached safety, before sinking her. Under the circumstances, this was clearly impracticable. In no way was it possible for Schneider to make arrangements for the safety of the huge number of people on board the trooper. Furthermore, several British warships were now in sight, and it would have been courting disaster to bring U-24 to the surface.

As he followed the progress of the *Amiral Ganteaume* through his periscope, Rudolf Schneider became more and more convinced that to allow this ship to pass unmolested with her reinforcements for France could well result in the slaughter of many hundreds of German soldiers at the front. Without further hesitation, he manoeuvred into position on the troopship's port bow, and fired his forward tubes.

One of Schneider's torpedoes went home, blasting a hole in the *Amiral Ganteaume*'s hull, and she slowly listed to port. Fortunately, help was close at hand. The South-Eastern & Chatham Railway's cross-channel ferry *The Queen*, under the command of Captain Robert Carey, was returning empty to Folkestone after landing troops in Boulogne, when she sighted the crippled *Amiral Ganteaume*.

The sea was too rough for *The Queen* to lower boats, but in a display of magnificent ship handling, Carey put the ferry alongside the liner, allowing her panic-stricken passengers to clamber aboard his ship. The crew of the *Amiral Ganteaume* stood by their ship, which was later towed into Boulogne by a French destroyer. Only when she was at anchor in the port was it discovered that thirty Belgian refugees, mostly women and children, and ten crew members had lost their lives as a result of *U-24*'s torpedo.

It was thus that Schneider became the first submarine commander to torpedo an unarmed merchantman without warning. He had also set a precedent, and from that night onwards no Allied merchant ship could expect to be afforded the courtesy laid down by the Prize Rules. The German High Command was not yet ready to authorise sinking without warning, but it was prepared to turn a blind eye when necessary.

Rudolf Schneider went on to sink forty-five Allied merchant ships totalling 126,000 tons gross, and for good measure, the battleship HMS *Formidable*. His deeds earned him the highest decorations, but his end was ignominious. In October 1917, he was swept overboard from the conning tower of *U-87* during a stormy night in the North Sea. He was hauled back on board, but his short immersion in the icy waters of the north had fatal results. He was buried at sea off the Shetland Islands.

Chapter Three

The Pace Quickens

In the wake of Germany's lightning invasion of Belgium in early August 1914, the fighting on the Western Front was spasmodic and largely inconclusive, the three main protagonists, Britain, France and Germany each intent only on testing the enemy's strength. Then, as autumn moved towards winter, General von Kluck made his bid for the French Channel ports.

Faced by an overwhelming superiority in men and guns, British, French and Belgian forces retreated into the coastal plain of Flanders, making a stand on 16 October near the ancient Belgium city of Ypres. The First Battle of Ypres lasted four agonising weeks, during which the opposing armies floundered in the mud of Flanders, advancing and retreating to the thunder of the guns. Territory gained or lost was measured in yards while men died in their thousands. The Allies, heavily outnumbered, suffered over 130,000 casualties, some 75,000 of them British, but they held the line. Eventually, both sides fought themselves to a standstill and began to dig in, thus setting the pattern for the demoralising trench warfare that was to prevail for the next four years.

At sea, autumn saw a rapid deterioration in the conduct of the war, the sinking without warning of the *Amiral Ganteaume* by Rudolf Schneider in *U-24* putting an end to any pretence of combat by Queensberry rules. On 2 November, London declared the North Sea to be a prohibited zone for all enemy merchant ships. Extensive minefields were laid, leaving only a narrow corridor of clear water off the east coast of England, through which neutral ships carrying cargoes for Holland, Denmark, Norway and the Baltic were allowed to pass under close supervision by the Royal Navy.

This effectively closed all access to Germany's few ports, and with her enemies all around her on land, her already faltering economy headed for disaster. Within a few days of the announcement of the British blockade, the German admirals were demanding retaliation, advocating that the U-boats be used to cut Britain's seaborne supplies by resorting to unconditional warfare. In 1914, the German Navy's U-boat strength stood at twenty-eight, of which twenty-one were in the North Sea, but not more than half a dozen of them at sea at any one time. For them to have any real effect on Allied shipping the Prize Rules would have to go overboard, something which the Kaiser, already smarting from accusations of atrocities committed in Belgium, was not prepared to authorise. For the time being, the U-boats were obliged to continue to fight under what their commanders regarded as an unwarranted disadvantage. As they saw it – and their logic made sense – the sole reason for the involvement of the submarine in war was its unique ability to attack from beneath the surface, unseen and unheralded. The Prize Rules clearly obliged them to surface and challenge, then see to the safety of a ship's crew before sinking her. As the North Sea and English Channel were crawling with British warships, the opportunities to surface and sink were few, leading to a virtual stalemate in the campaign. When the new year of 1915 opened, in four months of war the U-boats had sunk only 43,000 tons of Allied shipping, and as Britain's merchant fleet alone consisted of over 20 million tons, the policy was clearly not sustainable.

While the U-boats, hounded day and night by ships of the Royal Navy, and severely hampered by the need to observe the Prize Rules, were having little effect on Allied sea trade, German surface raiders continued to exact a significant toll. One of the most successful of these ships was the *Kronprinz Wilhelm*, a 23,500-ton ex-passenger liner of *Norddeutscher Lloyd*. A holder of the coveted Blue Riband of the Atlantic, this 23-knot armed merchant cruiser operated in the South Atlantic, far removed from the Royal Navy's main sphere of action. Her primary role was to disrupt Britain's meat trade with the South American ports, and despite difficulties in obtaining coal for her boilers in these remote areas, she achieved phenomenal success. Under the command of *Kapitänleutnant* Paul Thierfelder, she captured and sank fifteen ships totalling 56,000 tons, before being interned on entering a neutral port in the USA on 11 April 1915.

An extract taken from an article in the *New York Times* of 12 April, 1915 gives some idea of the ease with which the *Kronprinz Wilhelm* compiled her list of victims:

The first of the ships to fall victim to the *Kronprinz Wilhelm* was the British steamer *Indian Prince*, Capt Gray, bound from Bahia for New York with a valuable cargo of coffee and cocoa, with five passengers, thirty-two officers and seamen aboard. She was owned by the Prince Line Ltd., was 340 feet long, had a gross tonnage of 2846, and was built in 1910. The raider met and sank her on Sept. 4, just a month after escaping from Hoboken.

The British steamer *La Correntina*, bound from La Platte to London with 26 passengers, 95 officers and crew, and a cargo of 5,600,000 pounds of meat aboard, was sunk on Oct.7. She was a twin-screw steamer with a tonnage of 8,529, and was owned by the Houlder Line Ltd. She was built in 1912.

The French bark *Union*, Capt. Gregorio, bound from Port Talbot to Valpariso with a cargo of 3,100 tons of coal and twenty-four officers and crew aboard, was sunk on Oct. 28. The coal was transferred to the raider before the ship was sunk.

The French bark *Anne de Britagne*, Capt. Picard, bound from Fredrikstad for Sydney and Newcastle with a cargo of lumber and twenty-four officers and crew, was sunk on Nov. 21.

The British steamer *Bellvue*, Capt. Robertson, was the next victim. She was sunk on Dec. 4. The steamer had 4,000 tons of coal on board, and was bound from Liverpool for South America, and had thirty-four officers and seamen aboard. The Bellvue was built in 1896, and was owned by the *Bellvue* Steamship Company, Limited.

The French steamer *Mont Agel*, Capt. Vabre, bound from Marseilles for South America in ballast, was sunk on the same day. There were thirty-two officers and seamen aboard. The *Mont Agel*'s tonnage was 4,803. She was built in 1911 and owned by the General Transportation Society.

The British steamer *Hemisphere*, Capt. Roberts, with 5.500 tons of coal aboard, was accepted as a welcome Christmas gift on Dec. 28, and was sunk after her coal had been confiscated. She was bound from Hull for Rosario, with twenty-six officers and seamen aboard. The *Hemisphere* was built in 1897 and was owned by the Hemisphere Steamship Company, Limited.

On Jan. 10 the British steamer *Potaro*, Capt. Matthews, of the

Royal Mail Steam Packet Company, bound from Liverpool for the Argentine Republic for a cargo of meat, was sent to the bottom after her crew of forty-seven men and officers and her mascot, a kitten, had been taken off. She was built in 1904 and had a tonnage of 4,419.

The prize that pleased the German crew of the *Kronprinz* most was the next. It was the big English passenger steamer *Highland Brae*, of the Nelson Steam Navigation Company Ltd., built in 1910 and with a tonnage of 7,634. She was bound from London to Buenos Aires with 50 passengers, 91 officers and crew and, most welcome, a cargo of meats, shoes and boots flannels and other wearing apparel. The whole crew of the *Kronprinz* enjoyed a share of the clothing and food, it was said, and uniforms were made from the bolt cloth aboard. The officers, also, got champagne in quantities before the ship was sunk. The passengers taken from this ship, however, made such a noticeable increase in the demands on the larder that they were put ashore at Buenos Aires as soon as possible. It was on Jan. 14 that the *Highland Brae* was sent to the bottom.

Thierfelder was of the 'old school' of the German Navy, very much the officer and gentleman. The humanity he displayed in his treatment of those unfortunate enough to come under his guns was amply recorded in a diary kept by Samuel Hitchin, chief officer of the *Highland Brae.*

Thursday 14th Jany 1915: About 10 A.M. in lat 2° 46'N long 25° 55'W. Saw heavy smoke on the horizon to the S.E. which was found to be a cruiser approaching at high speed end on. She was alongside about 10.30 and swung round on starboard helm showing herself to be a four funnel three masted auxiliary cruiser flying the German Naval Ensign, name now visible '*Kronprinz Wilhelm*', he fired a gun across our bow, when we stopped our engines he sent an armed boat's crew on board with two officers who hauled down our Ensign and took charge and ordered us to steer East (true) cruiser following closely. Ordered us to swing out our boat ready for lowering which was commenced but the order was countermanded, the cruiser then left in chase of the 3 masted schooner *Wilfred M.* of Barbados.

Four weeks later, all prisoners on board the *Kronprinz Wilhelm* were transferred to the 5556-ton German supply ship *Holger,* which took them to Buenos Aires. Hitchin noted in his diary:

> Friday 12 Feby: AM. Wind and sea moderating. 9.30 A.M. '*Holger*' alongside bumping heavily, transferring baggage stores till 3.30 P.M. Transferred to '*Holger*', two dagos on bridge in private clothes wonder who they were, first gangway smashed as soon as put out, used '*Holger*'s' accommodation ladder turned upside down, Commander addressed Passengers apologising for inferior accommodation on '*Holger*' but begged their pardon and hoped they would get safe on shore, found that much pains had been taken for our comfort, Poop fitted out one compartment for married people and ladys, one for Capts and another for Officers and Gentlemen Passengers. Crew berthed in No 4 Tween Deck. '*Brae*'s' fittings used, Capt introduced to Capt of '*Holger*' who apologised for lack of accommodation, rather theatrical farewell to Cruiser flags hoisted and band played Der Wacht am Rhiem and Deutschland Uber Alle, might have spared us that. Speech by Commander through megaphone, someone called for three cheers for *Kronprinz* Commander and crew which might have been left out and was not universally responded to. Proceeding to W.N.W. *Kronprinz* following in distance, tea alfresco a scramble.

The above may make curious reading, but it does give a fair idea of the attitude prevailing on both sides of the conflict during the early days of the war. The majority of German U-boat commanders continued to obey the Prize Rules into 1915, but the patience of their commanders, angry at the handicap imposed on them by those ashore, was beginning to wear thin.

Thirty-year-old *Kapitänleutnant* Walther Schwieger was also typical of his breed. The tall, blue-eyed, aristocratic Berliner was 'old Navy', a gentleman officer, who ran a disciplined ship, and was popular with his crew. When, on 26 January 1915, Schwieger took *U-20* to war for the first time, he was determined to follow the Prize Rules to the letter.

U-20, built at the *Kaiserliche Werft* in Danzig and commissioned in August 1913, had an operational range of 5000 miles, and was armed with seven G-type torpedoes. She proved to be a successful hunter, but she was noisy, cramped, and in the opinion of her crew, downright dangerous.

Around about the same time as *U-20* cleared the lower reaches of the Ems and exchanged signals with the *Borkum Riff* lightvessel, her last link with Germany, the British steamer *Tokomaru* was running clear of the breakwaters of Santa Cruz, Tenerife and meeting the first of the long Atlantic swells. The 6084-ton *Tokomaru,* named for a bay on the east coast of New Zealand, owned by Shaw Savill & Albion of London, and commanded by Captain Francis Greene, was on the final leg of her long voyage home. Loaded with 6000 tons of frozen New Zealand lamb, butter and other dairy products, she had sailed from Wellington on 9 December, made a brief call at Montevideo for bunkers, and again at Tenerife to take on more coal. Before sailing from Santa Cruz, her hatch-tops had been piled high with crates and baskets of fresh fruit, oranges, bananas and tomatoes, green then, but ripening during the short passage to Europe.

The *Tokomaru* rounded Ushant late in the afternoon of 29 January, being challenged and identified by a French warship standing guard off the island. As the British ship set course up-Channel, 80 miles to the north *U-20* was off the Lizard, having just entered the Channel from the Atlantic. U-boat and merchantman, each completely unaware of the presence of the other, were on converging courses.

Walther Schwieger would have preferred to take the short route to the Channel via the North Sea and Dover Straits after leaving the Ems, but those shallow waters were strewn with British minefields and heavily patrolled by the Royal Navy. In view of the obvious risks involved, Schwieger had opted to go the long way round, passing to the north of Scotland and outside Ireland, before heading in for the Channel. By the time he reached the Lizard, having spent a great deal of time below the surface to avoid Allied patrols, Schwieger's attitude towards the Prize Rules, which obliged him to surface and challenge a potential victim, thereby putting his boat and crew at risk, had undergone a radical change.

The English Channel was as busy as ever, with the big ships jockeying for position in the deeper water, while fleets of fishing vessels, British, French and Spanish, blatantly ignored the rules of the road, trawling their nets across the designated sea lanes. Fortunately, the weather was good, and the visibility clear, but even so Captain Francis Greene had been obliged to spend the night on the bridge of the *Tokomaru*. It was with some relief that at around nine o'clock on the morning of the 30th Le Havre light vessel, its red and white striped hull conspicuous in the morning sun, came in sight. Greene reduced speed in preparation for meeting the pilot boat, which was usually on station near the light vessel.

The *Tokomaru*'s Second and Third Officers were on the bridge with Captain Greene, and all three men were searching to starboard, where they expected to find the pilot cutter. If any one of them had thought to turn their binoculars on to the port bow, U-20's periscope might have been seen just protruding above the surface of the water. Walther Schwieger had only in the last hour positioned his boat close to the light vessel, and already he had the first target in his sights, a deep-loaded British cargo ship with her decks piled high. The long, tedious voyage around the far north of Scotland suddenly seemed worthwhile.

Schwieger's carefully aimed torpedo slammed into the *Tokomaru's* port side between her forward holds and exploded with a muffled roar. A huge column of dirty water and assorted Canary Islands' fruit shot into the air and fell back on the merchantman's open bridge, drenching the astonished officers who, oblivious to the danger, were still diligently searching for the French pilot boat.

The *Tokomaru* leaned heavily to port and dipped her bows as the sea poured into her holds. Captain Greene was first to recover from the shock, quickly assessing the seriousness of the situation as he peered over the fore rail of the bridge onto the shattered deck below. What he saw was enough to make him stop engines and order the lifeboats to be swung out.

Damage reports coming to the bridge were bad, confirming Greene's worst fears. His ship, the sea already lopping over her forecastle head, was finished. He passed the word to abandon ship, and went below to his cabin to collect the ship's papers. His mission was fruitless: when he reached his cabin he found it under water.

It was fortunate that the *Tokomaru* had been on slow speed as she approached the pilot station, for by the time the boats hit the water she was almost at a standstill, and Greene was able to get all his crew away safely. They were picked up half an hour later by the French minesweeper *Saint Pierre*, and were able to watch their ship go down from the deck of the sweeper. It was a sad farewell for Captain Francis Greene and his men; they had lost a good ship, 6000 tons of precious cargo, and most of their personal belongings.

Although the British torpedo boats *Claymore, Foil, Pen* and *Pennant* were quickly on the scene, Walther Schwieger was able to dive deep and slip away. He had no regrets about torpedoing the *Tokomaru* without warning, having come to terms with his conscience on the grounds that to have surfaced would have put his boat and crew in imminent danger of being sunk. In these waters, the Prize Rules had no standing.

Still submerged, Schwieger took up a position to the north-west of the light vessel to await his next victim. He did not have long to wait. A little after midday, less than two hours after the *Tokomaru* went down, another ship was sighted approaching the pilot station from the west. She was the 2828-ton *Ikaria* of the Liverpool-based Leyland Line.

The *Ikaria,* commanded by Captain Matthew Robertson, was nearing the end of a long voyage from South America, loaded with 5000 tons of coffee, hides and general cargo. In preparation for picking up the Le Havre pilot, Captain Robertson, his chief and second officers were all on the bridge. At 12.30, the *Ikaria* was stopped, ready to take the towlines of the two tugs, which were then approaching with the pilot cutter. As she lay drifting, those on the bridge saw the track of a torpedo speeding towards the *Ikaria* on her port side.

For Captain Robertson this was a nightmare from Hell. He gave a double ring on the engine room telegraph, calling for emergency full speed ahead, but even as he did so he knew that there was no way he could avoid the disaster about to befall his ship. The fully loaded *Ikaria* had not even begun to get under way when the torpedo struck.

Schwieger's torpedo hit the *Ikaria* in her forward hold, and as with the *Tokomaru,* there was a loud explosion and a column of sea water carrying a mixture of cargo and broken hatchboards shot into the air. This then fell back on the bridge, adding to the confusion of the moment. With her hull blasted open to the sea, the *Ikaria* began to settle by the head.

This could have been a sad end to the British ship's 5000-mile voyage from South America, but fortunately for her, the tugs were nearby.

Towropes were passed, and the crippled *Ikaria* was towed into Le Havre. Unfortunately, she was so badly damaged that she sank in the outer harbour before she could be taken to a safe berth or beached.

In direct contravention of the Prize Rules, Walther Schwieger had now torpedoed two unarmed ships without warning. While in the case of the *Tokomaru* and *Ikaria* it could be argued that the presence of enemy warships in the area justified breaking the rules, the same could not be said of his next victim.

The 1484-ton *Oriole,* a new addition to the fleet of the General Steam Navigation Company of London, commanded by Captain Gale, had spent the previous week moored to a buoy in the upper reaches of the Thames loading a cargo of stores and provisions for British troops in France. She sailed on the afternoon of Friday 29 January 1915, bound for Le Havre, where she was expected to arrive at around nine o'clock on the morning of the 30th.

The *Oriole* failed to reach Le Havre on the 30th, or on any other day, and it seemed that at some point in her short passage down Channel she had disappeared off the face of the earth. A search was made when the *Oriole* was posted overdue at Lloyds, but no trace of the ship could be found. Then, a week later, two lifebuoys marked S.S. *Oriole* were washed ashore near Dover, indicating that she may have met her end in the narrows of the Dover Strait, run down by a bigger ship, perhaps. However, six weeks later, on 22 March, the mystery of the *Oriole* deepened when a salt-stained envelope embossed with the logo of the General Steam Navigation Company came ashore on Guernsey. Scribbled on the envelope were the two words 'Oriole torpedoed'. It was later learned that the *Oriole*, her cargo, and Captain Gale and his crew of twenty had been victims of Walther Schwieger's new 'sink without warning' strategy. Presumably, the ship had arrived off Le Havre within an hour or so of the *Ikaria* being torpedoed, and sailed straight into Schwieger's open arms.

Well pleased with his early run of success, Schwieger decided to remain in the vicinity of Le Havre, and when night fell on Sunday the 31st *U-20* was lying submerged 25 miles to the north-east of Cape d'Antifer. The English Channel was in a sombre mood, with a strong south-westerly wind blowing and a heavy sea running. At intervals, the moon broke through the scudding clouds, shedding its cold light on the wintry scene. On the horizon to the south-west, the lighthouse on Antifer winked its yellow eye once every twenty seconds, providing a useful navigational mark for Schwieger to hold position on.

At around ten o'clock, tiring of the uncomfortable rolling of the boat at periscope depth, Schwieger was on the point of looking for a sandy bottom to rest on, when the moon broke through the clouds to reveal a small ship coming down Channel.

The 468-ton British coaster *Lisette* had sailed from Poole early that morning, bound for Honfleur. Her master, Captain Tom Waterhouse, being a regular cross-Channel trader, was no stranger to rough crossings, but this one, on the last day of January 1915, he would remember for a long time. Running clear of the Dorset coast, and beam on to wind and sea, the tiny *Lisette* had all but rolled herself under, and Waterhouse had been forced to head back up Channel, before turning south for the Seine estuary. He was on this southerly leg, with the *Lisette* shipping green seas over her blunt bows as she fought to make headway, when Schwieger sighted her.

The *Lisette*'s second mate had the watch on the bridge, and at the wheel was 21-year-old Ordinary Seaman Arthur Brumby. At 10.30 the light on Cape d'Antifer was seen, and the lookout was sent below to call Captain Waterhouse. The lookout man had just left the bridge when the *Lisette* seemed to hit a brick wall. She shuddered and heeled over to port, then back to starboard, before coming upright and digging her bows into the oncoming sea again.

It could have been that the *Lisette* had slammed her bows into an unusually big sea, but the Second Mate was convinced that she had hit something more solid. He stopped the engines, and sent Arthur Brumby below to call all hands.

The helmsman was sliding down the starboard ladder to the main deck, when he saw a long dark shape lying almost under the *Lisette*'s starboard bow. Brumby was an ex-Navy man, and he knew a submarine when he saw one. He later reported, 'Her stem was lifted right up out of the water as though the fore part of the submarine was under our bow. She was in sight less than a minute when she sank and my vessel was righted. I saw part of the after deck on the submarine which is raised and I also saw one fin and the propeller race. I took her to be a German submarine trying to get across our stem or dive under us to leeward to speak to us and that she had either misjudged the distance or not dived deep enough and had come across our stem.'

Ordinary Seaman Brumby was not far wrong in his assessment of the situation. After examining the *Lisette* through the periscope, Walther Schwieger had thought her too small to warrant the use of a torpedo, and decided to surface and use his deck gun. But first he had to get between the coaster and the land, and in crossing the *Lisette*'s bow from starboard to port he misjudged her speed. The resulting collision damaged the German submarine's periscope, and caused her to spring several leaks in her pressure hull. Schwieger retired to lick his wounds, recording in his log that *U-20* had been the victim of a determined and unprovoked ramming by the British ship. Meanwhile, Tom Waterhouse continued on to Honfleur, wondering how on earth he was to explain to his owners the large dent in the *Lisette*'s bow.

Despite the damage to *U-20*'s periscope and the leaks in her hull, eighteen hours later, Walther Schwieger was to be found stalking the British hospital ship *Asturias* in the approaches to Le Havre.

The 1907 Hague Convention laid down that hospital ships should be immune from attack, providing they were clearly marked and their details and proposed employment were communicated to any potential enemy. Articles 4 and 5 of the Convention stated that hospital ships must be painted white, and clearly identified by a five-foot wide green or red band running around the hull from stem to stern on both sides. Additionally, they must fly the Red Cross flag, along with their own national ensign.

The *Asturias,* correctly marked as laid down by the Hague Convention, was on her way in to pick up wounded from the front, when Schwieger attempted to torpedo her. It was still light, and, fortunately, the torpedo was seen by a number of people on board the *Asturias* in time for avoiding action to be taken. The British Government made a strong protest against this illegal attack, prompting an apology, the gist of which was reported in the *New York Times* on 6 March:

> WASHINGTON, March 6. – The German Embassy issued tonight the following explanation of the recent attack on the British hospital ship *Asturias*:
>
> 'Government sorry to admit British hospital ship *Asturias* was

attacked on Feb. 1, 5.05 P.M. Coming up in twilight carrying lights as prescribed for ordinary steamers, ship was taken for transport conveying troops. Distinctive marks showing character of ship not being illuminated were only recognised after shot had been fired. Fortunately torpedo failed to explode. The moment ship was recognized as hospital ship, every attempt of further attack was immediately given up.'

The statement, signed by the Ambassador, Count Bernstorff, and in quotation marks as shown, has the appearance of a cablegram which had not been filled out on translation from code. No comment on the statement was obtainable.

The *Asturias* was about fifteen miles northeast of Havre, France, when she was attacked on Feb. 1. Press reports said her commander saw the torpedo fired by a submarine and succeeded in evading it.

Walther Schwieger, disillusioned by the futility of the gentlemanly approach to the enemy, had demonstrated what a lethal weapon the U-boat could be if the Prize Rules were ignored. It was largely due to his run of success off Le Havre that, on 4 February 1915, the German High Command made the following announcement:

1. The waters around Great Britain and Ireland, including the whole of the English Channel, are herewith declared to be in the War Zone. From February 18 onwards, every merchant ship met with in this War Zone will be destroyed, nor will it always be possible to obviate the danger with which passengers and crew are thereby threatened.

2. Neutral ships, too, will run a risk in the War Zone, for in view of the misuse of neutral flags by the British Government on January 31, and owing to the hazards of naval warfare, it may not always be possible to prevent the attacks meant for hostile ships from being directed against neutral ships.

After only six months of conflict, the restrictive Prize Rules had been consigned to the deep, and the war at sea was becoming a free-for-all. Three months later, Walther Schwieger entered the halls of infamy by torpedoing without warning the 30,000-ton passenger liner *Lusitania* off the south coast of Ireland. She went down in less than twenty minutes, taking 1,198 passengers and crew with her. The casualty list included 124 American citizens.

The news of the sinking of the *Lusitania* without prior warning raced around the world, and brought condemnation from all quarters. The Germans initially tried to brazen it out by claiming that the liner was carrying troops and ammunition, and was therefore a legitimate target. They also accused the British Government of deliberately exposing the *Lusitania* to danger, hoping that she would be sunk and the loss of American lives would bring America into the war. Far-fetched though this accusation may have been, Schwieger's supposedly unauthorised action did play a significant part in persuading the Americans to enter the war on the side of the Allies, although not until April 1917.

U-20 came to an untimely end in November 1916, when she ran aground in fog on the Danish coast. During an operation mounted to refloat her, the battleship *Kronprinz Wilhelm,* which was providing cover, was torpedoed by the British submarine J-1. The salvage operation was hastily abandoned, and *U-20* was blown up to prevent her falling into enemy hands.

After the narrow miss by Walther Schwieger's torpedo, the hospital ship *Asturias* continued with her humanitarian work, bringing home thousands of sick and wounded to Britain. Her luck finally ran out on the night of 20 March, 1917. She had left Malta six days earlier with 900 casualties on board, which she landed safely at Avonmouth, sailing for Southampton on the evening of the 20th with only her crew and RAMC personnel on board. She was correctedly marked with the Red Cross identification, and fully lit, but just before midnight, when she was off Start Point, she was torpedoed without warning by *UC-66*, commanded by Herbert Pustkuchen.

Pustkuchen's torpedo hit the *Asturias* aft in her engine room; all her lights failed, and she began to settle by the stern as the sea poured in through the great hole in her hull. With what little steam she had left in her boilers, she was taken inshore and beached. Of the total complement of 206 on board, which included twenty-nine nurses, forty-five lost their lives. The remainder reached the shore in the lifeboats.

Grudgingly, Berlin admitted responsibility for the loss of the *Asturias,* but sought to justify the sinking by claiming that, 'Even in spite of our warnings, wounded and sick have been sent into this sea zone and exposed to the dangers of being sunk. It would moreover be remarkable that the English in the case of the *Asturias* should have abstained from their customary practice of using hospital ships for the transport of troops and munitions; we are constantly receiving proofs that our enemies, as formerly, misuse hospital ships for the purposes of war.'

Chapter Four

Murder in the Western Approaches

The sun was setting over the Mersey when the Elder Dempster cargo/passenger liner *Falaba* sailed out of Liverpool on 27 March 1915. She left reluctantly, for, in the opinion of her crew, Saturday, when the lights are bright and the girls friendly, was no time to put to sea.

Only a half a dozen uninterested line handlers and a bowler-hatted marine superintendent were on hand to see the ship out, and when the last rope was cast off even they turned their backs. The superintendent, to give him his due, did doff his hat in farewell, but then, his duty done, he too hurried away to that cosy little house in Heswall, where his attentive wife and a hot meal awaited him.

On the bridge of the *Falaba,* Captain Frederick Davis looked back on the receding lights with no regrets. On this occasion he was not sorry to be saying goodbye to Liverpool, for this was a city not at ease with itself. While men were dying in the mud of Flanders and further afield in the Dardanelles, Liverpool's dockers had been on strike, turning the *Falaba*'s normally well-ordered loading operation into a chaotic rush. It was only after the intervention of Lord Kitchener that the men had gone back to work that morning, allowing the *Falaba* to close her hatches on a full cargo for West Africa. The 4086-ton *Falaba,* eight years old and one of ED's finest 14-knotters, carried a crew of ninety-five, which included one woman, Stewardess Louisa Tearle, a widow, whose husband, Henry Tearle, had lost his life in the service of the Company in West Africa in 1914. In addition to a cargo of manufactured goods, the *Falaba* had on board 147 passengers, most of whom were planters and civil servants returning to the West African colonies after a spell of leave in Britain. In their ranks was one American, 31-year-old Leon Thrasher, a mining engineer from Massachusetts.

Locked out ahead of the *Falaba,* and leading the way down river, was the White Star passenger ship *Cymric*, bound for New York with 245 passengers on board. The *Cymric*'s master, Captain F.E. Beadnell, had paid a social call on Captain Davis earlier in the day, and the two men spent an hour earnestly discussing the current situation at sea. Both had received reports of at least two enemy submarines operating in the South Western Approaches, with three British merchantmen being sunk off Land's End in the past two weeks – and right under the nose of the Royal Navy. The problem, as both captains saw it, was that even after seven months of war, the Admiralty still refused to give British merchantmen a fighting chance with a stern-mounted gun. And this despite the fact that the right of merchant vessels to carry defensive armament had been recognised for hundreds of years past.

While Davis and Beadnell drank their coffee, generously laced with Las Palmas brandy, yet another British ship was about to meet her end in the approaches to the Bristol Channel.

The 2114-ton *Aguila,* owned by the Yeoward Brothers of Liverpool and under the command of Captain Bannerman, was following her well-trodden path to Lisbon and the Canary Islands. She was 47 miles south-west of the Smalls, the tiny cluster of half-submerged rocks that lie off St. David's Head, when she was challenged and ordered to stop by the German submarine *U-28.*

U-28, one of a new class of submarines, laid down in 1912 and launched in 1914, had sailed from Emden on her first war patrol two weeks earlier. Displacing 870 tons submerged, she was armed with four torpedo tubes, two in the bow and two in the stern, and two 22-pounder deck guns. Her twin diesels gave her a speed in excess of 16½ knots on the surface, and she had a cruising range of 5,520 miles at 8 knots. Submerged, she was able to average a very respectable 9½ knots.

Under the command of 33-year-old *Kapitänleutnant* Georg-Günther Freiherr von Forstner, U-28 had achieved instant success in the North Sea by sinking the British ship *Leeuwarden* and capturing the *Batavier V* and *Zaanstrom,* both under the Dutch flag. Baron Forstner, well pleased with his new command, then took on the perils of the heavily guarded English Channel, eventually breaking through into the Atlantic.

For more than a week, Forstner, in company with Otto Weddigen, the scourge of the Royal Navy's cruiser squadrons, in U-29, lay in ambush off the Scilly Isles, one of the busiest shipping crossroads in European waters. Weddigen once again struck gold, sinking three ships in one day, but Forstner's vigil was in vain. This persuaded him to move further north to the Smalls. This 135-ft-high lighthouse was a favourite departure point for ships sailing out of Liverpool and the Bristol Channel ports.

Darkness was not far away when Forstner, acting in accordance with the Prize Rules, brought *U-28* out of the depths to challenge the southbound *Aguila*. Captain Bannerman, with no other means of defence, decided to make a run for it. Turning under full helm, he put the submarine astern and called for all possible speed from the engine-room.

Even in her heyday, the *Aguila* had never been capable of more than 13½ knots. Now, sixteen years old, she could not possibly hope to escape from Forstner's guns. Once *U-28* had worked up to full speed, she rapidly began to overhaul the fleeing ship, and in less than an hour she was within 300 feet of her. Forstner opened fire with both his 22-pounders, using shrapnel and solid shot.

There was carnage aboard the *Aguila*: her chief engineer, two crew members and a woman passenger were killed, while Captain Bannerman and a number of others were wounded. Realising the futility of continued defiance, Bannerman stopped engines and gave the order to abandon ship. But even when the way was off the ship and the boats were being lowered, Forstner continued to fire. In the confusion, one of the boats capsized on launching, and five more lives were lost.

The *Aguila* was hit by twenty shells before Baron Forstner completed her humiliation by firing a torpedo into her. She broke in two, and went to the bottom in a few minutes, leaving a sea of debris, on which four lifeboats crammed with survivors drifted aimlessly. Forstner then motored away, apparently leaving the survivors to arrange their own salvation. However, he went part way to redeeming his ruthless treatment of the defenceless *Aguila* by stopping the steam trawler *Ottilie,* which was fishing some miles away, and informing her skipper of the position of the lifeboats. The *Ottilie* found three boats containing nineteen survivors. It was assumed that the fourth boat, having the remaining survivors on board, must have foundered, but several days later it sailed into Fishguard harbour.

The barometer was falling, presaging a blow, when the two passenger ships *Cymric* and *Falaba* said their last goodbyes to the fading lights of Liverpool, and entered the Mersey buoyed channel. The *Cymric* was leading, with the *Falaba* following close on her flickering stern light. Both Captain Beadnell and Captain Davis were still completely unaware of the brutal sinking of the *Aguila*.

Four hours later, both ships dropped their pilots to the same cutter off the breakwaters of Holyhead. The *Cymric* then set course for the Tuskar Rock light, where she would make her departure for New York, while the *Falaba* continued on south for Las Palmas. As they parted company, the wind was keening in the rigging and the white horses were running, giving the promise of a dirty night to come.

U-28 rode out that night on the surface, rolling in a heavy westerly swell, her deck plates awash with angry green water as the rough Atlantic seas broke over her. Lashed by the icy spray, Baron Georg-Günther Forstner kept an uncomfortable vigil in the exposed conning tower with his watch officer and lookouts. But as the rain and spray streamed from his oilskins, the contemplation of *U-28*'s record so far, on this her first war patrol, did a lot to compensate for the foul weather. Since putting out from Emden only a fortnight earlier, she had sunk five ships and captured two others, a total of 12,697 tons of Allied shipping snatched out of service. And there would be more to come.

Dawn came reluctantly on Sunday 28 March, a slow transition from a black storm-tossed night into a grey sullen morning. The heavy seas were till running, the rain squalls continued to sweep in from the Atlantic, and despite the mugs of steaming black coffee, *U-28*'s conning tower remained a place of penance. When it was fully light, and he had established that the wheeling gulls were the only other inhabitants of this stretch of water, Forstner went below to recharge his batteries with a quick wash and a substantial breakfast. He was back in the conning tower within the hour to continue his watch for the enemy. His perseverance was rewarded at around 11.30, when the masts and funnel of a southbound steamer were sighted right ahead. He submerged with the intention of attacking underwater, but the sea was so rough that he found it impossible to hold *U-28* at periscope depth. He re-surfaced.

Traditionally, Sunday at sea in British merchant ships may not be a day of rest, but it is a relaxed day, with no unnecessary work being done. However, the watches must be kept, and the galley stoves continue to produce hot meals. And then there is the time-honoured ritual of the Captain's weekly inspection of the accommodation. On board the *Cymric*, which was by this time passing south of the Irish port of Waterford and plunging her bows into a rising sea, Captain Beadnell had finished his rounds. He was about to indulge in a pre-lunchtime beer with his senior officers, when the wireless operator appeared at his door. The message form he handed over to Beadnell contained the *Falaba*'s last communication with the outside world. It read: 'SUBMARINE ALONGSIDE. AM PUTTING OFF PASSENGERS INTO BOATS', followed by her position.

Captain Beadnell's first instinct was to reverse course and go to the *Falaba*'s aid, but he had specific orders from the Admiralty that in no circumstances was he to risk his own ship by entering a danger zone. Reluctantly, for he was acting in breach of the unwritten code of the sea, Beadnell decided to ignore the SOS and carry on westwards. Wisely, he refrained from informing his passengers of the *Falaba*'s call for help until the *Cymric* was 40 miles west of the Fastnet, and well away from the U-boat danger area.

At 11.40 that morning, the *Falaba* had been 38 miles west of the Smalls, and steaming southwards for the Canaries at 13 knots. In view of the reports received of German submarines operating in the area, Captain Fred Davis had foregone his weekly inspection, and was in his cabin below the bridge, attending to some neglected paperwork. When the bridge voice pipe shrilled urgently, he wasted no time in answering it, then left the cabin at a run.

When he reached the bridge, Davis found that the Third Officer, who was in charge of the watch, had sighted what appeared to be a British submarine overtaking on the starboard beam. Davis took the telescope from its rack and focused on the stranger. It was a submarine all right, and she was flying the White Ensign, but Davis, never one to take things at face value, had a gut feeling that she was not all that she appeared to be. The *Falaba* being unarmed, he took the only course open to him, turning the ship under full port helm to present her stern to the submarine, and sent word to the engine-room for all possible speed. His prompt action proved justified when the 'British' submarine lowered her

White Ensign and hoisted the black and gold ensign of the *Kaiserliche Marine* in its place. She gave chase.

At her acceptance trials on the Clyde in August 1906, the newly built *Falaba* had achieved a speed of 15½ knots, but now, after nine gruelling years pounding the trail to West Africa, she was reduced to a more comfortable 13 knots. In peril, and with Captain Davis' well-chosen curses booming down from the open engine room skylight, her engineers gave their all. The *Falaba*'s gleaming pistons threshed, black smoke poured from her tall funnel, and although she did not fly, her frothing bow-wave indicated that she was near to recovering her trial speed.

By this time *U-28*, her powerful diesels on full throttle, was making 18 knots. When, at 11.58 she was only about 200 yards astern of the *Falaba,* Forstner fired a gun and hoisted the two-letter flag signal for 'Stop and abandon your ship'.

Davis ignored Forstner's signal, and urged his engineers to pile on more speed. Two minutes later, Forstner hoisted a further flag signal, which after a hurried consultation of his code book Davis deciphered as 'Stop or I fire!'.

Much as he favoured defiance, Captain Davis was forced to accept that the odds were heavily stacked against him. The enemy submarine was plainly much faster than the *Falaba,* he had no gun with which to defend his ship, and he was carrying 147 passengers, the latter being the deciding factor. Davis consulted with his chief officer Walter Baxter, who agreed that, as it was impossible for the *Falaba* to escape, in the interest of the safety of their passengers they must surrender. With great reluctance, Davis gave the order to stop engines.

As *U-28* moved in closer, Forstner used a megaphone to hail the ship. 'Take to the boats,' he ordered, 'we are going to sink you in five minutes.' It would have been plainly impossible for Davis to have cleared his ship of her complement of 242 in just five minutes, but in order to gain time, he shouted back that he would comply. His next move was to instruct the wireless operator to send a distress message, and it was this message that Captain Beadnell of the *Cymric* received.

Unfortunately for those on board the *Falaba, U-28*'s operator also picked up her distress transmission, which was immediately passed to Forstner in the conning tower. At the same time, one of the submarine's lookouts reported smoke on the horizon, which Forstner took to be

British naval vessels arriving on the scene. This appears to have prompted what can only be described as an act of wanton inhumanity. *U-28* was now within 100 yards of the *Falaba,* and it must have been evident to Forstner that she was carrying a large number of passengers, who could be plainly seen assembling on her boat deck. Yet, at 12.10, five minutes after he had ordered the *Falaba* to stop, Forstner fired a torpedo, which hit the British ship abaft of her main accommodation on the starboard side. She staggered, and took a heavy list to starboard.

The *Falaba* was equipped with a total of eight lifeboats, all of which were carried swung outboard ready for lowering, and given reasonable circumstances it should not have been difficult to abandon ship quickly and in good order. Unfortunately, the circumstances were far from reasonable. The *Falaba* was leaning heavily to starboard, which made it very difficult to lower the port side boats, and furthermore there was a heavy sea running.

It would be wrong to say that chaos reigned aboard the *Falaba,* but with 147 passengers to evacuate, many of whom were frightened and confused, there was inevitably some disarray. This suddenly became panic when Forstner turned stern-on to the crippled liner and fired a second torpedo from one of his stern tubes. The torpedo slammed into the *Falaba*'s side as the boats were being lowered. One boat caught the full force of the explosion just as it reached the water, and was reduced to matchwood, killing many on board. Others, some badly injured, were thrown into the sea.

In the ensuing mayhem, other boats were smashed against the ship's side and capsized. Soon the sea around the doomed ship was dotted with bobbing heads as crew and passengers alike fought to stay alive in the icy water.

It is estimated that the *Falaba* took just eight minutes to sink, going down by the stern with a rush as her watertight bulkheads collapsed. The loss of life would have been greater, had it not been for the timely arrival of the steam drifters *Eileen Emma* and *Wenlock*, the smoke from which Forstner had mistaken for British warships racing to the defence of the *Falaba.* Between them, the two drifters plucked forty-eight persons from the water, eight of which later died on board the fishermen, among them Captain Fred Davis, who had remained on the bridge of the *Falaba* until she went down.

Of the total complement of 242 on board the *Falaba,* 104 lost their lives, 50 crew members, including the widowed stewardess Louisa Tearle, and 61 passengers. The one American on board, Leon Thrasher, a 31-year-old mining engineer from Massachusetts employed on the Gold Coast, earned the dubious distinction of being the first United States citizen to be killed in the First World War.

In sinking the *Aguila* and the *Falaba,* both unarmed merchant ships, Georg-Günther von Forstner showed a brutal streak not yet seen in German U-boat commanders. At the official inquiry held into the loss of the *Falaba* in London on 20 May, 1915, the Solicitor-General commented: 'A defenceless, unarmed, unoffensive vessel carrying passengers, the *Falaba* was torpedoed in broad daylight by a German submarine at a distance of not more than 100 yards. There are some deeds which speak louder than words, and the circumstances in which the *Falaba* was destroyed speak more strongly than any words I could use of the shame and disgrace of the people responsible for it . . . The submarine sent a torpedo through the struggling people already in the sea.' Eyewitnesses also claimed that crew members of *U-28* 'jeered at the drowning British men and women'.

Not surprisingly, Forstner had a different tale to tell. Questioned in Bremen by J.J. Ryan, a U.S. cotton broker, he assured Ryan that the *Falaba*'s officers must have been mistaken in thinking that the crew of the *U-28* laughed and jeered at the drowning passengers. 'Such an impression is most cruelly unjust to my men,' Forstner stated. 'My men were crying, not laughing, when the boats capsized and threw people in the water.' He also told Ryan, 'I warned the captain of the *Falaba* to dismantle his wireless apparatus, and gave him ten minutes in which to do it, and also to get out his passengers. Instead of acting upon my command, he continued to send out messages to torpedo boats that were less than 20 miles away to come to his assistance as quickly as possible. At the end of ten minutes I gave him a second warning about dismantling the wireless apparatus and waited twenty minutes. I then torpedoed the ship, as the torpedo boats were getting close up, and I knew they would go to the rescue of passengers and crew.'

No British warships were in the immediate area when the *Falaba* was sunk, and it seems likely that the 'torpedo boats' von Forstner feared so much were the harmless drifters *Eileen Emma* and *Wenlock.* Their skippers, George Wright and Denis Randleson, would have been more interested in hauling in a good catch than attacking *U-28*, even if they were armed – which they were not. As to Forstner's claim that the tough, highly disciplined German submariners were in tears at the fate of their victims, this is plainly ludicrous. However, it is equally unlikely that they were roaring with laughter. At this stage of the war, chivalry and respect for a brave enemy still to a large extent prevailed on both sides.

The official version of the sinking, circulated to German wireless stations, and received in London stated:

> Berlin April 14: Main headquarters reports as follows re the sinking of the British ship *Falaba*. It is reported from a reliable source that the *Falaba* refused to heave to, and that it drew away and even sent up rockets for assistance, thus exposing the submarine to danger from attack by ships coming to the rescue and that it also fired on the submarine.
>
> In spite of this the submarine did not shoot at once. From a distance of 530 yards the submarine ordered the crew to leave the ship within ten minutes. The crew took to the boats, but gave no help to the passengers who were in the water, who they might easily have helped.
>
> From the time that the command was given to the time when the torpedo was fired, not ten minutes but 23 minutes elapsed. When the shot was fired only the Captain could be seen on the ship, and the submarine could not take any passengers on board.
>
> It is a slander to say that the crew of the submarine laughed at the drowning victims.

Lord Mersey, President of the Board of Marine Arbitration, who chaired the London inquiry, commented: 'There was evidence before me of laughing and jeering on board the submarine while the men and women were on board the *Falaba* or struggling for their lives in the water. I prefer to keep silent on this matter in the hope that the witness was mistaken.'

German sources later attempted to justify the sinking of the *Falaba* on the grounds that she was carrying 13 tons of explosives in her cargo for West Africa, which indeed she was. But it was then the custom of the trade that most ships on this run carried small quantities of black powder and dynamite on the outward passage. This was legitimate commercial cargo for use in the West African mines, and had no connection with the war.

In the case the sinking of both the *Aguila* and the *Falaba, Kapitänleutnant* von Forstner was clearly in breach of the Prize Regulations, in that he opened fire on the ships and sank them before the passengers and crew had time to get clear. This he would no doubt have justified by pointing out that the ship refused to stop when challenged.

A German naval communiqué published in a Berlin newspaper shortly after the *Falaba* was sunk attempted just that:

> The prominence given to the sinking of the *Falaba* indicates, first of all, that the loss is sorely felt. The *Falaba* was not only a large and valuable vessel, but the first passenger ship overtaken by such a fate – a fate designed to undermine the customary feeling of security on liners. Hitherto even the English have acknowledged that we have given the occupants of doomed ships an opportunity to disembark. That is one of the demands of humanity which it goes without saying our submarine commanders respect as long as it is militarily possible, but, naturally, not a moment longer. The moment that England offers premiums to merchantmen which sink U boats and systematically trains them to ward the latter off, the exercise of such humanity by our U craft is narrowly made impossible. Since England has been so acting every English ship of commerce is not only legitimate booty, but subjects herself to the suspicion of belligerent action – namely, attack – and our submarines are compelled to exercise supreme vigilance.

Throughout history, the British merchant seaman has had the reputation of being fiercely independent, and even prepared to lay down his life for his ship. If the German Admirals expected meek surrender, then they were grossly underestimating their potential victims.

Although the loss of life in the sinking of the *Aguila* and *Falaba* was grievous, from the point of view of the British Government, the most significant casualty was the American Leon Thrasher, who died in the *Falaba*. His death aroused a storm of anger in the United States and was the subject of a memorandum sent to Berlin by President Woodrow

Wilson. This was the first step down the long road that would eventually lead to America entering the war on the side of the Allies in April 1917.

U-28's run of good luck continued throughout March 1915. Before the month was out Forstner had accounted for two more British merchantmen, Ellerman Papayanni's 3500-ton *Flaminian* and the 4505-ton Glasgow steamer *Crown of Castile.* Curiously, and contrary to the reports from the *Falaba,* Chief Officer Roberts of the Glasgow ship later said: 'The Germans treated us very decently. The commander was a big blonde man, and was by no means a bully. He handed cigars round to all of us.' On the other hand, some crew members of the *Crown of Castile* reported that the Germans jeered at them while they were in the lifeboats. To young Apprentice Harry Clark it was all a great adventure. He said: 'I was standing on the bridge when the submarine opened fire in earnest. A shell was aimed at the bridge, the Germans intention apparently being to place the officers hors de combat. A four-inch shell was fired, and actually went between my legs, striking the far side of the bridge. It was the narrowest shave I am ever likely to have. When I turned I found that a big hole had been made by the shell in the side of the bridge.'

Forstner met his match later that day, when he attempted to stop the Blue Funnel cargo liner *Theseus.*

The 6723-ton *Theseus* left Liverpool for Java on 27 March, and was 40 miles south-west of the Bishop Rock when she sighted the German submarine in pursuit. Forstner signalled her to stop and abandon ship, but this was no rusty old tramp. The *Theseus* belonged to the elite of the British merchant fleet, and although she was not armed, she was nearly ten times the size of *U-28*, and she had a top speed of 17 knots.

The chase lasted for three and a half hours, the *Theseus* zig-zagging away at top speed, with *U-28* in following her wake and lobbing shells after her. Forstner reluctantly abandoned the pursuit, but not until he had caused considerable damage on the Blue Funnel ship's decks. Of the seven shells fired by *U-28*, five struck the *Theseus.* Her mainmast was badly damaged, and the firemens' accommodation was wrecked. Fortunately, no one was killed or injured in the carnage.

As a result of these attacks, some British shipowners called on the Government to allow them to arm their ships. Their request was turned down on the grounds that this would turn merchant ships into men-of-war, and they could then legitimately be sunk on sight. However, the heavy loss of life involved in the sinking of the *Aguila* and *Falaba* aroused a storm of indignation throughout Britain, and the demand was made that the crews of German submarines be treated as pirates if captured.

Following her abortive attack on the *Theseus, U-28* withdrew from the Atlantic sphere, returning four months later in the summer 1915. She was then involved in a most bizarre incident that remains a subject for discussion in dockside pubs to this day.

On 30 July, 1915, *U-28* was lying in wait 9 miles south of the Fastnet Rock, where the Atlantic becomes the St. George's Channel, when the Liverpool-registered *Iberian* sailed into her ambush. The 5223-ton *Iberian,* owned by the Leyland Line, was on passage from Manchester to Boston with general cargo. What followed is described in an entry in Forstner's War Diary:

> On July 30 1915, our *U-28* torpedoed the British steamer *Iberian*, which was carrying a rich cargo across the North Atlantic. The steamer sank so swiftly that its bow stuck up almost vertically into the air. Moments later the hull of the *Iberian* disappeared. The wreckage remained beneath the water for approximately twenty-five seconds, at a depth that was clearly impossible to assess, when suddenly there was a violent explosion, which shot pieces of debris – among them a gigantic aquatic animal – out of the water to a height of approximately 80-feet.
>
> At that moment I had with me in the conning tower six of my officers of the watch, including the chief engineer, the navigator, and the helmsman. Simultaneously we all drew one another's attention to this wonder of the seas, which was writhing and struggling among the debris. We were unable to identify the creature, but all of us agreed that it resembled an aquatic crocodile, which was about 60-feet long, with four limbs resembling large webbed feet, a long, pointed tail and a head which also tapered to a point. Unfortunately we were not able to take a photograph, for the animal sank out of sight after ten or fifteen seconds.

The description of the creature Forstner and his officers claimed to have seen thrown high in the air closely resembled that of the Ichthyosaurus, a lizard or sea serpent which existed in the early Jurassic period. It is unthinkable that a man of *Kapitänleutnant* von Forstner's proven integrity would make a false entry in an official log book, so the entry must stand. The account has been investigated by experts in the field, and they have suggested that the monster, some form of prehistoric giant crocodile was swimming over the sinking *Iberian,* and was catapulted into the air when the British ship's boilers exploded. Whatever was seen from *U-28*'s conning tower was certainly very strange: one of those mysteries of the sea that will never be solved.

Georg-Günther von Forstner left *U-28* a year later to take up an appointment ashore, but his command continued with her run of successes. In all, the submarine sailed on five war patrols, sinking thirty-nine ships totalling 93,782 tons gross.

Chapter Five

The Horse Carrier

As the summer of 1915 progressed, the war on the Western Front approached stalemate. Exhausted by the initial blood-letting of 1914, which resulted in nearly a million casualties on each side, the Allied and German armies were content to consolidate their respective positions and prepare for a long and bloody war of attrition. Day and night, the battlefields of Belgium and Northern France, wrapped in endless coils of rusting barbed wire, reverberated to the thunder of a thousand howitzers and the malevolent rattle of massed machine-guns and rifles. The great adventure that had attracted millions of eager volunteer soldiers of all nations had turned into a Wagnerian nightmare from which, for so many, there was no hope of escape.

Out in the Atlantic, to the west of Ireland, there lay a very different world, where Sunday 4 July dawned fine and clear. Lulled by a ridge of high pressure stretching northwards from the Azores, the great ocean had ceased to rant and rage, and dozed content as the warm summer sun lifted from the horizon.

As the bells struck eight for the beginning of the forenoon watch, the British steamer *Anglo-Californian* was 70 miles south of the Fastnet Rock, and nearing the end of a long, but uneventful, voyage from Montreal. On her open deck, and below in the tween decks, she carried a cargo of 927 horses. The 7333-ton London-registered ship, owned by Lawther Latta & Company, and more usually engaged in the nitrate trade, was under charter to the Admiralty as a horse transport. The animals she carried, sturdy Canadian pack horses, were destined for the mud of Flanders, where man's wonderful new invention, the motor lorry, was proving to be singularly inadequate. As the war floundered in the sticky morass it had created, so more and more horses and mules were required to prevent complete stagnation. The *Anglo Californian* was already making her fifth delivery of animals from the Americas. For the crew of a ship built for the carriage of an uncomplicated bulk cargo like nitrates, animals on the hoof were an unwelcome departure.

In command of the *Anglo-Californian* was Captain Frederick Daniel Parslow, a 59-year-old Londoner, phlegmatic, independent, a good seaman and navigator; a typical British merchant captain of his day. His 44-man British crew included his son, also named Frederick, sailing as second officer in the ship. The welfare of the horses was in the hands of a team of fifty American and Canadian cattlemen.

Despite the deceptively benign mood of the sea around him, Captain Parslow was acutely aware of the dangers that threatened his ship as she approached British waters. Earlier in the year, on 4 February, the German Kaiser, incensed by the tight blockade imposed on his country's sea trade, had declared the seas around Britain a war zone, in which all Allied ships would be sunk on sight. In order to implement this threat, a force of twenty U-boats had been moved to Ostend, and ordered to carry out 'unrestricted submarine warfare'. The war on the merchant ships now began in earnest.

The Allies, clinging to the belief that, at sea at least, this was still a 'gentleman's war', fought according to the Prize Rules. They were completely taken by surprise, and appalled when the carnage began. Whereas in the early months of the war only one or two ships a week were going down, in March 1915, thirty-six Allied merchantmen of 79,369 tons, most of them British, were sunk, and six damaged. The U-boats claimed another 60,000 tons in April, sixty-three ships totalling 156,955 tons in May, and June saw the full horror of war at sea, with the sinking of 119 ships.

Among the Ostend-based U-boats was *U-39*, under the command of *Kapitänleutnant* Walther Forstmann. Built in Kiel and commissioned in January 1915, *U-39* was one of the new improved *U-31* class, having a top speed of 16½ knots on the surface, 9½ knots submerged, and a range of 4,440 miles at 8 knots on the surface. Manned by a crew of four officers and thirty-five ratings, she was armed with four 50-cm torpedo tubes, and an 88-mm deck gun. Thirty-two-year-old Walther Forstmann, who entered the Imperial German Navy as a cadet in 1900, was a cool, calculating, and sometimes ruthless, commander. He would go on to become one of Germany's top U-boat aces, but at the end of June 1915 he had accounted for only a handful of the enemy's ships, mainly off-shore fishing vessels. His fortunes were about to change.

Lying in wait off the Wolf Rock early on the morning of 3 July, Forstmann scored his first major triumph when the 3488-ton steamer *Renfrew* hove in sight, bound for the Bristol Channel port of Barry in ballast from Marseilles. Perversely, as Forstmann was to learn would be the case with most British merchant ships, Captain Stevenson refused to surrender the *Renfrew* when challenged. He turned stern-on and ran under a hail of shells from the U-boat, but was eventually forced to abandon ship. Forstmann then sank the *Renfrew*, but soon found himself the quarry, when two British destroyers, attracted by the gunfire, appeared over the horizon.

U-39 escaped by diving, resurfacing two hours later to challenge another merchantman. She was the 4355-ton *Larchmore*, inbound from Baltimore and under the command of a stubborn Welshman, Captain Isaac Jones. Seeing the submarine surface some 2 miles off, Jones attempted to escape, but *U-39*'s gunners opened up rapid fire. The shells began to hit home on the fleeing ship, and Captain Jones was injured. He stuck to his bridge, however, and the chase continued.

With one man killed and others injured, Jones was eventually obliged to stop and abandon ship. Walther Forstmann now showed his ruthless streak, continuing to fire as the *Larchmore*'s boats attempted to clear the stricken ship. Fortunately for the survivors, at this juncture a British cruiser appeared, and once again Forstmann was obliged to beat a hasty retreat, but not before he had sent the *Larchmore* to the bottom.

Having twice escaped the wrath of the Royal Navy, Walther Forstmann decided to seek a new hunting ground. When the sun came up on 4 July, *U-39* was at periscope depth off the southern coast of Ireland and, it was hoped, out of reach of the British guns. The horizon all round was empty, but Forstmann was confident that a potential victim would soon appear. His patience was rewarded when, at around 7.30 that morning, the tall masts and funnel of an eastbound steamer were sighted to the west. With a few quiet words Forstmann sent the U-boat's crew to their battle stations.

The *Anglo-Californian* was just twenty-four hours steaming from Avonmouth, her discharge port, and it was with some satisfaction that Captain Frederick Parslow paced the starboard wing of her bridge after an early breakfast. Very soon, his unarmed ship would come under the protective wing of the Royal Navy ships guarding the Western Approaches, who would relieve him of some of the heavy responsibility he had shouldered all the way across the Atlantic.

Parslow stopped his pacing, and surveyed the deck below, where the horses, quiet in their stalls, were being fed and watered by their handlers. This caused him to reflect on the progress of the war, which was not good. What little news had filtered through to the far side of the Atlantic indicated stagnation on the Western Front, with nearly five million men under arms facing each other across the barbed wire. Then there was Gallipoli, Winston Churchill's hope of an early victory, now turning into a bloody fiasco. The news from home was no better. Led by left-wing activists, workers in many of the vital industries were striking for more pay, not least in the Welsh coalfields. The miners had been out for some time, and although it was not widely known, stocks of coal were so low that the Grand Fleet was in danger of being confined to port. Parslow, who had already lost one son in France and had another lying wounded in hospital, was grateful that his remaining son, Frederick, had followed him into seafaring, and was sailing with him in the *Anglo-Californian* as second officer. He, at least, would be spared the horrors of the trenches. That might have been so, but unknown to them, the Parslows were about to face the ultimate challenge.

The *Anglo-Californian,* at 7,333 tons gross, was the first enemy ship of any great size to steam into Walther Forstmann's sights, and he was sorely tempted to remain submerged and torpedo her when she came within range. In view of the Kaiser's February declaration of 'unrestricted submarine warfare' he would have been fully justified in doing so, but after a quick sweep around the empty horizon, he decided to take the risk of surfacing to conserve his dwindling stock of torpedoes.

At 8 am, as the watch was changing on the *Anglo-Californian*'s bridge, Forstmann blew his tanks, and *U-39* broke surface 3 miles off the British ship's port beam. The submarine was sighted by an alert lookout, who raised the alarm at once. Captain Parslow crossed to the port wing of the open bridge and examined the submarine through his binoculars. He had already decided she must be German, and when she raised her ensign his worst fears were confirmed.

Frederick Parslow Senior, who had faced fire and tempest with equanimity so many times in his long seagoing career, now had to make a decision that would affect the lives of all on board. He had no means of defence against this powerful enemy, and the easy way out would have been to stop his ship and surrender. Then he thought about his sons and the sacrifice they had made in France, and the decision was made for him. He would run.

Ordering the helm hard over to starboard, Parslow showed his stern to the enemy, and gave a double ring on the engine-room telegraph, indicating he required emergency full speed.

The *Anglo-Californian,* built in 1912 by Short Brothers of Sunderland, was a no-nonsense British tramp. Owned by Lawther Latta & Company, also known as the Nitrate Producers Steamship Company, she was broad in the beam, blunt in the bow, and capable of paying her way in any trade. Her equally sturdy quadruple-expansion steam engine was designed to drive the loaded ship at an economical 12 knots, but she would never break any speed records. However, on this occasion, with only the horses on board, and the ship, in effect, part-loaded, Parslow hoped that his engineers would give him at least another 2 knots. With this, he might just be able to escape from the enemy submarine. Meanwhile, he instructed his wireless operator to attempt to contact any Royal Navy vessels in the area and ask for help.

With her firemen stripped to the waist and hurling coal into her roaring boiler furnaces, the *Anglo-Californian,* now on a southerly course, picked up speed, and slowly began to pull away from the enemy submarine. In the conning tower of *U-39*, Walther Forstmann, taken by surprise, was slow to follow, but when his wireless operator reported that the British ship was transmitting a call for help, the German commander was galvanised into action.

U-39 was designed for 16½ knots on the surface, and with her twin diesels hammering out a furious tattoo, she was soon closing the gap. It was Forstmann's intention to approach within a mile or so of the ship before putting a shot across her bows, but when his operator reported that the *Anglo-Californian* was in wireless contact with a British warship, he ordered his gunners to man the 88-mm at once.

The *Anglo-Californian*'s wireless operator had established communication with the Q-ship *Princess Ena,* an ex-London & South Western Railway Company's cross-Channel ferry. She was armed with three 12-pounder guns, and was racing to the threatened ship's aid, but as the *Princess Ena*'s top speed was only 15 knots, it was unlikely that she would arrive in time to intervene. However, as she steamed at full speed towards the *Anglo-Californian*, the Q-ship was in wireless contact with the two 28-knot destroyers *Mentor* and *Miranda,* which were close to the south.

With the knowledge that the Navy was on the way, Captain Parslow was more than ever determined not to surrender to the U-boat. He sent for his son, Second Officer Frederick Parslow, then cleared the bridge of all other personnel. Parslow Junior took the wheel, while his father, facing aft, conned the ship, keeping her at all times stern-on to the pursuing submarine, thereby presenting the smallest possible target. The chase was on in earnest.

For the next hour, Walther Forstmann was content to close the gap on his quarry, sending the occasional shell after her. At 9 o'clock, with the range down to about 1½ miles, he opened fire in earnest, aiming to cripple the *Anglo-Californian* and slow her down. As shell followed shell, dropping ever nearer to his ship, Captain Parslow responded by steering a zigzag course, sheering violently from port to starboard to spoil the German gunners' aim. For a while he was successful, but soon Forstmann's shells began to hit home. Parslow had ordered his crew to take shelter below decks, but he and his son had no protection on the *Anglo-Californian*'s open bridge, and with shell splinters scything through the air around them they were in mortal danger. The situation became so bad that they both dropped flat on the deck, young Parslow steering from the prone position, while his father raised his head from time to time to con the ship. It was *Boys' Own Annual* stuff.

At 10.30, Forstmann, close enough to make every shot count – and his gunners were doing just that – hoisted the International Code signal AH, meaning: *You should abandon your vessel as soon as possible.* This, Captain Frederick Parslow realised, was the point of no return for the *Anglo-Californian,* and the men under his command. If he continued to run, the enemy submarine, which was now very close, would systematically reduce his ship to a burning wreck, and many of those who put their faith in him would perish. With great reluctance, he rang the engines to stop and gave the order to lower the boats.

Satisfied that his quarry had stopped, and was about to abandon ship, Forstmann ceased fire. And that probably would have been the end of the matter, except that, as the boats were going down, the *Anglo-Californian*'s wireless operator appeared on the bridge and handed Captain Parslow a message. It was from the *Princess Ena,* urging Parslow not to give up, as the destroyers *Mentor* and *Miranda* were only just over the horizon, and would deal with the U-boat.

Frederick Parlslow needed no further encouragement. Ordering the boats to be brought inboard again, he sent the firemen back to their boilers, and once more rang for full speed. The chase was on again.

Walther Forstman was taken by surprise when the enemy ship he thought was within his grasp suddenly surged forward again. Surprise quickly turned to anger, and he ordered his gunners manning the 88-mm to open fire, aiming primarily for the *Anglo-Californian*'s unprotected bridge. As the submarine was now within 2000 yards, rifles and machine-guns joined in, and a veritable hurricane of shot and shell was hurled at the fleeing ship.

The chase is said to have gone on for another hour and a half, as bizarre and macabre a pursuit as any ever seen at sea. The *Anglo-Californian,* not a man in sight on her decks, her bridge apparently deserted, her helm unattended, steamed southwards, her propeller threshing the water, black smoke pouring from her funnel. After her ran *U-39*, straining every rivet in her hull, her thundering diesels leaving a trail of blue smoke hanging low on the water behind her . The two Parslows, as before, were lying prone on the deck of the bridge, young Frederick handling the wheel, while his father, occasionally getting to his feet to get a view of the enemy, called out the helm orders.

U-39's gunners had found the range, dropping their shells ever nearer to the unprotected bridge; shrapnel and bullets, ricocheting off the superstructure and deck, buzzed around the two brave men like swarms of avenging bees. The compass was smashed, several spokes of the wheel were splintered, and messages passed to the bridge by Chief Officer Harold Read reported that the hull was holed in several places and one of the holds was on fire. There was no sign of the Royal Navy.

The situation was hopeless, with only one possible end in sight, and for the second time that morning Captain Parslow decided to heave to and surrender, to give his men at least a chance to live. He rang the engine-room telegraph to stop, and once again gave the order to abandon ship.

Having already given the *Anglo-Californian* a chance to surrender and seen her make off again when he ceased fire, this time Walther Forstmann was determined not to be deceived. He passed the word to his gunners to keep up the bombardment. *U-39*, her 88-mm firing as fast as the ammunition could be passed, was now only 1,500 yards off the British ship, which was stopped and drifting. The destruction being wreaked aboard the *Anglo-Californian* was terrible to behold.

Under the direction of Chief Officer Read, the ship's four lifeboats were being lowered, an operation that, under a withering hail of shells and bullets from the U-boat, was rapidly turning into a rout. One of the davits on the port side received a direct hit, and the boat being lowered from its falls was upended, throwing its occupants into the sea. Other men panicked and threw themselves into the water, some without lifejackets, and another boat, already in the water, capsized. As the shells continued to rain down, the sea around the stricken ship was filled with struggling men, some of them dreadfully injured.

The bridge of the *Anglo-Californian* was still coming under heavy fire, and as the remaining boats pulled away from the ship a shell burst alongside Captain Parslow as he got to his feet, intending to take charge of the situation. He was blown from the bridge, and was dead before he hit the deck below. Frederick Parslow had not lived to see the arrival of the destroyers *Mentor* and *Miranda*, which as he died came racing over the horizon, guns blazing. Walther Forstmann, realising that his hour of victory had passed, took *U-39* down into the depths, and hurried away. The depth charge still being two years away, the destroyers could do no more than lob shells after the U-boat's diminishing trail of bubbles.

Due to the tenacity and bravery of her commander and his son, the *Anglo-Californian* survived to sail another day, but the cost of this achievement had been very high. Captain Parslow had lost his life, as had twenty of his men. Miraculously, Second Officer Frederick Parslow, who manned the bridge with his father throughout the chase, escaped without injury. Under the command of Chief Officer Harold Read, and escorted by HMS *Mentor* and HMS *Miranda*, the *Anglo-Californian* found refuge in Queenstown harbour early next morning. When her dead had been buried and her wounded taken ashore, she sailed for Avonmouth to land her cargo of horses, twenty of which had been killed in what, for them, must have been a frightening ordeal by gunfire.

On passage, the *Anglo-Californian* was diverted to Cardiff, where she berthed on 6 July. An interesting account of the action appeared in a local newspaper, given by a crew member, James Davies, who was described as 'a sturdy South Walian'.

> I had just had my breakfast and was walking along the deck when I sighted a grey object about 4 miles away. Shortly after I made out the conning tower of a submarine and minutes later a shot was fired at the vessel but passed over. We all rushed for lifebelts and stood in our allotted places by the boats. Shells burst all around us. Then I saw the sub signal by flags and I was told their message was, 'Get into your boats; you cannot get away.' The Captain, however, was determined not to abandon ship, whereupon another signal from the sub, 'If you do not want your lifeboats, we will shoot them away.' My boat was shot away. Then the Captain shouted 'Every man for himself', and I jumped into the water without a lifebelt and was swimming about 2½ hours before being picked up. When I was about to put my lifebelt on the Captain shouted to me to undo some ropes and I put my lifebelt down to carry out his orders. When I looked for it again it had gone. A minute later the Captain was blown to bits. I should say about 50 shots were fired at us and there were four big holes in the ship's stern. Another shot went through a ventilator on the port side and went down the hatch, while shrapnel struck the port side of the bridge. It is my belief that 11 men as well as the Captain were killed and 22 men, who had got into the boats, drowned, several being American and Canadian. About 30 horses were killed. This was my first trip to sea, but I have not had enough of it and am going to sign on the *Anglo-Californian* again.

Captain Frederick Daniel Parslow was buried in Queenstown Old Church Cemetery, near Cork, along with eight of his men who died with him in the *Anglo-Californian.* They had given their lives to save their ship, as had eleven of their shipmates whose only grave was the cold Atlantic.

Having displayed bravery of such magnitude in the face of the enemy it might have been thought that the Parslows, father and son, would have ranked amongst the great heroes of the Great War, worthy of the highest military awards. It was not to be, for then, as now, merchant seamen, even in war, were classed as civilians, and therefore not eligible for battle honours. Hitherto, ships' captains who defied the enemy had been awarded a suitably inscribed gold watch, but in this case, the Admiralty would not even agree to that. It has been said that the Admirals, fearful of setting a precedent, argued that official recognition of Captain Parslow's defiance of the enemy might invite repercussions against British merchant seamen held prisoners of war in Germany. In reality, Whitehall *was* fearful of setting a precedent, but it had nothing to do with the treatment of prisoners. The real fear was that merchant seamen should be ranked as equals with the fighting services. This would not do. Frederick Daniel Parslow, who had given his life for his ship and his country, was allowed to rest quietly and unrecognised in his Irish grave.

It was not until May 1919, with the war beginning to take its place in the history books, that justice was done to Captain Parslow and his crew. On 24 May, the following appeared in the *London Gazette*:

> Admiralty, S.W., 24th May, 1919.
> The King has been graciously pleased to approve of the posthumous award of the Victoria Cross to the undermentioned officers:
>
> Lieutenant Frederick Parslow, R.N.R.
>
> For most conspicuous gallantry and devotion to duty when in command of the Horse Transport 'Anglo Californian' on 4th July, 1915.

The report gave a description of the action, and concluded:

> Throughout the attack Lieutenant Parslow remained on the bridge, on which the enemy fire was concentrated, entirely without protection, and by his magnificent heroism succeeded, at the cost of his own life, in saving a valuable ship and cargo for the country. He set a splendid example to the officers and men of the Mercantile Marine.

It will never be known how Captain Frederick Parslow, a master mariner and shipmaster of great experience, would have viewed his apparent demotion to Temporary Lieutenant of the Royal Naval Reserve in command of a Horse Transport. He had never, at any time during his life, been a member of the Reserve, and while the *Anglo-Californian* may have been on charter to the Admiralty, she was by no stretch of the imagination a warship, auxiliary or otherwise. But this was the Admiralty's way of overcoming an embarrassing situation, and that being done, the way was clear to award the Distinguished Service Cross to Second Officer Frederick Parslow, after first generously presenting him with a commission as Sub-Lieutenant in the Royal Naval Reserve.

Frederick Parslow followed in his father's footsteps, remaining in the service of Lawther Latta, and eventually gaining command. He was master of the 5455-ton *Anglo-Australian* when she sailed in ballast from Cardiff on 8 March 1938, bound for Vancouver, via the Panama Canal. On the evening of 14 March, Captain Parslow passed the following radio message to his owners:

> PASSED FAYAL THIS AFTERNOON AT 9 KNOTS, 26 TONS BUNKER CONSUMPTION. ROUGH WEATHER, ALL WELL.

There was nothing in Parslow's message to indicate that anything was amiss. The wind in the Azores area at the time was reported to be force 8 to 9, not unusual for the North Atlantic at the time of the year. And yet, that was the last ever heard of the *Anglo-Australian* and her crew of thirty-eight. No wreckage was ever found, no bodies sighted. The sea had finally claimed Frederick Parslow, D.S.C.

The *Anglo-Californian,* which had been sold to the Cunard Steamship Company in 1915 and renamed *Vandalia*, met her end off the Smalls on 9 June 1918, when she was torpedoed and sunk by *U-96*, under the command of Heinrich Jess. So ended the career of a ship that made the history books by being commanded by the first merchant seaman ever to be awarded the Victoria Cross.

Following the debacle of the attack on the *Anglo-Californian, U-39* moved to the Mediterranean, where Walther Forstmann would reap a rich harvest of unsuspecting Allied merchantmen. Her place in the Western Approaches was taken over by *U-20*, under the command of another proven submariner, the now infamous Walther Schwieger, responsible for sinking the transatlantic liner *Lusitania* with the loss of 1,198 lives. For three days Schwieger's immediate horizon remained empty, then on 9 July, when *U-20* was idling on the surface 50 miles south-west of the Tuskar Rock, the 2750-ton British steamer *Meadowfield* hove in sight. The *Meadowfield,* commanded by Captain Thomas Dunbar, was on her way from Huelva to Glasgow with a cargo of copper ore.

Captain Dunbar was on the bridge of the *Meadowfield,* sweeping the horizon ahead with his binoculars, hoping for a first sight of the Tuskar, when he heard the crack of a gun from astern. He swung around to see a submarine on the port quarter, a puff of blue smoke drifting away from the gun on her casing. Dunbar was focusing his glasses on the submarine, when her gun banged again, and seconds later the *Meadowfield*'s bridge erupted in smoke and flame. It was a direct hit.

With other enemy shells exploding close alongside, Dunbar fought his way into the smoking ruin of the wheelhouse, where he found the helmsman, Able Seaman Neil McLean lying dead in the wreckage. The wheel and compass were still intact, and Dunbar considered running away from the U-boat, then he thought of the five passengers he carried, two of them women and two children. Resistance would almost certainly put their lives in danger, and this he could not do.

Confident that his attacker would cease fire if he was aware of women and children on board, Dunbar ordered the engines to be stopped, and then called his passengers out on deck, where they must have been clearly visible to those in the conning tower of the U-boat. This appeal to Walther Schwieger's better nature had no effect, and the shells continued to rain down on the helpless *Meadowfield.*

It could only be a matter of time before others died in the *Meadowfield,* and Thomas Dunbar had no choice but to abandon his ship. In a statement later made under oath, he reported:

> Deponent [Dunbar] ordered the boats out, and the Mate and 14 hands got into the port boat and deponent and the remainder of those on board, who included two lady passengers, one male passenger and two children, got into the second boat, which was the starboard lifeboat. As the port boat was being lowered the submarine ceased firing, but as soon as she got clear recommenced, and continued firing during the time the deponent's boat was being lowered and got away.

The two lifeboats were so crowded that it was difficult to man the oars, but they finally pulled clear of the ship, which was being slowly reduced to a smouldering wreck by Schwieger's gunners. When safely out of range, Dunbar ordered his men to lay back on their oars, and they watched their ship go down. When the waves had closed over the *Meadowfield, U-20* motored away without so much as a backward glance at the two overloaded lifeboats, now adrift more than 40 miles from the nearest land. It seemed that Walther Schwieger, who had entered this war determined to play by the rules, was already so hardened by the power he wielded that he was losing all respect for the common decencies by which seamen of all nations live their lives.

U-20 remained on station covering the entrance to the St. George's Channel, and later that day Walther Schwieger's patience was rewarded by the appearance of the *Ellesmere*, a 1170-ton steamer commanded by Captain C.W. Heslop. The *Ellesmere* was 48 miles off the Smalls, bound Liverpool, when she sighted *U-20* some 2 miles off on her starboard bow.

As was now routine in British ships, Captain Heslop immediately presented his stern to the U-boat, and attempted to run away. Predictably, Schwieger opened fire with his deck gun, carpeting the retreating ship with shells. His second shell carried away the davits of the starboard lifeboat, quickly followed by four others that slammed into the superstructure.

Heslop held his nerve, and called for more speed, but the little ship's engine, already pushed beyond its absolute limits, could give no more. *U-20* was gaining rapidly, and more of her shells were finding their mark. One went home on the bridge, reducing the wooden structure to matchwood, killing one man and severely injuring another. With no place left from which to navigate, Captain Heslop stopped the ship and lowered his ensign.

On this occasion, Walther Schwieger held his fire while Heslop got his men away in the boats. The *Ellesmere* was then torpedoed and sunk, her surviving crew being picked up by the armed trawler *Osprey II*. In his report to the Admiralty, Captain Heslop, echoing the cry of many of his fellow shipmasters, declared that if the *Ellesmere* had been fitted with a stern gun, she would have lived to sail another day. To be fair to the Admiralty, they were doing their best to arm the merchantmen, but such was the demand from France for guns, that by the end of July 1915 only a few hundred of the most vulnerable ships had been armed.

Chapter Six

The Ordeal of the Clans

Since the days of Nelson, the Royal Navy had reigned supreme over the waters of the Mediterranean. With the narrows of the Gibraltar Strait, the mid-way island of Malta and the Egyptian coast all firmly under British control, few hostile surface ships would dare to venture into this landlocked sea. Then, out in the deep Atlantic, another new page of history was turned.

On 1 May, 1915, the 35,500-ton Cunard liner *Lusitania* sailed from New York, bound for Liverpool. She carried a crew of 700 and 1,257 passengers, 124 of whom were citizens of the United States of America. Her cargo, carried in two holds in the fore part of the ship, was manifested as copper ingots, auto parts, dental equipment, machinery, sheet brass, cheese, beef, bacon and confectionery. Not manifested were 4,200 cases of small-calibre rifle ammunition, 1,250 cases of artillery shells and eighteen cases of percussion fuses, the later containing highly explosive fulminate of mercury. It has since been claimed – but never proven – that the *Lusitania* actually had on aboard some six million rounds of ammunition, bullets and shells, and 323 bales of gun cotton. Some sources say that she also carried six million dollars in gold bullion in her strongroom.

With 26 knots at his disposal, the *Lusitania*'s master, Captain William Turner, was confident that no enemy could harm his great four-funnelled vessel as she ploughed across the Atlantic. The Admiralty had warned him that U-boats were active off the southern coast of Ireland, but as he was to rendezvous with the cruiser HMS *Juno* in the Western Approaches, which would then escort the *Lusitania* to the Mersey, Turner's mind was as at rest as it would ever be.

The 'U-boat activity' detected by the Admiralty was in fact Walther Schwieger's *U-20*, then patrolling to the north-west of the Fastnet. Since his initial foray into the English Channel in January 1915,

Schwieger had enjoyed moderate success. Returning to sea in March, he combed the waters from Liverpool Bay to the Longships, sinking three British merchantmen with a total tonnage of 9,006. Still in *U-20*, he appeared again in May off the southern coast of Ireland, where on the 5th and 6th he sank two trawlers and two 5000-ton cargo ships. His intention then was to pass through the St. George's Channel into the Irish Sea. He was unaware of the approach of the *Lusitania*.

U-20 was briefly sighted off the Fastnet on the morning of the 5th, and the Admiralty, fearing for the safety of the 20-year-old *Juno*, which had a top speed of only 18 knots, ordered the cruiser to return to Queenstown. Two destroyers were called in to take her place as escort to the *Lusitania*, but they failed to arrive.

On the evening of the 6th, Captain Turner, then approaching the Fastnet from the west, was alerted to the danger, and fully expected to be diverted north-about Ireland, but the order did not come. Consequently, the *Lusitania* and *U-20* were then on similar courses to pass south of the Fastnet and on into the St. George's Channel. Needless to say, the 26-knot liner was rapidly overtaking the U-boat.

Walther Schwieger sighted the *Lusitania* overhauling him on the afternoon of the 7th. He submerged, and waited at periscope depth for the British ship to come within range.

It required only one torpedo to sink the *Lusitania*. This struck her forward of the bridge, close to where the ammunition was stowed, resulting in a devastating explosion that blew a huge hole in her side. The great liner sank in eighteen minutes, taking 1,198 of her total complement of 1,957 with her. Of the 785 passengers who lost their lives 124 were American. The reaction in the United States was a mixture of shock and indignation. Berlin, fearful that America might be dragged into the war, ordered the German Admirals to move some of their U-boats into the Mediterranean, where there was less chance of American citizens being involved.

A small force of Austrian submarines, based in Pola at the northern end of the Adriatic, were already operating against Allied ships supporting the ill-fated Dardanelles campaign, but with little effect. Then, between August and November, 1915, five German boats slipped through the Straits of Gibraltar to join the Austrians.

The German Mediterranean Flotilla consisted of *U-33*

(*Kapitänleutnant* Konrad Gansser), *U-34* (*Kapitänleutnant* Claus Rücker), *U-35* (*Korvettenkapitän* Waldemar Kophamel), *U-38* (*Kapitänleutnant* Max Valentiner) and *U-39* (*Kapitänleutnant* Walther Forstmann). The boats were all of the new 'Thirties' class; 870 tons displacement, with a surface speed of 16½ knots, and armed with four 50-cm torpedo tubes and a 105-mm deck gun. They were stationed at the Austro-Hungarian naval base at Cattaro on the Adriatic coast of Montenegro, and their primary role was to attack Allied shipping passing through the Mediterranean to and from the Suez Canal. The introduction of these U-boats to the Mediterranean paid handsome dividends. By the end of November they had sunk sixty-five Allied merchantmen, totalling 213,855 tons gross.

Captain Harry Southward, commanding the British steamer *Clan Macleod*, was well aware of the increasing dangers in this hitherto untroubled sea, and was taking what precautions were open to him. The 4796-ton cargo liner, owned by Clan Line Steamers Ltd. of Glasgow and London, was homeward bound from Chittagong and Calcutta to London and Dundee with a full cargo of jute and tea. She was not armed, so could offer little resistance if attacked. Captain Southward's only weapon was vigilance, and to this end he could do no more than post extra lookouts, which he did.

On the morning of 1 December, the *Clan Macleod* was some 100 miles east-south-east of Malta and steering to make a landfall on the island. At 7.45, the Chief Officer, who had the watch on the bridge, was in the process of writing up his log. When he walked aft to read the thermometers, he noticed a smudge of smoke on the port quarter. Captain Southward was also on the bridge, and after examining the smoke through their binoculars both men concluded that they were being overtaken by another ship, possibly, by its low profile, a destroyer.

The routine of the morning went on, the watch was changed, and then, at about five minutes past eight, the crack of a gun was heard, and a shell hit the water close astern of the *Clan Macleod.*

Southward was still unable to identify the overtaking vessel, but this was certainly no friend. He immediately put the stranger stern-on, and rang for more speed. The engine room was made aware of the situation, and all available firemen were sent below to man the furnaces. The *Clan Macleod*'s triple-expansion engine responded enthusiastically, and the ship surged forward. Harry Southward was not about to give up his ship easily.

The British ship's attacker, now clearly seen to be a submarine, was closing in on the port quarter, firing as she came. Southward was zig-zagging furiously, and the enemy's shells were dropping wide. For the time being, it seemed that the *Clan Macleod* would survive, but no matter how hard her sweating firemen hurled coal into her roaring boiler furnaces, she was still a heavily-laden cargo ship, and a fraction over her normal 12 knots was all she could manage. Relentlessly, the submarine – it was Konrad Gansser's *U-33* – was overtaking, and by 10 o'clock was within half a mile, and scoring hits on the *Clan Macleod*. Captain Southward later reported:

> About this time I realised that I could not save the steamer, hoisted international signal of surrender, stopped the engines, and rounded to, bringing the submarine on the starboard side. The crew were sent to boat stations, but to my surprise the submarine started to shell the bridge, doing considerable damage. I was struck by the first shell. He then started to shell the boats and boat crews, killing nine men, wounding six (three fatally), and smashing the starboard boats. During this shelling the crew had all been sent to the port boats, which were manned and lowered without any casualty. After the boats were lowered the chief officer and myself had a look around the decks, but could not see anyone alive, so we then left the steamer.
>
> After the boats left the steamer, the gun of the submarine was pointed towards the lifeboat and the commander shouted for me. As the second officer told him I was in the other boat, he turned the gun away and told him he need not be afraid. The submarine was flying the German naval flag. When the other boat appeared in view of the submarine, I was ordered to go on board. I did so, and found the commander and lieutenant in a furious rage with me because I had not stopped sooner. The commander rushed down from the conning tower, shook his fist in my face, and said, 'Why did you not stop?' I replied that I wanted to save my ship. He then said, 'Why did you not stop when I fired?' I replied that my instructions were to escape if possible. The commander said,

'Never mind your instructions; you must obey my orders.' I replied that I did not know anything about his orders. His next remark was, 'I can shoot you as a franc-tireur. I said, 'I don't think so.' He said, 'You are assisting my enemy.' I replied, 'I am your enemy.'

The commander than said, 'Had you stopped when I fired three shots you would not have had this,' pointing to a wound in my hand. I replied that it was my misfortune.

I was then ordered back into the boat, and the submarine at once proceeded to sink the steamer by shellfire. After firing a couple of shots into every compartment, he returned to the boats and I was again ordered on board. I was asked for my instructions, which I said I had destroyed. I was also asked for the register, and told him that was on board the steamer.

The lieutenant dressed my hand, pointed out that my foot was wounded, and gave me packets of dressing for my foot and for some of the wounded. Before I left the submarine he told me to inform all captains I met that they would be fired upon if they tried to escape. I told him that that would be their business and had nothing to do with me. He also asked me the position, and I said I had not had a position for some time.

Konrad Gansser's arrogant belligerence contrasted sharply with Captain Harry Southward's coolness in the face of adversity. In firing on the *Clan Macleod*'s lifeboats, killing twelve men who had already surrendered to him, the German commander was guilty of a heinous war crime. His actions were also a clear indication of the way the submarine war was going.

U-33 moved on, and Southward, and his men, crowded into two boats, one lifeboat and a small cutter, were left to watch the sad end of their ship. The *Clan Macleod,* on fire from stem to stern, and holed below the waterline, made a dignified exit, going down on an even keel, leaving only a cloud of steam and smoke and a few scraps of blackened wreckage to mark her grave.

When the ship had gone, Southward searched for other survivors, finding only two injured men, Egyptian stowaways who were ruing the day they concealed themselves aboard the *Clan Macleod.* The two boats, the lifeboat carrying fifty men and the cutter nineteen, then set sail for Malta. The lifeboat was sighted by the westbound Liverpool steamer *Lord Cromer* on the following evening, and the survivors were landed at Algiers on 5 December. The cutter's crew were less fortunate, spending three days adrift before being picked up and landed in Malta. One of the injured men died of his wounds after rescue, and Captain Southward spent several months in hospital recovering from his injuries.

Throughout the remainder of December, the U-boats of the Mediterranean Flotilla continued to enjoy success in this new sphere of operations, culminating on the 30th of the month in the sinking of another of Clan Line Steamers' fleet, the 4823-ton *Clan Macfarlane.*

The *Clan Macfarlane,* which first took to the water in 1898, was a relic of the early days of the Suez Canal. Dues for transiting the canal were charged on the breadth of the ship at the upper deck, and one of the shipowners' answers was to build ships with a narrow upper deck, which was no more than a trunk for the cargo holds. These were known as 'whaleback' or 'turret' ships. Their hulls being box-like in construction, they were good cargo carriers, but inevitably slow and cumbersome. They also had a tendency to capsize without warning. The *Clan Macfarlane* was one of thirty turret ships built for the Clan Line. Due to judicious loading, she had lasted well, but at seventeen years old she rarely exceeded 10 knots, given a fair wind.

The *Clan Macfarlane* had sailed from Birkenhead on 16 December, down to her winter marks with a general cargo of 7,400 tons for Bombay. Her master was Captain James Whyte Swanston, who commanded a crew of eleven British officers and sixty-three Lascar ratings.

The voyage had gone well, Malta being passed on Christmas Day, and noon sights on the 30th put the *Clan Macfarlane* 60 miles south of Cape Martello, the southernmost point of the island of Crete. The weather was fine, and the ship was making a steady 10 knots. Having passed through the dangerous waters around Malta without incident, and with Alexandria, where the *Clan Macfarlane* was to call for coal bunkers, only thirty-six hours steaming away, Captain Swanston had good cause for optimism. There was, in fact, a general feeling of all being well when, at 4 pm, Chief Officer Fred Hawley climbed the bridge ladder to take up his watch. As he reached the top of the ladder and set foot on the well-scrubbed teak deck, the quiet of the afternoon was shattered by a loud explosion, and the *Clan Macfarlane* staggered and came slowly to a halt.

The *Clan Macfarlane*'s unseen attacker was *U-38*. Under the command of 32-year-old *Kapitänleutnant* Max Valentiner, she had entered the Mediterranean on 3 November 1915. Living up to the reputation he had already built in the Atlantic, Valentiner quickly made his mark by sinking the 3584-ton British steamer *Woodfield* 40 miles south-east of Gibraltar, this only a few hours after slipping through the Straits. Before the month was out, Valentiner had sunk another fourteen ships, totalling 48,000 tons gross. He also caused a major diplomatic incident by sinking two Italian ships while *U-38* was flying the Austria-Hungary flag, Italy at that time not being at war with Austria-Hungary. Moreover, forty Americans were lost with these ships, which immediately resulted in such a threatening protest from the United States Government that Berlin ordered the U-boats in the Mediterranean to abandon the 'sink without warning' policy.

Undeterred, after a brief lay-up in Cattaro, Max Valentiner resumed operations towards the end of December, and confirmed his contempt for international protocol by sinking without warning the P&O passenger liner *Persia*.

The 7974-ton *Persia*, commanded by Captain W.H.S. Hall, sailed from Tilbury, bound for Bombay, via the Suez Canal, on 18 December. Her total complement was 518, made up of 317 crew members and 201 passengers, many of whom were women and children. She had on board a full general cargo, and she mounted a small gun on her poop for defensive purposes.

Having made calls at Gibraltar, Marseilles and Malta, the *Persia* was passing south of Crete on the afternoon of 30 December, when she appeared in the crosswires of *U-38*'s periscope. Remaining submerged, Max Valentiner fired a single torpedo, which hit the liner in her stokehold on the port side. The violent explosion of the torpedo was closely followed by a second explosion as the boilers blew up. Her hull was laid wide open to the sea. The *Persia* sank within five minutes, taking with her 121 passengers and 213 of her crew, including Captain Hall.

The 167 who survived the brutal end of the *Persia* escaped in four lifeboats, and were picked up by the minesweeper HMS *Mallow* at around 7 o'clock on the following evening. *U-38* remained in the vicinity of the sinking, waiting for her next victim to come along. No more than two and a half hours elapsed before the *Clan Macfarlane* walked into Max Valentiner's ambush. A single torpedo stopped her in her tracks.

Captain James Swanston and Chief Officer Fred Hawley, were on the bridge of the *Clan Macfarlane* when the torpedo hit, and Swanston immediately sent Hawley on deck to make a quick assessment of the damage. This showed that the ship had been hit in way of No.5 hold, where a huge hole had been blasted in the ship's side. The sea was pouring into the hold, and cargo was floating out through the gaping hole. The slope of the deck showed that the *Clan Macfarlane* was sinking by the stern.

Returning to the bridge, Hawley reported to Captain Swanston, who instructed him to lower the lifeboats to the level of the harbour deck and assemble the crew ready for boarding. Swanston and Hawley then searched the accommodation to make sure no one had been left behind. Only then did Swanston give the order to abandon ship.

The sea being relatively calm, the six boats were lowered without incident, the last boat leaving the ship's side shortly after 5 o'clock, just as the sun was setting. There was still a faint possibility that the *Clan Macfarlane* would stay afloat, and Swanston took the boats half a mile to the north, where they lay to await whatever might transpire.

After half an hour, with darkness setting in, the survivors heard a loud rushing sound, and *U-38* surfaced close on the other side of their doomed ship. Men appeared on the submarine's casing, and she opened fire with her 105-mm deck gun. Six shells were fired in quick succession, each of which went home on the *Clan Macfarlane.* And that was the last James Swanston and his men saw of their ship. The night had closed in to hide her last death throes.

Not one to cry for a lost cause, Captain Swanston brought the six boats together, and discussed a plan of action with his officers. Masts were stepped, sails hoisted, and, lashed together in line astern, the small flotilla set out for Crete, which lay some 60 miles to the north.

There was a light westerly wind blowing, and with sails close-hauled, the boats made fair progress. By mid-afternoon a smudge of land was sighted ahead. This could not be identified, but the survivors were by now cold and wet, ready to grasp at the slightest straw. It was decided that the dark shadow on the horizon – and it was no more than that –

must be the mountains of Crete, and the sagging morale in the boats began to recover. An early end to the ordeal was anticipated.

Then, cruelly, in the early hours of next morning, the first day of 1916, the wind dropped right away, and the boats lay rocking in the swell, their sails hanging lifeless. With the agreement of his officers, Captain Swanston decided to separate the boats and proceed under oars.

Handling the heavy wooden lifeboats under oars was backbreaking work, but some slow progress was made. Fortunately, at 10 o'clock that morning, a light wind sprang up, and it was possible to proceed under sail again. When darkness closed in that night, all six boats were lashed together again, with the Captain's boat leading.

Captain Swanston was aware of a current flowing to the east off Crete, and he was not surprised when, at sunrise on the 2nd, the eastern end of the island, possibly Cape Sidero, came in sight. Unfortunately, at the same time the wind started to blow hard, and the tops of the waves were breaking. There was no possibility of landing on the south coast, so Swanston decided to shorten sail and attempt to get in the lee of the eastern end of Crete, where a sheltered beach might be found.

By this time the *Clan Macfarlane*'s survivors had been in their boats for three days and three nights; they were suffering from exposure and exhausted by the constant struggle to stay alive. In the late afternoon their troubles increased when two towropes carried away in the rough seas, and the boats in charge of Third Officer Whyte and Third Engineer Ballingall drifted away into the gathering gloom. Captain Swanston at once cast off his boat and went after them, leaving Chief Officer Hawley in charge of the remaining three boats.

The weather had by now deteriorated further, and Hawley decided to heave to for the night. The hours that followed took on a nightmarish quality, with the waves breaking right over the boats, and the men were forced to keep bailing to stay afloat. It was all too much for six of the Lascar seaman, who died of exposure during the night.

Captain Swanston's boat rejoined at daylight on the 3rd, having failed to make contact with the two missing boats. Third Officer Whyte and Third Engineer Ballingall and their crews were never seen again. Swanston had also lost three Lascars during the night.

The remaining four boats were made fast to each other again, and they again set off, but after a few hours battling the wind and waves it was realised that the Fourth Engineer's boat was sinking. It was abandoned and its crew transferred to the other boats. No sooner had the transfer been made, than Captain Swanston's boat lost its rudder. Chief Officer Hawley then took over in the lead of the procession, while Swanston, using a steering oar, tagged on astern.

That night, the survivors' fourth night at sea, the wind rose to a full gale, and the boats were all in danger of being swamped. Swanston and Hawley decided to lay to with sea anchors out, and throughout the night the boats were battered by the breaking seas. It was necessary to bail continuously to avoid the boats being swamped, and by the time daylight came on the 4th, the crews were totally exhausted. Captain Swanston's boat was again missing, and although Hawley caught sight of it several times during the day, when darkness closed in again he lost sight of it. Captain James Whyte Swanston, his boat and his crew were not seen again.

There was no let-up in the weather, and the two remaining boats lay hove to all night, battered by the waves and making no progress in any direction. Early on the 5th, one boat was wallowing with her gunwales awash, and it was obvious that it would soon sink. Hawley made the decision to abandon it, and all the thirty-one remaining survivors were crowded into the last boat. They were packed so tight that it was almost impossible to handle the boat. The rudder was lost, and for the rest of that terrible night Fred Hawley rode the waves with a steering oar, fighting to stop the boat broaching to, for if she went beam on to the seas they would all drown.

Then they began to die. The second cook went on the morning of the 6th, followed by a deck boy and a fireman in the afternoon. There was no fuss; they just lost the will to live, and slipped quietly into oblivion. During the night, two more Lascars succumbed, and for the first time Hawley began to wonder if any of them would survive. Then, miraculously, the wind eased, and at last they were able to steer a rough course. Alexandria lay only 250 miles to the east, and Hawley decided to hoist all sail, and run before the wind.

Two more men died the next day, and as the wind had shifted and freshened again, even Fred Hawley was losing hope. Then, when all seemed lost, a ship was seen to be bearing down on them. She was the British steamer *Crown of Aragon,* bound for Malta, and thanks to the vigilance of her lookouts the survivors were soon wrapped in blankets and sipping hot drinks.

Of the *Clan Macfarlane*'s total crew of seventy-eight, only twenty-four, six Europeans and eighteen Lascars, were landed in Malta, two more of the survivors having died on the passage.

Clan Line had a number of refrigerated vessels which carried frozen mutton and wool from Australia via the Cape of Good Hope. One such was the 5816-ton *Clan Mactavish,* which sailed from Fremantle under the command of Captain W.N. Oliver on 9 December 1915. She carried a cargo of wool, frozen mutton, copper, wheat, leather and tinned meats. Having rounded the Cape, she called at Dakar, where a 6-pounder quick-firing gun was mounted on her after deck, and two Royal Navy gunners were shipped to man and maintain the gun.

This was an early gesture by the Admiralty to fit defensive armament to British merchant ships. And it was no more than a gesture. A 6-pounder is a pathetically small gun, and this one was so mounted on the *Clan Mactavish*'s port quarter that it gave no cover to the starboard side.

The *Clan Mactavish* sailed from Dakar on 13 January, and Captain Oliver set course to pass outside the Canary Islands. He passed west of the island of Palma early on the morning of the 16th, and late that afternoon sighted two ships on the port bow, apparently crossing ahead. Oliver examined them through his binoculars and decided they were no threat, probably from South America and bound in through the Straits of Gibraltar.

Under the Steering and Sailing Rules, which govern the conduct of ships at sea, the *Clan Mactavish* was the 'stand on ship', and it was the duty of the other ships to get out of her way. Captain Oliver held his course.

By the time dusk began to close in, the nearer of the two ships was very close, and quite obviously was not going to give way to the *Clan Mactavish.* In order to avoid a collision Captain Oliver was forced to alter to port and go under her stern. As the two ships passed, the stranger's morse lamp flashed, 'What ship is that?' Oliver, whose suspicions were now aroused, replied by questioning the other ship's identity. The reply came back, 'the *Trader* of Liverpool.' As Oliver was familiar with the *Trader,* one of Harrisons' of Liverpool, his suspicions were satisfied, and he gave his ship's name. Little did he realise that he was about to be molested by the German armed merchant cruiser *Möwe.*

The two ships were now steaming on parallel courses, about 300 yards apart, and minutes later the *Möwe*'s lamp flashed, 'Stop at once! I am a German cruiser.'

Captain Oliver calculated the odds, and as he could see no guns visible on the German ship, he decided to try to run away. He sent his gunners to man the 6-pounder, gave a double ring for emergency full speed, and ordered his wireless operator to send out a call for help.

When the raider realised that the *Clan Mactavish* was not going to surrender, she dropped her canvas screens, exposing her guns, four 150-mm and one 105-mm, huge weapons in comparison with Oliver's puny 6-pounder.

The first shot went across the British ship's bows, and when this had no effect, the *Möwe*'s guns spoke in earnest. A shell exploded on the *Clan Mactavish*'s foredeck, killing the forward lookout man, and this was followed by a rain of shells directed at the bridge, one of which crashed into the stokehold, killing seven Lascar firemen. Others hit the bridge accommodation, destroying two officers' cabins, and reducing the ship's gig to matchwood. The end came when the main steam pipe was hit, and the *Clan Mactavish* slowed to a halt. Captain Oliver, already having eighteen men dead and six wounded, was left with no alternative but to cease fire and surrender his ship.

Oliver and his surviving men were transferred to the *Möwe,* from the deck of which they were sad witnesses to the destruction of their ship by scuttling charges. Most of the crew of the *Clan Mactavish* were landed in a neutral American port, but Captain Oliver and his two gunners returned to Germany with the *Möwe,* and ended up in a prisoner of war camp.

It would have been no consolation to Oliver, as he rotted in his prison camp, to learn that his cry for help transmitted by the *Clan Mactavish*'s wireless operator ('I am in imminent danger of capture by the enemy in lat. 30° 40' N, long. 17° 10' W – *Clan Mactavish.*') was received in the wireless office of HMS *Exeter,* but not passed on to the bridge. As the result of this omission, the *Möwe* continued her piractical career unchecked.

An unnamed officer of the *Möwe* later wrote:

> The *Clan Mactavish* – as we later found out the ship was named – had cleared her after deck for action and was aiming a heavy gunfire at us, of course, without any result. This was sufficient for Count Dohna to proceed again parallel to the steamer and rake her, not caring where our shots landed. Every salvo hit the mark. Soon we heard explosions on board and the ship was in a helpless position. Then her captain morsed: 'We stop,' at the same time ceasing fire. The *Möwe*'s guns were also silenced, and our prize crew went aboard the ship. The men were taken off her, and a Captain and two sailors of the British Navy, who were in civilian clothes, added to the number of our prisoners of war.
>
> The value of our prize was more than eleven million marks because the cargo consisted of skins, cotton and meat. The steamer had been on the way from Sydney to London. Here in the middle of the ocean her trip was unexpectedly halted. At 9 o'clock that evening the *Clan Mactavish*, 4693 tons, was under the Atlantic. Of the seventy natives of India on board the ship, some had been killed by gunfire, to our regret, and four others died shortly afterward. The night was quiet, and the natives buried their countrymen in the ocean. We now had more than five hundred people on board.

Captain Oliver's determination to resist capture made a deep impression on the *Möwe*'s commander, *Korvettenkapitän* Count Dohna-Schlodien. He wrote in his log:

> When the master reports to me, I take him severely to task for his criminal behaviour. The master states that he disclaims all personal responsibility – he had received orders from his Government to get his ship through to England. Furthermore he had been provided with a gun, and he regarded it as his obvious duty to use it . . . I must own that I appreciate the loyalty with which this old Scottish seadog stuck to his principles, and I shook him by the hand.

Captain Harry Southward, having recovered from his ordeal when the *Clan Macleod* was sunk under him in December, 1915, returned to sea, and served throughout the rest of the war. In March 1918, he was in command of the 4710-ton *Clan Macdougall*, homeward bound in convoy. She had sailed from Naples on the afternoon of the 14th, and at 7 o'clock on the morning of the 15th was 60 miles south of Sardinia when she was torpedoed and sunk by Hans von Mellenthin in *U-49*. Captain Southward and thirty-two others lost their lives.

Chapter Seven

Out of the Frying Pan

Contrary to popular belief and the unwavering optimism of the holiday travel brochures, the Mediterranean does not always resemble a millpond basking under a cloudless blue sky. Winter happens here – just as it does elsewhere throughout the globe – and all too often this largely landlocked sea can stage vicious and prolonged gales fit to match anything met with in the North Atlantic. This applies particularly to the eastern approaches to the island of Malta, where the comparatively shallow water produces a short, steep sea sufficient to give any deep-loaded ship a very uncomfortable ride.

In the opinion of the majority of her crew, the British ship *Coquet* committed an unpardonable sin when she sailed from the Spanish port of Terrevieja on New Year's Eve, 31 December, 1915. The London-registered *Coquet,* owned by the Mercantile Steamship Company and commanded by Captain Arnold Groom, was loaded with 6,200 tons of bulk salt, and bound for Rangoon via the Suez Canal. Built in 1904 in a Middlesbrough shipyard, she was a typical British tramp, a slow plodder, but of solid construction and powered by a reliable engine. Captain Groom anticipated arriving at Port Said on about 7 January, and allowing a full day for the canal transit, expected to reach Rangoon at the end of the month.

The ship being at sea, the New Year was ushered in with appropriate restraint aboard the *Coquet.* The celebrations were limited to the traditional ringing of sixteen bells at midnight – eight for the old year, and eight for the new – while only those off watch raised their whisky glasses.

Three days later, the *Coquet* was passing south of Malta, wallowing awkwardly in a heavy beam swell, which indicated there was bad weather in the offing. Captain Groom was keeping a close eye on the steadily falling barometer, and clinging to the hope that they would reach the protection of the breakwaters of Port Said before the worst of the blow hit them. He was also uncomfortably aware that another enemy was about to show his hand.

Before sailing from Terrevieja, Groom had been well briefed on the increasing threat posed by German U-boats in these waters. The German Mediterranean Flotilla, now based in Constantinople, Pola and Cattaro, had been substantially reinforced, and with British and French naval forces heavily committed in the Dardanelles there was little protection on offer for merchant ships sailing alone. The deep-loaded *Coquet* was slow, manoeuvred like a Thames barge, and was unarmed. Under the circumstances, Captain Groom had taken what precautions he could, which did not amount to much. A lookout was posted in the bows day and night, the two lifeboats were swung out ready for launching, and crew members had been warned to keep their lifejackets handy.

U-34, under the command of *Kapitänleutnant* Claus Rücker, had entered the Mediterranean in August, 1914, and in four busy months had sunk over 46,000 tons of Allied merchant shipping. Rücker had found his last victim only twenty-four hours after the *Coquet* set out from Terrevieja. She was the 9395-ton British ship *Glengyle,* sunk some 240 miles to the east of Malta. Although she was armed, the *Glengyle* was laden down with 14,000 tons of produce from the Far East, and, caught unawares, fell an easy victim to Rücker's unannounced torpedo. Her loss would be sorely felt in the markets of London.

After the *Glengyle, U-34* remained to the east of Malta, awaiting the next enemy ship to come along. The weather was foul, with rain squalls, angry seas, and a short, steep swell. Clinging to the compass binnacle in his wildly oscillating conning tower, Claus Rücker began to regret his posting to *'das schöne Mittelmeer'*, and found himself longing for the wide open spaces of the broad Atlantic.

On Tuesday, 4 January, the *Coquet* had reached a position 200 miles to the east of Malta, and although still plagued by a persistent northerly swell, was making good progress. There was a moderate north-westerly blowing, and the clouds were lowering ominously, but Captain Groom remained confident of picking up the Port Said pilot before dark on the 7th. Just before noon, Groom was in the officers' saloon discussing fresh provisions required with the Chief Steward, when he heard the distinct crack of a heavy calibre gun.

Groom sprinted for the bridge, and was taking the ladder two steps at a time, when two more shots rang out followed by a shrill whistling as shells passed over his head. Two tall waterspouts erupted on the *Coquet*'s starboard bow.

When Groom reached the wheelhouse, the Third Officer pointed out the unmistakeable silhouette of a submarine on the port quarter. At almost the same moment, the lookout reported another submarine on the port bow.

Confronted by only one enemy submarine, Arnold Groom would certainly have been tempted to run away. But to defy two U-boats armed with deck guns and torpedoes would be to invite a messy annihilation of his unarmed tramp. Groom stopped his engines, and ordered the lifeboats to be made ready for lowering. That done, he went below to burn his confidential papers and books in the galley stove.

Returning to the bridge, Groom found that one of the U-boats had disappeared. The remaining enemy submarine, which was Claus Rücker's *U-34*, was now flying the two-letter flag signal 'A.G', which in any language carries the clear message, 'You should abandon your vessel as quickly as possible'.

The wind was rising, stirring up a boisterous sea, which combined with the heavy swell to make putting the *Coquet*'s two lifeboat's into the water an extremely difficult operation. However, when danger threatens, the urge for survival conquers all difficulties. Within minutes, both boats, containing all thirty-one crew, were pulling away from the ship's side. No sooner were they clear than *U-34*'s deck gun opened up, hurling a vicious fusillade of shells at the helpless *Coquet*. The German gunners' aim was either upset by the rolling of their boat, or they needed more training, for of the eight shells they fired, not one scored a hit on the British ship.

Claus Rücker moved in closer, and hailed the boats to come alongside. The submarine was lying low in the water, her casings being awash most of the time, and bringing the oar-propelled boats alongside her was, in Captain Groom's words, 'a dangerous procedure', in the circumstances a gross understatement.

It was useless for Groom to prevaricate, for Rücker was becoming more and more frustrated every time he screamed the order to come alongside. By dint of some excellent boat work, which did great credit to the discipline and ability of the *Coquet*'s crew, both lifeboats were laid alongside *U-34*. Captain Groom was then ordered aboard the submarine, where he was interrogated at length by Rücker. Groom gave little away, posing as a not very bright British tramp master, which was probably in line with Rücker's opinion of him.

While Groom was in *U-34*'s conning tower under interrogation, armed men boarded the lifeboats and forced them to return to the *Coquet*. There the survivors were allowed to gather up a few personal belongings while the boarding party ransacked the ship for anything that might be of use to *U-34*. Charts, binoculars, books, chronometers and provisions were loaded into a small jolly boat that had been left hanging from the falls. Scuttling charges were then laid in the *Coquet*'s forward holds, and all three boats left. As they rowed across to the U-boat, two loud explosions were heard, and the doomed ship began to settle by the head. Five minutes later, she lifted her stern high in the air and slid into the depths. Another ship and her cargo had been lost to the Allied cause.

When the *Coquet*'s lifeboats returned to *U-34*, they were both leaking badly, some of their planks having been sprung by the battering received while being thrown against the side of the ship and the U-boat. Seeing this, Captain Groom dropped his dimwit act, and proceeded to read the riot act to Claus Rücker, informing him that it would be nothing short of murder to leave thirty-one men adrift in leaking boats in deteriorating weather, and so many miles from land. Rücker laughed in his face, promising that he would spare the next Allied ship that came along, and send her to their rescue. With that, the British lifeboats were then stripped of their charts and every scrap of paper that might be used to draw up a crude chart. This was to condemn the British survivors to drift directionless in the rising seas. Groom was ordered to take his place with his men, and the boats were cast off. *U-34* then motored off into the gathering dusk.

The prospects for the survival of Captain Groom and his men were not good. Their boats were so badly damaged as to be near breaking up, and required constant bailing. They had no navigational charts, no means of establishing their exact position, which Groom estimated to be some 200 miles east-south-east of Malta, a similar distance from the Greek islands to the north-east, and the coast of Cyrenaica to the south.

The heavy wooden ship's boats of the day were notoriously difficult to handle under sail, and with the wind in the north-west, attempting to make either Malta or the Greek islands was out of the question. The only way to go was south, running before the wind. The coast of North Africa was largely unknown territory, and reported to be inhabited by some very fierce tribesmen. The consolation was that, in heading south, the boats would be sailing across the tracks of ships bound to and from Port Said. It seemed more than likely that they would be rescued by a passing ship before they reached the coast.

Captain Groom consulted his officers, who agreed with his assessment of the situation. Masts were stepped, sails hoisted, and with Groom in charge of one boat, and Chief Officer Griffiths the other, they set off for Africa.

With the wind astern, the boats made good speed, and much to the surprise and delight of the survivors, they sighted their first ship just as night was closing in. She was westbound, and quite close, but although the boats burned red distress flares, their would-be rescuer steamed past without giving the slightest sign of having seen them.

This was a crushing blow to the morale of the survivors, and their spirits fell lower when the wind increased in force as the night came on. Seas began to break over the gunwales of the crowded boats, and soon the men were up to their thighs in icy water. As the night wore on, cold, wet and thoroughly miserable, some of them reached the point where they were ready to give up and die. Groom eased their suffering by streaming the sea anchors, so that the boats rode head to wind and sea, and their motion was less severe. Unfortunately, the net result of heaving to was that the boats drifted out of sight of each other in the storm-filled darkness.

Captain Groom recorded in his log:

> Heavy weather, with a cold northerly and westerly wind, continued all that night. 'Allowance' of biscuits and water was started right away that night, viz., two and a half biscuits and two gills of water per man, per day; latterly I increased the water allowance, finding it was not enough with so much salt spray about. All the able-bodied men had to take their turn at bailing, two at a time; the steward, who firstly was old, and secondly ill, I made exempt from this work, also the four boys I had, who were very young, also seasick and somewhat frightened, I fancy. The

> boat was very overloaded with seventeen in it, and was ankle-deep in water, in spite of the vigorous bailing with the two buckets. The next day, the 5th, I got the carpenter to take out three of the watertight tanks on the side where the plank was split, and caulk it roughly from the inside with bits of shirt; this stopped the leaking a little.

Throughout that day, and the night that followed, the weather continued to deteriorate, the visibility being sometimes completed obscured by flying spray; even if the boat had been in the thick of a fleet of passing ships, it had little hope of being seen. Then, just before dawn on the 6th, as his boat lifted on the crest of a wave, Groom caught a glimpse of a dark shadow to the north, which he took to be a ship. There was a mad scramble to set off a distress flare, and when this was answered by another red flare, rescue seemed certain. Hopes were again dashed, when it was realised that the answering flare was from the *Coquet*'s other boat, which had closed up during the night.

As much Groom would have welcomed the Chief Officer's boat keeping company, he realised that by keeping the two boats well apart, their chances of rescue were greatly increased. He hailed Griffiths, and told him to keep his distance, and the other boat soon faded out of sight in the murky dawn. That was the last ever seen of Chief Officer Griffiths and his boat's crew.

Groom's log continued to record the worsening nightmare:

> The weather got a little worse that night and we used the oil-bag with good effect in keeping the breaking seas flat. No change in the day or night of the 7th; everybody chilled to the bone with that northerly wind blowing right through our saturated clothes; we all used to look forward to the daylight coming, in the hopes of seeing a little sun; but it was nearly always covered with clouds. Several of us had excruciating pains in the ankles, knees and wrists; the poor little Italian boy was crying all one night with them in his sleep, and, of course, I could do absolutely nothing for him; I had them badly myself.

Early on the morning of 8 January the agonies of the survivors were eased by an improvement in the weather. The wind moderated sufficiently for the mast and sails to be raised again, and estimating that by now they must have crossed the steamer lanes, Groom decided to head south for Africa. As his only navigational aid was a distinctly unreliable boat compass, Groom had no means of knowing how far off the coast lay, but with the food and water now running dangerously low, he could only pray that they would make a landfall soon.

The boat made fair progress throughout that day, but before nightfall the wind was backing to the west, and by daylight on the 9th holding a southerly course was proving nigh on impossible. Once more, the seas were slamming against the boat's side, and icy spray was lashing the unprotected occupants, bringing back the misery of the previous days and nights. Then, mercifully, as the night wore on, the low clouds cleared away, and the moon broke though, bathing the tumbling seas in a silvery light. All the horrors of the voyage were forgotten when, just after midnight, the low outline of the land was seen dead ahead. So grateful for this miracle were the weary, battered men that they managed to raise a cheer – although this came out as little more than a hoarse croak.

Unfortunately, their ordeal was far from over. Within the hour the wind backed all the way to the south and freshened, and the boat could make no headway towards the land. Groom was forced to lower the mast and sails again and stream the sea anchor. Thereafter, the heaving boat, head-on to a rough and dangerous sea, resembled a half-tide rock. There were no cheers now.

At about 5 a.m., with just over an hour to dawn, the wind moderated enough for the sails to be broken out again. Throughout the rest of the day, Captain Groom waged a constant battle with the wind, steering as close-hauled as he possibly could, edging towards the land on a diagonal course.

When, at last, the land was tantilisingly near, the wind they had been fighting suddenly dropped away to a dead calm, and the boat was left wallowing in the ground swell. Now, Arnold Groom had to call on his men for a last desperate effort. Even though they had suffered six days of unimaginable misery, short of food and water, lashed by wind and waves, they responded to their captain's call.

The oars were shipped, and those who still had the strength, put their backs into rowing for the shore. Progress was painfully slow, and at times it seemed that they were being pulled backwards by a sea reluctant to let them go, but at last, even as night was falling, the boat clawed its way into a small sheltered bay with some houses just visible beyond the beach. At the last moment, the boat broached to in the surf, and was almost swamped, but with a final magnificent effort by the exhausted oarsmen, they grounded on the beach, and crawled ashore. Captain Groom later described the disappointment of the landing after six days of misery in the open boat:

> We slept on the sands that night, after having slaked our thirst with some well water and eaten a quantity of limpets from the rocks with our biscuits. There were a quantity of cave-dwellings around the bay; but they were all so damp and smelly that we deemed it wiser to sleep in the open on the sandy beach, thinking that the sand would have retained some of the sun's heat. This conjecture proved faulty, however; there was a chill dampness which struck up through the sand, and, having only our wet clothes to cover us, we woke up chilled through and through, with every bone aching; we slept, owing to the fact that it was the first opportunity we had had of sleeping since leaving the ship. The buildings we had seen from the sea proved to be long-deserted ruins, and there was no sign of life anywhere. The two engineers, the second mate, and I kept watch by turns during the night.

When morning came at last, Groom took stock of their situation, which in the light of day proved to be not as hopeless as he had thought. They had a good supply of drinking water in the well, and the shellfish were abundant, if not very appetising. Furthermore, the ruined houses offered shelter from the wind, and there was plenty of driftwood on the beach for fires. They would survive.

Groom was aware that they had landed somewhere on the coast of Cyrenaica, but he had no idea of their exact location. The boat had, in fact, come ashore in the Gulf of Sirte, a wild and desolate coast under tenuous Italian rule. In reality, the area was dominated by the fierce Senussi Berbers led by Sayed Ahmed Sherif. The Senussis, fanatical followers of Islam, regarded all Christians, Jews and Turks as infidels to be cut down with the sword.

After consulting with his officers, Captain Groom decided to explore

Memorial to Captain Charles Fryatt at Liverpool Street Station. (*Wikipedia*)

Otto Weddigen (centre) with the crew of *U-9*. (*Bundesarchiv*)

Falaba's lifeboats approaching rescue ship. (*Colliers Photographic*)

Wreck of the *Brussels* in Zeebrugge harbour. Captain Fryatt inset. (*Postcard*)

The *Glitra* was the first merchant ship to be sunk by a U-boat. (*Source unknown*)

The raider *Möwe* sinks the *Clan Mactavish*. (*The Great World War*)

The collier *Thordis*, which retaliated by ramming *U-6* when attacked.
(*Amalgamated Press*)

Kapitänleutnant Walther Forstmann, who in *U-39* failed to sink the *Anglo-Californian*.
(*Axis Biographical Research*)

Le Petit Journal

ADMINISTRATION | 5 CENT. | SUPPLEMENT ILLUSTRÉ | 5 CENT. | ABONNEMENTS

27me Année | Numéro 1.714

DIMANCHE 27 FÉVRIER 1916

LE CHATIMENT DU PIRATE

Au retour d'un raid sur l'Angleterre
le Zeppelin " L-19 " sombre dans la mer du Nord

Zeppelin *L-19* down in the North Sea. Trawler *King Stephen* approaching. (*Le Petit Journal*)

Lieutenant Commander W.E. Sanders, VC, DSO, RNR, commander of the Q-ship *Prize*. (*Royal Navy 'Q' Ships*)

New Zealand Shipping Company's *Otaki* (Captain Archibald Bisset-Smith, VC). (*Old Ship Picture Galleries*)

The Q-ship *Prize* turns the tables on *U-93*. (*W.E. Sanders Archive*)

The *Falaba* sinks while her attacker, *U-28*, looks on. (*The Nations at War*)

The wreck of SMS *Koenigsberg* in the Rufiji River, August 1915. (*Der Weltkrieg 1914-18*)

Chief Officer Samuel Hitchin of the *Highland Brae* with family. (*Mark Hitchin*)

U-9, which sank the British cruisers *Aboukir, Hogue* and *Cressy.* Otto Weddigen inset. (*Postcard*)

further inland, in the hope that some human habitation might be found. Accompanied by two others, he set off to get help. For men who had been cooped up in a small boat knee deep in cold water for almost a week, the going was hard. The sandy ground was littered with small jagged rocks, which very soon cut their feet to pieces, and they staggered along in agony. Groom kept his party moving until noon, seeing nothing but the harsh, barren desert. Then, when they were on the point of turning back, an Arab appeared out of the haze.

The stranger appeared to be friendly, but he spoke no English, and Groom and his companions knew no Arabic. Using hand gestures, Groom persuaded the Arab to return to the camp with them. There, one of the *Coquet*'s two Greek firemen, who spoke Arabic, acted as translator, and the Arab eventually agreed to go to a nearby fort to get help. The two Greeks, one of whom spoke Italian, went with him. After they had left, a catastrophe struck the remaining survivors. Captain Groom recorded in his log:

> That night the rest of us – fifteen – slept in one of the cave dwellings with a big wood fire; we had dried our clothes somewhat during the day and the fire helped to keep us warm during the night; the floor, however, was very hard and damp. After 'breakfast' we began looking out longingly for signs of a boat coming; some of us had a wash in a muddy river-bed. I was just going off to this pool about 9.45 a.m., thinking to have a bathe, when we were all surprised by several bullets whizzing around us. On looking, we found that they came from two Arabs on a hill some distance inland, who, between shooting at us, were dancing wildly and laughing and yelling. Thinking they were two Arab boys who had got hold of rifles somehow and were just amusing themselves, I told our people to take cover, which we did in a deep trench formed by the ruins of some old building right at the water's edge; in fact the sea came well up in the trench at one end. I could watch the two Arabs from where we were, and they soon went away, but I thought it wise to keep down there for a bit.
>
> Half an hour after that about fifteen Arabs, with rifles, suddenly appeared over the edge of our trench and, after giving a preliminary yell, began jabbering hard in Arabic at us. The two

> closest had their rifles all ready to fire. I held up my hands to indicate that I was unarmed; one of them still jabbered at me, but the other took careful aim at my head; I ducked forward and to one side a little at just about the same instant that he pulled the trigger, so the bullet took a track through the flesh across the back of my shoulders, instead of hitting my head. The Arab was only about six feet from me when he fired; the force of the shock knocked me backwards. I remember falling and my head hitting the sand. After that I must have lost consciousness, as when I awoke everything was quiet except for the groaning of the carpenter, who was rolling between me and the edge of the water, about six feet. I found that he was horribly mutilated, but still alive. He asked me to drag him away from the sea; I tried to, but he was a big man and my wound was very painful. A little way out in the water the steward was floating face downwards; whether he was shot or drowned, or both, I do not know. Farther up the beach the little Italian messroom boy was lying dead. I could see nothing of anybody else, and was afraid to go out of the trench, thinking that if the Bedouins saw me alive they would come back to finish me off.

Arnold Groom remained in his desert trench, his only companion the *Coquet*'s mortally wounded carpenter, until a cloud of smoke appeared on the horizon, heralding the arrival of a small steamer. When she steamed into the bay and Groom could see she was flying the Italian flag, he cautiously emerged from his hiding place.

The Italian ship anchored, and dropped a boat containing an Italian officer and a party of Arab soldiers. When they landed, Groom learned that the two Greek firemen sent to get help had reached the Italian fort of Marsa Susa, and persuaded the authorities there to send a rescue party by sea.

Before leaving the beach, Groom discovered one of his seamen, a man named Lord, lying in the dunes. Lord had been shot and bayoneted by the Bedouin, and probably left for dead. But he was still conscious, and was able to tell Groom that ten men who had survived the attack had been taken prisoner by the Arabs.

The Italian officer and his men searched the surrounding area for several miles inland, but they found no sign of the Bedouin or their prisoners. They then returned to the beach and ferried Captain Groom, Lord, the wounded carpenter, Alexander Wiklund, and the bodies of the *Coquet*'s steward and messroom boy, back aboard the steamer. It was too late for Wiklund, who died shortly after being lifted on board ship.

As for the ten men taken by the Arabs, their ordeal was only just beginning. After being stripped of anything of value, they were marched at bayonet point towards the distant hills. It was a nightmare journey that lasted for more than three weeks, during which they were forced at a half-run over the stony ground with only brief stops for meals of rice and rancid goat's meat. There was no rest until darkness fell, and they were roused again at dawn to stagger on in agony.

Eventually, exactly one month after they had abandoned their sinking ship, the ten survivors reached Jedabiah, an abandoned and partly ruined Italian fort about 120 miles from Benghazi. One of the British survivors kept a rough diary on the way. He wrote:

> We were first housed in a room with four walls, a roof, and a concrete floor, and were quite well looked after for a few days. A party of Italian prisoners were brought in on the fourth day, and that evening we were all put together in a compound. Our party, comprising twenty-three men, were lodged in another hut facing us across the courtyard. Of course, we got into communication, as one of the Italians spoke French very well, and we could understand that. They asked us if we had been made to do any work, and were surprised to hear that we had not. Next day, however, an Arab guard came and took us all out to work together, and that was the beginning of our troubles.
>
> That same evening two Italians prevailed upon our Greek sailor to try to escape, to which he agreed. So about midnight they all climbed the wall of the compound, which was right on the outskirts of the fortified blockhouse of Jedabia. They climbed to the top all right, with much puffing and blowing, and the first man to drop down on the other side fell on some rusty tins and rubbish, making a frightful row, and we all thought that the whole lot would be caught, but nothing stirred, so they set off on foot. Of course the next day the Arabs discovered the escape, and some of them

set off in pursuit on fast racing camels, and soon came up with the fugitives and brought them back.

Then all we prisoners, British and Italian, were lined up and given a lecture by the Commandant of Jedabia upon the evils of trying to escape. He asked who was the instigator of the attempt, and all the blame was put on the poor Greek sailor. The two Italians were given twenty lashes with the *kurbash* and the Greek was given fifty lashes and condemned to be chained to a six-foot chain pegged into the ground for six months, and he was also handcuffed. Whenever he wanted to move about, the second mate had to take a turn round his (the Greek's) neck with the chain and keep hold of the peg, and peg him up securely when he came back. The Commandant also warned us that the next person or persons attempting to escape, would, if caught, be shot.

Needless to say, there were no further escape attempts, but the treatment of the prisoners continued to be harsh, stopping only just short of brutality. They were set to work rebuilding parts of the fort, commencing at sunrise, and with the exception of a two-hour siesta in the heat of the day, worked right through until sunset. It was hard labour, designed to wear down their spirits and health, and consisted of collecting and breaking stones for the Arab masons to lay. The prisoners were given two meals a day, usually boiled goat's meat and rice made into a kind of soup. At best, it was sustaining, but there was never enough meat. At night, exhausted, they lay down on grass mats spread over an earthen floor, with a flat stone for a pillow. Their blankets – it was invariably cold at night – were date sacks made of camel's hair, smelly and full of voracious ticks.

Quite unexpectedly, in April, their plight improved with the arrival at the fort of several German officers, who said they had landed from a submarine 15 miles along the coast. With the Germans came Nuri Bey, brother of the Turkish general Enver Bey. Nuri Bey claimed that he had been captured by British forces, but escaped to take refuge with the Berbers. Both Germans and Turk treated the British survivors with surprising kindness. It may be that they felt some sort of solidarity with the bearded, skeletal white men in this alien land. Each week, they gave the survivors money to buy tobacco and tea, which helped to make life a little easier.

In July 1916, when the *Coquet* survivors had been prisoners of the Berbers for seven months, their ordeal suddenly came to an end. One day, Nuri Bey called them to his tent, and gave each man thirty Turkish francs, which he said was payment for work done for the Turkish Government, which was to take possession of the rebuilt fort at Jedabiah. On that same day, a parcel arrived from the British Consul containing money, cigarettes, and letters.

Two days later, the survivors were taken before a number of high-ranking Egyptians, who informed them that they were to be sent home next day. After so long in captivity and so far from home, the *Coquet*'s men were highly sceptical, expecting their hopes to be dashed at any moment. Yet, when morning came, their rags were exchanged for full Arab dress, and they left the fort mounted on camels and escorted by outriders. Twenty-four hours later, they arrived at a fort manned by Italian troops, where they rested for two days. They were then put aboard a small coastal steamer, which took them to Benghazi. There they were given into the charge of the British Consul, who provided them with European clothes, and cared for them for ten days, at the end of which they boarded a ship bound for Malta. On the morning of 29 August, 1916, seven months and twenty-five days after the *Coquet* was sunk by Claus Rücker, the survivors arrived in London to tell their extraordinary tale.

Chapter Eight

The New Enemy

Towards the end of January 1916, the air war over Britain took on a much more worrying aspect. Until then, raids by German Zeppelins had been sporadic and not pressed home with particular zeal. London was raided on one memorable occasion, but the main targets were ports on the East Coast, which were easily accessible across the North Sea. Some civilians had been killed, which was not good for morale, but little damage had been done to the British economy.

The brainchild of Count Ferdinand Zeppelin, a German army officer, the first Zeppelin, a flimsy wood and canvas contraption, took to the air in 1900. By the time war broke out in 1914, Count Zeppelin had produced an impressive airship 540 feet long with a maximum speed of 84 mph, capable of flying at 14,000 feet and carrying a bomb load of 4,400 lbs. Properly employed, this was a weapon to be feared, but for some reason, the German High Command was reluctant to fully commit the Zeppelin to war.

The first tentative sortie by the Zeppelins against England took place on 19 January 1915, when two airships attacked Great Yarmouth and King's Lynn, killing four people. London was attacked five months later, when on 31 May a lone Zeppelin dropped over 100 small bombs on the city. Seven civilians lost their lives, and thirty-five were injured. The material damage caused in both raids was not great.

In October 1915, Berlin decided to broaden the scope of the Zeppelin war, and ordered *Korvettenkapitän* Peter Strasser, commanding the Naval Airship Unit, to prepare for a raid on Liverpool. The weather was unsuitable throughout the rest of the year, and it was not until the end of January 1916 that conditions were right. At about midday on the 31st, a fleet of nine Zeppelins, all of the latest type, took off from bases in northern Germany, their target the port and city of Liverpool. This was to be the most ambitious and far-reaching air raid ever carried out on Britain, the round distance to fly being almost 1000 miles, much of it over very hostile territory.

The airships, each carrying a full bomb load, were led by *Kapitänleutnant* Max Dietrich in L-21. Dietrich crossed the Norfolk coast near the Wash at 5.50 pm, just as darkness was closing in. L-21 was flying at 13,000 feet, where conditions were almost unendurable. It was bitterly cold, compasses and instruments were freezing up, and ice building up on the airship made it difficult to control. An inadequate oxygen-breathing system did not help.

At first, the weather was fine, with good visibility, although smoke generated by forests of chimney pots below was beginning to obscure the larger towns. There was high cloud, and no stars were visible to give sights, so navigation was by dead reckoning, after crossing the coast. As there was no wireless communication between the Zeppelins it was imperative that they all followed closely in L-21's slipstream.

At about 8 pm, the lights of a large city were seen below. Dietrich calculated this must be Manchester. Adjusting his course slightly, he flew on towards Liverpool, supposedly a mere 30 miles away, which he was confident of identifying as soon as the River Mersey was visible below.

With the other airships following, L-21 continued on a course a little south of west, but much to Max Dietrich's consternation, the expected bright lights of Liverpool failed to appear. Looking down from his gondola, Dietrich could see only darkness, no river, no town. By 8.50 he accepted that he must have overshot Liverpool and was somewhere over the Irish Sea. He turned south, and then turned inland again. Ten minutes later, two clusters of lights emerged from the haze below, the larger one to port, with a dark strip separating them. Dietrich was now satisfied that he had found Liverpool, the dark strip being the River Mersey, and the smaller cluster of lights to the south being Birkenhead. He sent his crew to their attack stations, and began his descent. The other Zeppelins followed his cue.

Fortunately for the citizens of Liverpool, Max Dietrich's navigation was seriously in error. The lights he had earlier identified as Manchester had in fact been those of the town of Derby, 50 miles to the south-east. Again, when he had assumed he was over the Irish Sea, he was actually flying over the thinly populated counties of North Wales.

When L-21 began her bombing run, she was nowhere near Liverpool, but had arrived back over Derby. The Zeppelins had by pure chance arrived above one of the great industrial centres of England, where everything from fine porcelain to Rolls-Royce engines was manufactured. That night, much to their consternation, the good citizens of Derby, Burton, Tamworth, Walsall, and the surrounding areas for the first time found themselves facing the full horrors of the war. High explosive and incendiary bombs showered down, resulting in a great deal of peripheral, though not serious, damage. The human cost was far greater, seventy civilians being killed and over 100 injured.

As it had up until that night been considered impossible for the Zeppelins to fly so far inland, there was no resistance to the German raid. The area possessed no anti-aircraft guns, and no fighter aircraft were available. Dietrich's squadron was completely unmolested, and when they had finished their odious work, he led them home.

The last Zeppelin to make her bombing run was L-19, under the command of *Kapitänleutnant* Odo Loewe. L-19 was a new airship, on her first operational flight, and she had been experiencing engine problems from the time she crossed the North Sea. As Loewe turned for home, three of his four engines were faltering, and he still had much of his bomb load on board.

When, on the last day of January 1916, Max Dietrich led his Zeppelins out into the North Sea, bound for Liverpool, the British collier *Franz Fischer* was setting sail from Hartlepool with a full cargo of coal for Cowes, in the Isle of Wight. Such were the pressures of war, that the 957-ton *Franz Fischer*, seized by the Royal Navy and handed over to British owners, still retained her German name, much to the disgust of those appointed to man her.

Making her way down the east coast of England, keeping close inshore to avoid the attention of her previous owners, the *Franz Fischer* reached the Thames Estuary at around 10 o'clock on the evening of 1 February. As she steamed southwards inside the Gabbard Banks, she was hailed by a Royal Navy patrol launch and warned that there were mines in her path some miles ahead. It was a very dark night, and rather than risk running into the minefield, the Master of the collier prudently decided to anchor until daylight came. He chose an anchorage some 8 miles north of the Kentish Knock buoy, where a number of other ships were already at anchor.

The overnight stop provided a welcome break for the *Franz Fischer*'s 16-man crew, who had already spent an exhausting day and a half at sea trimming cargo, battening down hatches, and hosing the decks to get rid of the invasive coal dust. Of all the occupations a seafarer might wish to take up, life aboard a short-sea collier is perhaps the ultimate test of a man's endurance.

Having anchored the ship and seen her snugged down for the night, the Master of the *Franz Fischer* retired to his cabin, where he was later joined by his Chief Engineer, John Birch. A bottle was produced, and the two senior men sat yarning. They had been relaxing for no more than half an hour, when they were disturbed by a strange growling noise that seemed to come from the sky overhead. They went out on deck, where they found the First Mate and a seaman gazing up into the sky, equally puzzled by the noise, which was growing louder. The seamen remarked later, 'The sound was like several express trains crossing a bridge together.'

The sky was heavily overcast and full of dark shadows, and no matter how hard the men searched, they could not pinpoint the source of the noise. The average seaman of the day was not over familiar with the sound of aero-engines, but it was agreed on the deck of the *Franz Fischer* that a large aircraft of some description was passing low overhead. Then the noise suddenly stopped.

Five hundred feet up in the night sky, *Kapitänleutnant* Odo Loewe was fighting what seemed to be a losing battle to keep L-19 in the air. Throughout the long and hazardous flight back across the waist of England three of the airship's four engines had been firing badly, and now they had cut out altogether. L-19 was drifting with the wind on one engine, and losing height rapidly. Having already jettisoned all his ballast, Loewe was left with one last card in his pack. Most of his bomb load was still on board, and although his orders were not to bomb indiscriminately, he now assumed he must be over the water, and little damage could be done by emptying his racks. He had no idea that the *Franz Fischer* was immediately below him.

Aboard the collier, just as the four men were about to leave the deck, the First Mate and the seaman to return to the bridge, and the Master and Chief Engineer to enjoy a final nightcap, there was a tremendous explosion, and a sheet of flame and smoke shot up from the port side of the *Franz Fischer*'s engine-room.

The tall column of water thrown up by L-19's jettisoned bombs fell back on the deck of the collier, knocking the Master and Chief Engineer off their feet. When they recovered from the shock, they both ran for the bridge. At this juncture, no one knew exactly what had happened, but it did not appear that the *Franz Fischer* was badly damaged. However, as a precaution, it was decided to muster all hands, and swing the boats out ready for lowering. No sooner had this been done than the collier listed heavily to port and capsized, throwing all those on deck into the water.

Unceremoniously tossed into the black, icy water, Chief Engineer John Birch fought his way back to the surface, and searched around in the darkness for some means of support. He could hear frightened voices calling, but could see nothing. Then, he saw a shadow bobbing on the waves, and swam towards it. The shadow turned out to be a large wooden lifebelt box, normally kept on the *Franz Fischer*'s bridge. For Birch it was a safe haven in the midst of a hostile sea. He clung on to a handrope which ran around the box, grateful for his deliverance. He was soon joined by seven other survivors. While the box was buoyant enough to support all eight men if they remained in the water holding onto the handrope, when one of them tried to clamber aboard, it rolled over, spinning like a barrel. This happened several times, and each time a man tried to ride the box, he was thrown off, and disappeared into the darkness.

Eventually, John Birch decided to go his own way, swimming off into the night, where he found a cork lifebelt, which kept him afloat. He left the others still trying to climb aboard their box, but their numbers were dwindling fast. Soon, only one man, Able Seaman Hillier, was left clinging to the box, and he was by then very near to death.

Anchored close to the *Franz Fischer* at Kentish Knock was the small Belgian steamer *Paul*. The explosion of L-19's jettisoned bombs was heard on the *Paul*'s bridge, but no one saw the flash. It was only when the heart-rending cries of the sunken collier's men struggling in the water were heard that it was realised that a tragedy had occurred. The *Paul*'s master immediately sent away a boat.

The *Paul*'s rescue boat was manned by her first mate, boatswain and two seamen. The darkness was complete, and with no lights to guide them they rowed around calling out to any survivors that might still be alive. It was a forlorn hope, for the voices heard in the night had now fallen silent. It was purely by chance that the boat came across Chief Engineer John Birch, Able Seaman Hillier, and the *Franz Fischer*'s steward, all of them more dead than alive when they were found.

The three survivors, all that was left of the *Franz Fischer*'s crew of sixteen, were hauled aboard the rescue boat, but their ordeal was not yet over. With a total of seven men on board, the *Paul*'s tiny dinghy could make little headway against the tide, now ebbing at 3-4 knots and carrying the boat down Channel away from the *Paul.* It was fortunate that the master of the Belgian ship realised that all was not well with his boat, and he weighed anchor and came looking for it. Another three hours passed before the boat was found, by which time the three British survivors, cold, wet and miserable, had abandoned all hope of living. Once aboard the *Paul*, wrapped in blankets and given hot drinks, they slowly recovered. Although they were not then aware of their place in the history books, they were the survivors of the first British merchant ship ever to be sunk from the air. And they owed this distinction to the sheer bad luck of being in the wrong place at the wrong time.

To add to *Kapitänleutnant* Loewe's troubles, L-19 encountered a strong head wind after she cleared the Thames Estuary. She was still on one engine, with the other three functioning intermittently, and continued to lose height. Over the North Sea, she ran into mist. Loewe, who was steering to cross the Belgian coast near Antwerp, soon became hopelessly lost.

At about 3 o'clock on the morning of the 2nd, Loewe sent a wireless message to base, reporting: 'Radio equipment at times out of order. Three engines out of order. Approximate position Borkum Island'.

L-19 was, in fact, 40 miles west-south-west of Borkum, and crossing over the Dutch island of Ameland. She was flying very low, and was an easy target for the Dutch batteries, which opened fire on her with every gun they could bring to bear. L-19 was last seen by the Dutch gunners on fire, and drifting helplessly before a strong south-easterly wind.

A little before dawn on 2 February, the British trawler *King Stephen* was approaching the Dogger Bank fishing grounds with her trawl down. The mate, George Denny, was in the tiny wheelhouse, idly scanning the horizon, and savouring the possibility of a hearty breakfast when the sun came up. When he saw a distress rocket arc into the sky his appetite was forgotten.

Denny called Skipper Bill Martin to the bridge, by which time wreckage was in sight. Martin was wary of approaching in the half light, but when full daylight came he recognised the wreckage as that of a downed Zeppelin. He hauled in his trawl and moved in closer, intending to see if there were any survivors; but when he realised that there were at least twenty men, all in German uniform, clinging to the wreckage, he had second thoughts about going to their rescue. His total crew amounted to only nine men, and although they were hard-bitten trawlermen, they did not have as much as a pop-gun between them. The Germans, outnumbering them more than two to one, would undoubtedly be well armed. Taking them aboard the trawler would be a very risky business.

Martin was later interviewed by a reporter from the *Daily Mail*. He said that the German commander offered him twenty-five dollars if he would send a boat. Martin added:

> He was a gentleman and behaved as one; he was nice and polite. He spoke good English, too. I thought a bit, and then said: 'Well, if there wasn't so many of you I would take you off, but there's too many.'
>
> The officer straightened himself up and said: 'There is nothing in that.'
>
> I thought again, and said: 'But supposing we take you, and you sling us overboard and navigate the trawler to Germany? That will be another decoration for you, but it won't be much for us.'
>
> He said: 'I pledge you my word we will not do anything of the kind.'
>
> He took his dying oath he would not interfere with us, and I could have plenty of money if I saved them.
>
> I took another thought. They were thirty, and we were nine. They were armed, and we had not as much as a pistol aboard, and I could not take the risk. If there had been another ship standing by to help me, I could have chanced it, but there was nothing in sight. Besides, I remembered what the Huns have done, and what they might do again.

> I ought to tell you that I could see three iron crosses painted on the Zeppelin – two on one side and one underneath the wooden nose, which was tilted up. I suppose they were for some daring deed and did not want me and my crew to be part of a fourth. As we drew away some of the German crew at first shouted, 'Mercy! Mercy! Save us!' and then shook their fists at us as they saw it was no use.

The *King Stephen* then backed away. Martin had no wireless, so he concluded his best action would be to make for the nearest British port, in this case Harwich, and there report to the Royal Navy, who would rescue the stranded Zeppelin crew. Unfortunately, long before the trawler reached port, the remains of L-19 had sunk, taking all her surviving crew with her.

A few days later, the Norwegian newspaper *Gothenburg Handelstidende* reported that fishermen at Marstrand had picked up a bottle containing a dispatch from Commander Loewe of the wrecked Zeppelin L-19 to his superior officer, in which he had written:

> With fifteen men on the platform and no gondola, L-19 is going very slowly. I am unable to save the airship. In foggy weather, we, on our return from England, passed Holland and were bombarded by Dutch sentinels. At the same moment three motors failed. 1 p.m.

The newspaper reported that the bottle also contained fifteen letters from the crew of L-19 to their relatives.

This last poignant message, written by the hand of Odo Loewe, and the farewell letters of his crew, were the only traces ever found of Zeppelin L-19 and the men who manned her.

Skipper Bill Martin was vilified by Berlin – and by some of his own – for abandoning the crew of L-19 to the North Sea, but his first duty was to his own men. Who can honestly say that, under the same circumstances, they would have decided otherwise? It might also be fairly argued that the sacrifice of the sixteen Germans was fair retribution for those killed in the raid on the Midlands towns and those lost with the *Franz Fischer*.

Bill Martin never recovered from the trauma of taking the decision to leave the Zeppelin's crew to drown. Full of remorse, he died a few days after reaching port. His trawler, the *King Stephen*, never fished again. She was commandeered by the Admiralty, and fitted out as a 'Q' ship. On 24 April, 1916, under the command of Lieutenant Tom Phillips R.N.R., she was on patrol in the North Sea, when she ran into the German High Seas Fleet. Phillips and his crew were taken prisoner, and on reaching Germany Phillips was charged with the war crime of refusing to rescue the crew of L-19. It was only when a British newspaper produced a photograph of Skipper Bill Martin that Berlin realised they had the wrong man. Nevertheless, Tom Phillips and his men spent the rest of the war in a German prisoner of war camp.

The *Franz Fischer* was the first of only seven Allied merchant ships to be sunk from the air in World War I. She was also – although this would not have been dreamt of at the time – the harbinger of an age when wars would be largely won and lost in the air. Meanwhile, the submarine, and German U-boats in particular, continued to create havoc in the shipping lanes. Throughout the remainder of that year the monthly tonnage lost to the U-boats steadily escalated, reaching an incredible 350,000 tons by December.

One ship caught up in this orgy of destruction was the 5620-ton oil tanker *Conch,* owned by the Anglo Saxon Petroleum Company of London. Commanded by Captain Edwin Stott, with a crew of twelve British officers and forty-four Chinese ratings, the *Conch* was homeward bound with 7,000 tons of benzine from Rangoon.

As cargoes go, benzine, with a flash point of below 23° C – the temperature at which vapour given off will ignite – is one of the most volatile and dangerous cargoes to carry. It was therefore with some relief to Captain Stott and his crew that, early on the morning of 7 December, the *Conch* entered the English Channel on the final leg of her voyage.

The weather in the Channel was good, as it often can be in December, and the *Conch*, steaming in bright moonlight, was off Portland Bill by 8 o'clock that night. The Thames pilot was only hours away, but the experienced Captain Stott was not about to relax his vigilance. He remained on the bridge with the Third Officer, the wheel was doubled up with two quartermasters, a lookout was on the forecastle head, the gunner and wireless operator were stood by the gun on the poop, and a zig-zag course was being steered.

All Stott's precautions were of no avail. The fair weather and bright moonlight also favoured *Oberleutnant* Heinz Ziemer, who was lying in wait off the Isle of Wight. At sea in *UB-23* for four weeks, Ziemer had sunk only two small sailing vessels, a collier, and a coastal ore carrier. He was looking for bigger fish.

At about 10.15 pm, the *Conch* was abeam of Anvil Point and clearly visible each time the powerful beam of the lighthouse swept out to sea. Ziemer bided his time, and when the moment was right, fired a single torpedo at the tanker.

Chief Engineer Raffray was in his cabin in the after accommodation of the *Conch* warming his hands on a scalding hot mug of cocoa, and contemplating whether he might snatch an hour's sleep before the busy hubbub of the Straits of Dover began. At precisely 10.30 the decision was made for him. He felt the ship shudder violently, list to port, then heave upright again.

Raffray, fearing that the worst had happened, ran for the engine-room and skidded down the ladders into the steamy depths. The Fourth Engineer was on watch, and strangely unconcerned. He said he had felt and heard nothing untoward. The bridge telegraph was still calling for full speed ahead, and the engine was churning out revolutions for 10 knots.

Puzzled, Raffray sent the Fourth Engineer to call the other engineers. When he reached the deck, the young watchkeeper found that the whole forward part of the ship was on fire, a raging inferno with flames leaping high into the sky. He succeeded in rousing the other engineers, but in the process was caught by the advancing flames and severely burned about the hands and arms.

Below, in the depths of the engine-room, Chief Engineer Raffray was attempting to make contact with the bridge, but with no success. He was not aware that the bridge had been engulfed by the flames, and everyone on watch, including Captain Stott, had been burnt alive.

Joined by his other engineers, Raffray was appraised of the situation on deck, but uncertain of what was happening on the bridge, he decided to keep the engine running.

Several times during the hours that followed, the engineers tried to reach the deck, but each time they were driven back by the flames, which by now had spread to the after accommodation. And so, the *Conch,* with 7000 tons of flaming benzine consuming her, burning oil trailing in her wake, and presumably a ghost at the wheel – for she was steering a straight course – ploughed on up Channel. To the onlookers – and there were plenty at large in the Channel that night – she must have resembled a fugitive from Hell itself.

It was after midnight when the four engineers escaped from the engine-room to reach the open deck, which was by then a disaster area. The bridge house had been reduced to a pile of smoking rubble, all four lifeboats had been burnt to cinders, and as they stood wondering at the devastation, so the flames began to advance on them. Their only hope lay in a small dinghy, which appeared to be still intact, but to lower this when the ship had so much headway on her was to attempt the impossible.

Raffray tried to get back down into the engine-room to stop the engine, but already the flames were barring his way. It now only remained to attempt the seemingly impossible.

As they struggled to swing the dinghy out, the engineers were joined by four Chinese ratings, who appeared out of the smoke like ghosts seeking reincarnation. Working together, the eight survivors swung the dinghy outboard, and lowered it to the water, where it was held alongside by a rope painter, bouncing wildly on the wave-tops as it was towed by the burning tanker. The Chinese ratings, who were by now in a state of panic, threw caution to the winds, and slid down the rope falls into the tossing boat. The Fourth Engineer followed them down, but his hands were so badly burned that he lost his grip on the falls, and dropped into the sea. He was never seen again.

Time was running out for those few still alive on the blazing ship. Raffray called to the two engineers to follow him, and went hand over hand down the boat fall to join the Chinese in the dinghy. He was not a moment too soon, for as he dropped into the boat it broke adrift from the ship and drifted astern. Those left on the deck of the doomed *Conch* looked on in horror as their only hope of survival disappeared into the darkness astern. The blazing tanker, the beat of her engine only just audible above the roar of the flames that were consuming her, thundered on towards her final destination.

Raffray found that the dinghy, which had sustained severe damage by being slammed against the ship's side, was half full of water and in danger of sinking. As the burning pyre of what had once been their ship pulled away from them, Raffray drove the petrified Chinese literally to bail for their lives. Fortunately for the five men, by then the naval inshore patrol vessel *Rattray Head* was chasing after the burning *Conch* with every knot her engines could muster, and as she began to gain, an alert lookout sighted the drifting dinghy. Soon, Raffray and his companions were being helped aboard the patrol vessel.

By now, the bizarre spectacle of a ship enveloped in flames charging through the night had attracted a great deal of attention, and several other ships had given chase. A trawler was first to catch up with the runaway, picking up the two remaining engineers, who were persuaded to jump over the side. Then, in the early hours of the 8th, the destroyer HMS *Nymphe,* commanded by Lieutenant Grough Scott, arrived on the scene. Scott could see small clusters of men still alive on the *Conch,* most of whom would soon have no escape from the dancing flames. At the risk of setting fire to his own ship, Scott moved in close to the stern of the tanker, where most of the survivors appeared to have taken refuge.

The terrible predicament of the men urged Scott to put the destroyer alongside the tanker, but this would be to tempt providence too far. He did, however, edge in closer, where he dropped liferafts, lifebelts and lifebuoys, calling on the Chinese to jump into the water.

Three times Lieutenant Scott carried out this dangerous manoeuvre, on the last occasion finally prevailing on the terrified Chinese on the poop to jump, and be rescued from the water. He then discovered that another group of nine were in the bows of the *Conch,* and surrounded by flames. No matter how much Scott called on them to jump, they refused. Fear had frozen them to their burning ship.

In the end, not wishing to see these men die, Scott took the enormous risk of laying his ship alongside the bows of the tanker. This called for the utmost in courage and ship handling, and Lieutenant Grough Scott lived up to the Royal Navy's proud reputation of dealing with impossible situations. Steaming parallel with the *Conch,* he slowly edged in on her weather bow, which, for the moment, was free of flames. Fenders were lowered over the side, and handling the *Nymphe* like a ship's cutter, Scott laid her gently alongside the *Conch,* bow to bow. After a great deal of forceful persuasion, the trapped Chinese seamen were finally cajoled into dropping down, one by one, onto the deck of the destroyer. Only then did Scott sheer away and leave the burning ship to her fate.

Other ships had by now homed in on the rescue effort, and more survivors were picked up from the sea. When the final head count was made, it showed that of the *Conch*'s total complement of fifty-six, twenty-eight had been saved, namely Chief Engineer Raffray, his second and third engineers, and twenty-five Chinese ratings. The others, including Captain Edwin Stott and all his deck officers, had died in the fire that raged through their ship as she steamed up Channel with no human hand in control. Providentially for other shipping in this busy waterway, the *Conch* sank in a cloud of hissing steam before she reached the shallows of the Straits of Dover.

The destruction of the *Conch* was the crowning glory of Heinz Ziemer's short wartime career. He sank only one more ship, the 1,410-ton French coaster *Gabrielle,* before being relieved of his command, bringing his total contribution to the German war effort to eight ships of 12,015 tons. *UB-23*, under a new commander, did not survive long after Ziemer. Damaged by depth charges from the patrol boat HMS PC-60 off the Lizard on 26 July, 1917, she took refuge in the Spanish port of Corunna, and was interned for the duration of the war.

Chapter Nine

A Martyr to War

By the time 1915 opened, the Admiralty had reluctantly concluded that there was an urgent need to fit defensive armament to all merchant ships. Not surprisingly, however, at this early stage of the war, suitable guns were in short supply. As an admittedly poor substitute, the following clandestine orders were issued to all British shipmasters:

> No British merchant ship would ever tamely surrender to a submarine, but should do its utmost to escape. If a submarine comes up suddenly with obvious hostile intentions, steer straight for it at maximum speed, altering course as necessary to keep it ahead. The submarine will probably dive, in which case you have ensured your ship's safety, as the enemy will be compelled to surface astern of you.

This perhaps not being specific enough for him, Winston Churchill, then First Lord of the Admiralty, elaborated:

> 1. All British merchant ships to paint out their names and port of registry, and when in British waters to fly the flag of a neutral power (preferably the American flag).
> 2. British vessels are ordered to treat the crews of captured U-boats as 'felons' and not to accord them the status of prisoners of war.
> 3. Survivors should be taken prisoner or shot whichever is the most convenient.
> 4. In all actions, white flags would be fired upon with promptitude.

Churchill's orders to merchant ship captains faced with attack by U-boat were quite clear and unambiguous. They were to immediately engage the enemy, either with their armament if they possessed it, or by ramming if they did not. He added, 'Any master who surrenders his ship will be prosecuted.' Later, Churchill admitted, 'The first British countermove made on my responsibility was to deter the Germans from surface attack. The submerged U-boat had to rely increasingly on underwater attack and thus ran the greater risk of mistaking neutral for British ships and of drowning neutral crews and thus embroiling Germany with other Great Powers.' Even then, the Great Schemer was busy manipulating the levers of war.

All this was probably completely illegal in the light of the Prize Rules, but it was welcomed by British shipmasters who, fiercely protective of their commands, were delighted at being given a chance to hit back at the enemy. Thirteen days after the edict was issued, Captain John Bell, commanding the 500-ton collier *Thordis,* demonstrated that British merchant ships were quite capable of defending themselves.

On the morning of 28 February, the *Thordis* was bound down Channel to Plymouth, and when passing off Beachy Head, she sighted a submarine's periscope. Seconds later, Captain Bell saw the wake of a torpedo speeding towards his ship. With the helm hard over, he easily avoided the torpedo. Then, angry at the attack on his ship, he followed Churchill's orders and steered directly for the enemy periscope at full speed.

Bell's attacker was Reinhold Lepsius in *U-6*. Watching the progress of his torpedo through the periscope, *Oberleutnant* Lepsius saw no reason to seek cover and was stunned when he saw his intended victim suddenly turn and come charging at him. He tried to go deep, but it was too late. The collier's blunt stem struck the conning tower, and *U-6* rolled over to starboard. Miraculously, apart from losing both her periscopes, the U-boat was not seriously damaged, and was able to limp away.

The *Thordis* was dry-docked on arrival in Plymouth, where she was found to have one blade of her propeller missing and significant damage to her keel plate. The Admiralty, prematurely as it turned out, claimed that *U-6* had been sunk, and for his determined engagement of the enemy Captain Bell was awarded the Distinguished Service Cross and presented with a gold watch. The shipping newspaper *Syren & Shipping* presented Bell and his crew with a prize of £660, while a grateful British public voiced their appreciation of such unprecedented bravery. The *Thordis* had changed the face of the U-boat war for ever.

On a blustery evening in late April 1929, with the wind rattling the warehouse doors of Albert Edward Dock, in the west coast port of Preston, a tired old ship eased away from the quayside and lined up on the harbour entrance. Her hull was streaked red with rust, and her scuppers still ran brown with the effluent of her final cargo of Irish cattle on the hoof. The *Lady Brussels* had reached the end of a long and useful life, and was setting out on her last voyage, which would end in a breaker's yard on the Clyde.

Built and engined by Gourlay Brothers of Dundee in 1901 for the Great Eastern Railway Steamship Company, the 1380-ton *Brussels,* as she was then named, had been the pride of the North Sea ferry service. Twin-funnels, twin-screws, an operating speed of 18 knots, and the last word in luxury accommodation, with her sisters, *Colchester, Cromer* and *Wrexham,* she ran a fast service between Harwich and Rotterdam, covering the 100-mile sea crossing in just six hours. She was among the elite.

When war came in the summer of 1914, with the entire Belgian coastline in German hands overnight, the southern North Sea was suddenly infested with marauding U-boats based in Ostend and Zeebrugge. Allied merchant ships hugged the east coast of England, seeking the protection of the shallow waters, while most of the North Sea ferry companies withdrew their ships, leaving only the Great Eastern Railway boats to show the British flag.

The busiest North Sea route was that between Harwich and Rotterdam, which in more peaceful days had been jointly operated by British and Dutch ferries. When war came, Holland being neutral, the Dutch ferries were taken out of service, and it was left to the Great Eastern steamers to keep open this vital doorway to Continental Europe. One of the mainstays of this service was the *Brussels,* then under the command of 43-year-old Captain Charles Algernon Fryatt.

Fryatt was already known to the Germans, and to the Admiralty, for his actions when in command of Great Eastern Railway's *Wrexham.* On 2 March 1915, when challenged by a U-boat, Fryatt refused to surrender, and presented his stern to the enemy. The 40-mile chase across the North Sea that followed, with the 12-knot *Wrexham* pushed to her utmost limits, had ended with the ferry finding safety in neutral Dutch waters, the U-boat being only yards behind. The grateful shipowners presented Charles Fryatt with a gold watch for saving his ship, an award that did not go unnoticed in Berlin.

After her narrow escape, the *Wrexham* was taken off the North Sea service, and Fryatt was given command of the bigger and faster *Brussels*. He was still coming to grips with his new ship when he had his second brush with the enemy.

Early in the afternoon of 28 March, the *Brussels* was approaching the Maas light vessel, inward bound from Harwich to Rotterdam, when her lookouts sighted a large submarine on the starboard bow. This was Konrad Gansser's *U-33*, which had completed a fruitless patrol in the northern North Sea, and was on her way south to look for victims in the English Channel. In a report covering the incident that followed, Fryatt informed his employers of the sequence of events:

> I beg to report that on Sunday afternoon on the 28th instant, when from Parkeston to Rotterdam, I sighted a German submarine. I sighted him about 2 points on my starboard bow at a distance of 4 miles steering to the southward. As I got closer to him he turned round very quickly of his port helm and steered towards me, very fast from starboard to port. I at once altered my course E by S to ESE, which brought him on my port bow about one point. I could see it was no use trying to get away from him as by steering my course to the southward he could easily have torpedoed me and his speed was far greater than mine. He hoisted two flags for me to stop but I did not like the idea of giving up my ship so I decided to ram him.
>
> I starboarded my helm and sent down to the Engineers to give her all speed possible, and sent all the crew aft out of the way in case he fired at me and I got the Chief Officer to fire three of the socket rockets to make him think I had a gun and I steered straight for his conning tower. He was then about 100 yards from me and when he saw me ignore his signal and heard the reports from the rockets he immediately submerged. He was approximately 20 yards ahead of me when he submerged and I steered straight for the place where he disappeared and when I considered that I was on top of him I then gave the order 'hard-a-port' to sweep over his

> periscope. His periscope came up under our bottom abreast of the fore gangway doors about two feet out of the water and came close along our port side. I could not feel the ship strike her but one of the firemen felt a bumping sensation under the bottom. I think I must have damaged him if I have not sunk him as I consider it was impossible for him to get clear according to the position of his periscope when it came to the surface.
>
> After it had passed our bridge it came further out of the water showing a decided list, after which it disappeared. Although a good lookout was kept, I saw nothing further of him.
>
> I still kept my course, going as fast as the Engineers could drive her, until I reached the Examination Boat inside the three mile limit.
>
> I should think according to my opinion she was quite 300 ft long, very high bow and very large circular conning tower and no distinguishing marks. I must highly commend my Officers and Engineers and crew for the way my orders were carried out.
>
> Time when first sighted – 1.10 pm. On top of submarine 1.30 pm. Lat. 51° 58' N Long. 03° 41' E.

Understandably, *Kapitänleutnant* Gansser had a different view of events. The entry in *U-33*'s war diary covering the incident read:

> 28.3.15. North Sea, light northerly breezes, visibility eight miles. 2.20 pm. Steering for the Noord Hinder Lightship. Sighted a steamer . . . heading for the Maas Lightship at full speed and showing no flags. At a distance of four miles I signalled, 'Stop immediately or I fire!' – at the same time altering my course towards the steamer. At a distance of one mile I cleared one tube for action. The steamer neither altered its course nor speed. *U-33* making direct for the steamer. At a distance of 500 M [metres], and only a few seconds before the shot was to have been fired, the steamer put her helm over, and came at *U-33* with the manifest intention of ramming us. In view of her high speed and the large arc described by the steamer, it was not possible for me to make sure of striking her with a torpedo. As observed through the periscope, the steamer passed us at a distance of twenty to thirty metres, after which she resumed her course at high speed . . . 2.40 came to the surface.

The time differences in the two reports are due to the *Brussels* keeping Greenwich Mean Time, while *U-33* was on Mid-European Time (one hour ahead of GMT).

Captain Fryatt's action in defying Gansser and attempting to run him down caused outrage in Berlin. Fryatt was branded as a dangerous pirate, and it was made quite plain that if he was caught he could expect no mercy. And yet Fryatt was doing only what any self-respecting British shipmaster would be expected to do under similar circumstances. It seemed that, in German eyes at least, there was one law for the U-boats and another for their victims.

The Admiralty certainly had no reservations concerning Fryatt's conduct. He was congratulated on the courage and skill he showed in defying the enemy and defending his ship, and was presented with a gold watch. Fryatt's name was also mentioned in the House of Commons, and at a civic ceremony in Harwich the Mayor presented him with yet another gold watch. In all, Charles Fryatt, now known on the North Sea as the 'Pirate Dodger', had collected no less than three gold watches for his defiance of the U-boats on the road to Rotterdam. German fury knew no bounds.

Despite the notoriety of the ship and her master, the *Brussels,* with Charles Fryatt in command, continued her regular shuttle between Harwich and Rotterdam. But she was a marked ship, weaving her way carefully through the frequent ambushes set for her by German destroyers, torpedo boats and U-boats. She was not invincible, and a number of times came very near to capture or sinking, but always the 'Pirate Dodger's' luck held. Moreover, this luck seemed to rub off on the other G.E.R. ferries, the *Colchester* and *Cromer* which operated the North Sea service with the *Brussels.* By the summer of 1916, the Germans appeared to have given up their attempts to close the Harwich-Rotterdam service.

On 22 June 1916, Captain Fryatt set out on his ninety-eighth crossing in the *Brussels*, sailing from Rotterdam in the late afternoon, bound for Tilbury. The ferry had on board 390 tons of general cargo and 100 Belgian and Russian refugees, whose untidy bundles of belongings littered the decks. There was only one fare-paying passenger, believed to be an American. Prior to sailing, the British Consul General handed Fryatt a diplomatic bag containing highly sensitive papers, which he was told must under no circumstances be allowed to fall into enemy hands.

On her way down river, the *Brussels* called at the Hook of Holland to pick up mails, sailing from there at 11 o'clock that night. It was a beautiful warm summer's evening, with clear visibility, light winds, and a cloudless starlit sky. Fryatt and his Chief Officer Bill Hartnell were on the bridge as they steamed down the New Waterway towards the open sea, and both witnessed the rocket that went soaring up from the coast line to starboard to burst with a shower of white stars over the sea. It was later said that this could have been some sort of signal sent up by a British agent on shore to warn Fryatt that enemy ships were about. At the time, however, it was such an idyllic night that neither Fryatt, nor anyone else on the bridge of the *Brussels* attached any sinister meaning to the show of pyrotechnics.

It was not until the *Brussels* was 12 miles west of the Maas Lightship that Fryatt began to suspect that all was not as it should be. The bridge lookout reported a small craft just visible in the darkness ahead. Both Fryatt and Hartnell swept the horizon with their night glasses and distinctly saw 'a very small craft, probably a submarine not submerged'. As they drew closer, the unidentified craft was seen to be using a signal lamp, flashing to seaward the morse letter 'S'.

Friend or foe, Fryatt was unable to tell, but by now his suspicions were aroused. He had a growing feeling that his ship was being watched, perhaps even stalked, by a predator. He gave the order for all lights to be extinguished and the passengers to be sent below decks for their own safety. He then passed the order to the engine room for all possible speed.

Once the lights of the shore had fallen astern, the darkness that closed around the bridge of the *Brussels* was all but complete, relieved only by the dim light of the compass binnacle reflecting on the helmsman's face. Charging through the night, her pistons pounding furiously, the ferry was steaming blind, her fate in the hands of the two men, Fryatt and Hartnell. Conversing in hushed tones, they strained to penetrate the darkness ahead, sweeping with their binoculars, but seeing nothing but the empty night. Yet they both knew that there was something out there, something they might at any minute run headlong into with devastating results.

At thirty minutes past midnight, Fryatt felt he could no longer risk a collision with another ship in this busy shipping lane, and told Hartnell to switch on the sidelights for a few minutes. The sudden transformation from total darkness to a diffused glow, red to port and green to starboard, was almost blinding to eyes grown accustomed to the dark. Taking a quick look around to see if there were any answering lights – of which there were none – Fryatt ordered the sidelights to be doused.

Fryatt's primary motivation in using his navigation lights may have been a wise precaution to prevent a collision with other ships in the busy approaches to Rotterdam, but he had not bargained for the German destroyers lurking in the darkness as the *Brussels* headed for home. Fifteen minutes after switching off his lights, Fryatt found his ship hemmed in on all sides by German warships – no less than nine sleek, very businesslike destroyers.

Captain Fryatt, his ship being unarmed, had no other option but stop and offer surrender. This he did, and leaving Hartnell in charge of the bridge, he hurried below, retrieved the secret code books and the diplomatic mail bag from his cabin, and fed them to the boiler furnaces.

Returning to the bridge, Fryatt found that his ship had been taken over by a boarding party of German officers, all armed with revolvers. None too gently, he was ordered to join Hartnell and the helmsman, who hands on heads, were backed up against the after bulkhead of the wheelhouse. The rest of the crew had been herded on to the destroyers.

The *Brussels* was taken under escort to Zeebrugge, and after five hours at the quay, was moved up the canal to Bruges, where her crew and the refugees were landed. It was significant that the only fare-paying passenger, the mysterious American – who incidentally was heard to speak fluent German – was treated with a great deal of respect by the Germans. He may, or may not, have been involved in the taking of the *Brussels*, but there were certainly some very suspicious characters on the fringes of the event. A report written by the British Consul in Flushing and sent to the Foreign Office via the British Ambassador in the Hague, commented: 'It appears that the information about her capture was brought in by a fisherman by the name of Schroevers of the V46. This is the boat which had previously been suspected of taking supplies to German subs, but no concrete evidence has been obtainable up to now. It is a fact, however, that she often puts to sea when no other boats are out, and comes back after 36 or 38 hours with no fish on board.'

The forty-five crew members of the *Brussels* were packed into cattle trucks and transported to Germany, being publicly exhibited and humiliated in many of the towns they passed through on the way. But the saga took a more sinister turn when Captain Fryatt and Chief Officer Hartnell were separated from the others and sent to a prisoner of war camp at Ruhleben in the suburbs of Berlin.

On 30 June, Fryatt and Hartnell were taken out of Ruhleben under escort, and put aboard a train returning to the west. They arrived back in Bruges on 2 July, and were immediately thrown into jail and treated like common criminals. The two men were separated and subjected to intense interrogation. Fryatt made no secret of the fact that he had attempted to ram *U-33* fifteen months earlier, as he believed he had done nothing wrong. However, the Germans seemed already convinced that his actions were those of a *franc-tireur*, or civilian saboteur, a most serious military offence.

Towards the middle of July, the Foreign Office was notified by the British Consul-General in Rotterdam that Captain Fryatt would shortly be tried by court martial. The news caused a considerable stir in London, and the Foreign Secretary, Sir Edward Grey, immediately contacted James W. Gerrard, the American Ambassador in Berlin, and asked him to engage a competent defence counsel for Fryatt. Gerrard in turn approached the German Foreign Office, but he was given no guarantee that Fryatt would be properly defended.

On 28 July, Reuters in Amsterdam received the following official telegram from Berlin:

> On July 27, at Bruges, before the court martial of the Marine Corps, the trial took place of Capt. Charles Fryatt of the British steamer Brussels, which was brought in as a prize. The accused was condemned to death because, although he was not a member of a combatant force, he made an attempt on the afternoon of 28 March 1915 to ram the German submarine *U-33* near the Maas lightship. The accused, as well as the First Officer and Chief Engineer of the steamer received at the time from the British Admiralty a gold watch as a reward for his brave conduct on that occasion, and his action was mentioned with praise in the House of Commons. On the occasion in question, disregarding the U-boat's signal to stop and show his national flag, he turned at the critical moment at high speed on the submarine which escaped the

> steamer by a few metres only by immediately diving. He confessed that in doing so he acted in accordance with the instructions of the Admiralty. The sentence was confirmed yesterday afternoon and carried out by shooting. One of the many nefarious franc tireur proceedings of the British merchant marine against our war vessels has thus found a belated but merited expiation.

Few details were ever released of the court martial in Bruges, and the trial was clearly a farce, a macabre production staged to make an example of Charles Fryatt, and to deter other British merchant captains from following his lead. Records that were made available showed that Admiral Ludwig von Schröder, officer commanding the Marine Corps in Flanders, was solely responsible for setting up the court martial, and for overseeing the proceedings. Von Schröder was the archetypal Prussian officer, self-opinionated, humourless and ruthless. Before the trial, he was heard to declare in public that he wished to see Fryatt dead.

The request made by the American Ambassador for proper legal representation for Captain Fryatt was ignored. Meanwhile, Fryatt was held in solitary confinement, unable to communicate with anyone but his jailers.

At 9 o'clock on the morning of 27 July, Fryatt, his chief officer Bill Hartnell and four other members of the crew of the Brussels, were taken to a large house in the centre of Bruges, where they found the court martial had assembled. The president of the court was a Dr. Zäpfel, a qualified barrister, and sitting with him were five unnamed officers and a secretary, or note-taker.

As Fryatt entered the court house, he was introduced to an elderly German officer in the uniform of the Army Reserve. Major Naumann, who was said to have once held a junior position in the Imperial Courts, told Fryatt that he had been ordered to defend him, and would do so 'to the best of his ability'. This was hardly reassuring for Fryatt, who had been expecting a defending lawyer of some substance and independence appointed by the American Embassy.

The charge against Fryatt, which seemed to be largely based on the inscribed gold watch he had received from the Admiralty, was that he was 'strongly suspected of having attempted to cause injury to the forces of Germany.' That being the case, he was charged under a proclamation issued by the Imperial German Government, which stated: 'All persons not being members of the enemy forces, including civil servants of the enemy government, render themselves liable to the death penalty if they undertake to advantage the enemy state or to do injury to Germany or her allies.' This was plainly ludicrous, as was the attempt to pin the label of *franc-tireur* on Charles Fryatt, when all he had done was to attempt to save his ship by forcing his attacker to dive. In reality, his action had been completely logical.

Before the trial began, Dr. Zäpfel read out a telegram from the Foreign Office in Berlin asking for the trial to be postponed. It must be assumed that Berlin, fearful of antagonising the Americans, who were now watching the proceeding closely, had had a change of heart. Major Naumann, perhaps realising the hopeless task he had been given, enthusiastically seconded the postponement, and called for the American Embassy to be allowed to appoint a defence lawyer. The court did retire to consider Berlin's proposal, but returned after a few minutes to reject it. It was then revealed that von Schröder had already informed the Foreign Office that the trial must go ahead, and as the Admiral appeared to have been given complete jurisdiction over the prosecution of Captain Fryatt, there was no objection from Berlin.

The travesty that Ludwig von Schröder called a fair trial descended further into farce when the prosecution called its only two witnesses, *Leutnant-zur-See* Wieder and *Vollmatrose* (Able Seaman) Richter. Both were said to have been on board *U-33* on 28 March 1915 when Fryatt was accused of trying to run them down, but in giving evidence they contradicted one another, and their statements should have been ignored. The only other evidence the prosecution produced was a written statement made by Konrad Gansser, but not witnessed, and extracts from Dutch and English newspapers. No unbiased court would have dared to convict Captain Fryatt on such flimsy and questionable evidence, but there were some dark forces at work here. At 4 o'clock that afternoon, after deliberating for only a few minutes, the court returned a verdict of guilty against Charles Fryatt. He was sentenced to death by shooting, the sentence to be carried out on the following day. This ludicrous show trial, a matter of a man's life and death, had lasted less than four hours.

And still von Schröder was not satisfied. Fearing that the American intervention might persuade the politicians in Berlin to have second thoughts on the verdict, he ordered Fryatt to be put to death without delay. That evening, only two hours after he was convicted and sentenced, Fryatt was taken from his cell to an army barracks in the suburbs of Bruges, where his executioner, Colonel von Bottelar, waited impatiently, puffing on a cigar. Without further delay, Fryatt was tied to an execution post in the corner of the barrack yard next to a pile of manure, and shot by the firing squad, dying with twelve bullets in his chest. Half an hour after he died, a telegram was received from the Foreign Office in Berlin ordering the sentence to be postponed.

Charles Fryatt's body was hastily buried in the communal cemetery at Bruges, next to thirteen other people executed by the Germans. Later, a black cross appeared on his grave inscribed in white with the words, 'Here lies Captain Fryatt, Master of the S.S. *Brussels* of glorious memory. R.I.P.'

The news that Captain Charles Fryatt had been taken to a piece of waste ground and shot like a dog shocked the whole of the civilised world. Not since the execution of Nurse Edith Cavell in October 1915 had the international telegraph wires hummed so loud.

In London, the Foreign Office, slow to act when Fryatt needed it most, claimed that 'the act of a merchant ship in steering for an enemy submarine and forcing her to dive is essentially defensive.' Prime Minister Asquith said, 'His Majesty's Government have heard with the utmost indignation of this atrocious crime against the law of nations and the usages of war.' He pointed out that, even under Germany's own Prize Regulations, in the case of a merchant ship under attack offering armed resistance, should her crew be captured they were entitled to be treated as prisoners of war.

In America, headlines in the *New York Herald* protested against a 'CROWNING GERMAN ATROCITY', while the *New York Times* called the shooting of Captain Fryatt 'a deliberate murder – a trifle to the Government that has so many thousands to answer for.'

The Dutch newspaper *Nieuwe Rotterdamsche Courant* in its edition of 29 July condemned the outrage in no uncertain terms:

> At the time that the Captain of the *Brussels* made his unsuccessful attempt, the submarine war was being carried on in the most brutal manner in contempt of all rules of humanity. The mere sighting of a German submarine meant death for hundreds who

> are now called '*franc-tireurs*' in the German communique. To claim for oneself the right to kill hundreds of civilians out of hand, but to brand as a *franc-tireur* the civilian who does not willingly submit to execution, amounts, in our opinion, to measuring justice with a different scale, according to whether it is to be applied to oneself or to another. This is, in our view, arbitrariness and injustice. And that touches us all even in the midst of all the horrors of the war. It shocks the neutrals, and arouses fresh bitterness and hatred in the enemy.

The Swiss *Journal de Genève* wrote of 'a German crime', and said: 'It is monstrous to maintain that the armed forces have a right to murder civilians but that civilians are guilty of a crime in defending themselves.'

The death of Captain Charles Fryatt evoked a great surge of world opinion against Germany, which would eventually contribute much to her defeat and subsequent humiliation. Charles Fryatt did not die in vain.

After the war, in July 1919, Fryatt's body was exhumed and brought back to England on the deck of a British destroyer, escorted by vessels of the Dover Patrol. His coffin was landed in Dover and borne on a gun carriage to the railway station accompanied by a naval escort and representatives of the civil authorities. After a memorial service in St. Paul's Cathedral, the gallant captain was finally laid to rest at Dovercourt, overlooking the port of Harwich which had been journey's end to him for so many years.

The unwarranted killing of Captain Fryatt aroused intense anger in Britain. In the House of Commons, Prime Minister Asquith declared that his government would not agree to a resumption of diplomatic relations with Germany after the war until reparation had been made for the 'murder of Captain Fryatt'.

Today, Charles Algernon Fryatt is all but forgotten, his name living on only in an obscure fund set up in his memory by the Imperial Service Guild to bring succour to British mariners incarcerated in foreign jails.

Chapter Ten

Raider Under Sail

She first appeared on the horizon to starboard as a tiny white cloud, possibly the top of one of the fair-weather cumulus clouds that were bubbling up all around the steamer *Gladys Royle* as she steamed south into the Trades. The day wore on and the cloud became a beautiful three-master, fully rigged, with her sails billowing taut in the fresh westerly breeze.

On the bridge of the *Gladys Royle*, Captain William Shewan steadied his telescope against an awning stanchion and studied the stranger, marvelling at her clean lines and her graceful roll as she breasted the swells. She was on a similar course to the *Gladys Royle* – making good her easting before rounding the Cape of Good Hope, Shewan surmised. The steamer, the measured thump of her pistons echoing across the water, would soon overtake her, but she would never match her beauty.

Not that the 3268-ton *Gladys Royle* was herself completely lacking in grace. Owned by James Westoll of Sunderland, and registered in that port, the 22-year-old British tramp had unusually fine lines for one of her class. On that warm but blustery Tuesday morning, 9 January 1917, she was 120 miles south of the Azores, outward bound from Cardiff to Buenos Aires with 4,300 tons of best Welsh steaming coal. She was completely unarmed, but to Captain Shewan that was of little consequence now that they were well out of the range of the German U-boats.

Shewan continued to run his telescope over the tall three-master he was steadily overhauling, concluding that she must be one of the last great windjammers flogging her way around the southern oceans. Had he been able to take a closer look at the object of his admiration, he would have been unpleasantly surprised. The elegant three-master, with her fine spread of white sail, rolling easily on the *Gladys Royle*'s starboard bow was in fact a heavily armed German sea raider.

Raider Under Sail

In June 1915, the ex-British barque *Pass of Balmaha*, then owned by the River Plate Shipping Company of New York, sailed from that port with a full cargo of cotton for Archangel. Built on the Clyde in 1888, she was, even then, one of a dying breed: proud ships rapidly being superseded by the tall-funnelled steamers spreading their foul black smoke across the oceans of the world.

Eighteen days after clearing American waters, the *Pass of Balmaha* was passing north of Scotland's Cape Wrath, when she was stopped and boarded by a British naval patrol. Although an innocent neutral going about her legitimate business, she was arrested and ordered into Kirkwall in the Orkney Islands, with a prize crew on board. She had not yet reached the Pentland Firth, when she was again stopped, this time by the German submarine *U-36* under the command of *Kapitänleutnant* Ernst Graeff. For some reason not recorded, the British prize crew offered no resistance, and the *Pass of Balmaha,* now under the command of one of *U-36*'s midshipmen, ended her voyage in Bremerhaven.

In Germany the ex-American barque underwent an extensive refit, during which two 105-mm guns were mounted concealed behind drop-down false bulwarks, one on each bow. Two heavy machine guns were similarly hidden on the bridge. A powerful wireless transmitter was installed, and her sail power supplemented by a 1,500 hp diesel engine driving a single propeller, which was designed to give the barque a speed of 14 knots over short distances. To help with boarding her prizes, she carried two powerful diesel launches, while in anticipation of successful raiding, one of her cargo holds had been converted into accommodation for up to 400 prisoners.

On 21 December, 1916, the *Pass of Balmaha* returned to sea as the *Seeadler* (Sea Eagle), the only armed merchant cruiser under sail. In command was the charismatic 35-year-old *Kapitänleutnant* Felix Graf von Luckner, a German naval officer with considerable experience in sailing ships. With him Luckner had a crew of six officers and fifty-seven ratings, all experienced naval men, and many of them ex-Cape Horners.

The *Seeadler* was a completely new concept in sea warfare, and the German Admiralty expected great things of her. Being sail-driven, and free of the need to constantly search for coal to fill her bunkers, it was envisaged that she would roam far and wide with complete independence. Should she be challenged by an enemy patrol, her innocent appearance would carry her through. Von Luckner decided for much of the time to masquerade as a Norwegian ship, and to this end many of his crew were fluent Norwegian speakers, a language which he himself spoke well.

Four days before Christmas 1916, the *Seeadler,* sailing under the name *Hero*, and purporting to be a Norwegian timber-carrier bound for Melbourne, slipped out of the River Weser into the North Sea. The fogs of winter provided perfect cover, and the disguised raider made her way up the Norwegian coast without difficulty, eluded the ships of the Royal Navy's Northern Patrol, and broke out into the Atlantic via the north of Scotland.

The first three days in the open ocean were spent battling a howling westerly gale, but by the morning of the 25th the *Seeadler* was 180 miles south of Iceland, and in improving weather. Unfortunately, the proposed seasonal celebrations were postponed by the sudden appearance of the British armed merchant cruiser HMS *Avenger*. An armed party boarded the barque, but found her papers apparently in order, her crew friendly Norwegians, and plenty of evidence scattered around in the accommodation to confirm that she was indeed out of Norway. As final proof of her nationality, a young, beardless deckboy had dressed up in woman's clothes and gave a credible performance as the Captain's wife, it then being common practice for Norwegian captains to carry their wives on the voyage. After a cursory examination of her deck cargo of timber, the *Seeadler* was allowed to go on her way. Never had *Stille Nacht, Heilige Nacht* been sung with such feeling as aboard the *Seeadler* that Christmas night.

After his brush with the British Navy, von Luckner sailed south into the steamer lanes looking for an early conquest. He had no success, and by the time the first week of January 1917 had passed with no ships, enemy or otherwise, being sighted, all the great hopes he had held for a successful voyage of piracy were beginning to fade. Then, soon after dawn on the 9th, the *Seeadler*'s lookouts sighted a smudge of black smoke on the horizon astern.

Before sailing from Germany, it had been made quite clear to von Luckner that the *Seeadler*'s primary role was to harass, and where possible sink, any sailing vessels still carrying cargo for the Allies.

Steamers he was to keep well clear of. But Felix von Luckner, a great-grandson of Nicolaus von Luckner, Marshal of France and Commander-in-Chief of the French Army of the Rhine, was very much his own man. When the smoke of the overtaking ship was reported to him, he ran up his Norwegian ensign and discreetly reduced sail to allow the steamer to draw closer.

Captain Shewan lowered his telescope, and adjusted the *Gladys Royle*'s course to bring her closer to the three-master, which, out of sheer curiosity, he was anxious to take a good look at. As the distance between the two ships narrowed, Shewan was able to make out the large Norwegian flag painted on the side of the stranger's hull, and then the Norwegian ensign flying at her stern became visible. He had nothing to fear from this ship.

Shewan was not surprised when, as they drew near, the Norwegian hoisted the International Code signal indicating that she required a chronometer check. At a time when very few sailing ships were fitted with wireless, it was common practice for them, when out of sight of land for long periods, to approach a steamer and request a time check.

Accordingly, the *Gladys Royle* hoisted her ensign at the yard arm, and stood by to lower it at the precise time agreed. It was an old and well-tried procedure, with Captain Shewan, who had more than a sneaking regard for the beauty of sail, partaking willingly. He reduced speed to allow the Norwegian to move in closer.

Judging the moment to be right, von Luckner lowered his false Norwegian colours, then sent the German Imperial Navy ensign, with its Hohenzollern Eagle, claws unsheathed, soaring to the *Seeadler*'s gaff. At the same time, the gunnery officer, *Leutnant* Kircheiss, ordered the false bulwark hiding the starboard 105-mm gun to be dropped.

Captain Shewan, mystified by the sudden appearance of the German flag, was for the moment unwilling to believe his own eyes. When the *Seeadler*'s 105-mm barked, and a shell whistled across the *Gladys Royle*'s bow, sending up a tall column of water close to starboard, the German ship's intentions became clear.

Shewan recovered quickly, reacting instinctively to the danger. He carried no guns to answer this challenge, but he could run. He ordered the helm over, brought the *Gladys Royle*'s bows into the wind, and called for more speed. He was assuming that his adversary was relying on sail only, and that by heading into the wind he would easily outstrip her. He was not to know, however, that the *Seeadler* had auxiliary power, and when he saw her furl her sails Shewan felt confident of showing this enemy a clean pair of heels.

Much to Shewan's surprise, the *Seeadler* did not fall astern, but appeared to be giving chase, the tell-tale wake churned up by her hidden propeller stretching out astern as she gathered way. Von Luckner closed the distance between the two ships to about half a mile before opening fire again. At that range, *Leutnant* Kircheiss would have been hard pressed to miss, and his first three shells went home, one landing amidships and setting the Captain's cabin on fire, while the other two hit aft.

Despite the three hits on the *Gladys Royle*'s superstructure, there were no casualties amongst her crew, but William Shewan realised it could only be a matter of time before the blood began to flow. Wisely, he stopped his ship, and at 11 am, some two hours after the chase had begun, he hauled down his ensign in surrender.

If the *Seeadler* had been a normal run-of-the-mill raider with coal-fired boilers, the capture of the *Gladys Royle* and her cargo of best Welsh steaming coal would have been a prize well worth having. But the German raider had no use for her victim's cargo. After taking Captain Shewan and his men prisoner, and transferring any usable stores to the *Seeadler,* von Luckner ordered the *Gladys Royle* to be sunk with scuttling charges. As darkness fell, the British ship, her voyaging ended at last, slid into the cold depths of the Atlantic.

Next morning, the *Seeadler* sighted another steamer. She was the 3095-ton *Lundy Island,* owned by the Glynafon Shipping Company of Cardiff, and bound from Mauritius to Nantes with a full cargo of sugar for the French Government. She had sailed from Port Louis on 29 November 1916, and after calling at Durban and the Cape Verde Islands for coal bunkers, was on the final leg of her long voyage to Europe. Her master was Captain David Barton, who was no stranger to the world of German surface raiders.

In January 1916, Barton was in command of the 3687-ton *Corbridge,* owned by the Cambridge Steamship Company. The *Corbridge*, carrying a full cargo of coal from the Bristol Channel to Brazil, was 150 miles west of Cape Finisterre when she was sighted by the German raider *Möwe.*

The *Möwe,* masquerading as an Ellerman Line ship, gave chase, but although the raider had the advantage of at least 2 knots on her quarry, the distance between the two ships was great, and the gap closed only very slowly.

By late afternoon, it seemed very likely that the *Corbridge* might escape into the advancing darkness. Then the *Möwe*'s lookouts reported a second merchantman close to port and on a converging course. Abandoning the *Corbridge*, the raider reduced speed and altered course towards the newcomer.

The unlucky ship was the 3146-ton *Farringford*, homeward bound with a cargo of copper ore. Unarmed, she could offer no resistance to the *Möwe*'s guns, and after her crew had been taken off, she went to the bottom, along with her precious cargo of ore.

Meanwhile, the unsuspecting Captain Barton had continued to hold his course, and early next morning the *Möwe* caught up with the *Corbridge*. The raider fired a gun and signalled the British ship to stop, at which Barton perversely increased speed and attempted to get away. The *Möwe*'s superior speed told, and soon she was bracketing the *Corbridge* with shells. Realising the futility of further resistance, Barton stopped and surrendered his ship. Her cargo of coal was used to replenish the *Möwe*'s bunkers. Captain Barton and his crew were taken prisoner, and later released on parole after agreeing not to engage in 'any further war activity', an undertaking which would, in effect, bar them from returning to sea again. Barton, having no intention of throwing away a career he had followed for so many years, applied to return to sea just as soon as he reached a British port. After a short period of 'survivor's leave', he took command of the *Lundy Island*.

As might be expected, having broken his parole, albeit in the pursuance of his lawful occupation, Captain Barton viewed the approach of any unidentified ship with extreme caution. When, at around 9 o'clock on that January morning in 1917, he saw the big windjammer showing Norwegian colours bearing down on him from the west, he was immediately suspicious.

Under the rules that govern the conduct of ships at sea, steam must always give way to sail, and it was the turn of *Kapitänleutnant* von Luckner to be apprehensive when, as he neared the *Lundy Island*, the steamer kept resolutely to her course. Barton's suspicions were growing, and when von Luckner used his usual ploy of requesting a chronometer check, the British captain did not answer.

When less than 300 yards separated the two ships, von Luckner realised that he was in imminent danger of being rammed, and he was forced to bear up. Angry, the German commander lowered his Norwegian ensign, dropped canvas screens over the flags on his hull, and ran up the German flag. A string of code flags hoisted to the yardarm called on the *Lundy Island* to heave to.

Barton, fearing that he might well be hung from that same yardarm if he surrendered, rang for more speed and sheered away from the *Seeadler*. Von Luckner cleared his guns and opened fire, his first shots dropping well astern of the fleeing steamer. He then furled his sails, started his auxiliary engine, and gave chase.

The *Lundy Island*, unarmed except for a few ancient rifles, could not hit back, but by zig-zagging violently Barton made his ship as difficult a target as possible. The chase continued for more than forty-five minutes, during which time the *Seeadler*'s gunners fired thirty-one shells at the *Lundy Island*. Barton's evasive action was so good that only three enemy shells hit his ship. However, one of these shells holed her below the waterline, and another carried away one of her steering chains. Taking in water, and unable to steer, Barton was obliged to heave to.

As the *Seeadler* approached, now using her machine-guns to sweep the decks, Barton ran below to his cabin, gathered up all his confidential papers and books, and burned them in the galley stove. When he returned to the bridge, he found that his crew, probably thinking him to be dead, had taken the two lifeboats and abandoned him. The two ships were now very close, and von Luckner, on seeing Barton stranded on his doomed ship, sent a boat across for him.

After boarding the *Seeadler*, David Barton began to regret his rescue. The first man he came face to face with was the raider's surgeon, Dr. Pietsch, who had been serving in the *Möwe* when Barton had been taken by her in the *Corbridge*. Pietsch recognised Barton but, fortunately, von Luckner chose to take no action with regard to the captain's broken parole, other than to send him to join Captain Shewan of the *Gladys Royle*, then keeping a lonely vigil in captivity below decks.

Capturing and sinking the two steamers, although they were unarmed, had not been easy, and Felix von Luckner was beginning to come around to the way of thinking of his superiors in Berlin. Sail, even when equipped with an auxiliary engine, was no match for steam. Although the steamers were rapidly dominating the trade routes, the wind was free, and most shipowners being by nature parsimonious, there was still a considerable number of merchant ships under sail, particularly on the long ocean passages. Von Luckner decided that he might have better luck if he moved south of the Azores and west of the Canaries, where the sailing ship routes to Cape Horn and the Cape of Good Hope criss-crossed. There, the *Seeadler* could sit like a spider at the centre of a huge web, waiting for the Allied windjammers to come to her.

Von Luckner reached his desired position in mid-Atlantic on the morning of 21 January, and shortened sail to await his prey. He did not have long to wait. His first victim sailed into the net within hours. She was the 2199-ton French three-masted barque *Charles Gounod*, loaded with a cargo of corn. Her log book was a mine of valuable information for von Luckner, giving details of other ships met and their intended routes.

Three days then passed with an empty horizon, but on the 24th, when the *Seeadler* was some 150 miles north-east of the lonely outpost of St. Paul's Rocks, another sail was at last sighted. This proved to be the 364-ton Liverpool schooner *Perce,* bound Santos with a cargo of timber and fish in barrels. Von Luckner stopped her with two shots across the bow, and ordered her crew to abandon ship. He was not pleased when he found that the *Perce*'s master, Captain Kohler, had been recently married and was carrying his new wife with him. The *Seeadler* had acquired her first female prisoner, and in the early 20th century, when chivalry was still held in high regard, this promised complications. Von Luckner solved the problem by accommodating Captain Kohler and his wife in a spare stateroom.

Over the following three weeks, the *Seeadler* sank only two more ships, both sailing vessels loaded with saltpetre from Chile. Nevertheless, two more ships sunk meant two more crews to feed and water, and the raider's supplies were running low. Then, ten days later, on 19 February, a four-master was sighted and chased. She turned out to be the 2431-ton British ship *Pinmore,* commanded by Captain James Mullen, and homeward bound from Buenos Aires, also with a full cargo of saltpetre. It so happened that Felix von Luckner had served in this ship fifteen years earlier, and he knew her well. Typical of the man, he 'borrowed' the *Pinmore*, and impersonating Captain Mullen, took her into Rio de Janeiro with a prize crew to pick up supplies.

Returning to the *Seeadler* three days later, von Luckner disposed of the *Pinmore* with scuttling charges, and continued to cruise between the Azores and St. Paul's Rocks, sinking three more large sailing barques, two French and one British. In the seven weeks he had been avoiding steamers and adhering to Berlin's orders to attack only sailing vessels, he had accounted for only eight, in all a total of 16,235 tons of shipping. He decided to return to his own policy of attacking anything that came along. Six days later, the *Horngarth* obligingly hove in sight.

The 3609-ton, Cardiff-registered steamer, *Horngarth*, under the command of Captain I.N. Stainthorp and carrying a crew of thirty-two, was on passage from Montevideo to Plymouth with a cargo of 5,650 tons of maize. On the morning of 11 March 1917, she was 220 miles east-north-east of St. Paul's Rocks and, urged on by a fresh south-easterly breeze, was making good speed to the north-east. At about 8.30, the masts of a sailing ship were sighted at four points on the starboard bow.

She also appeared to be on a north-easterly course.

Throughout the day the *Horngarth* slowly overtook the stranger, which by 3 o'clock in the afternoon was recognisable as a fully rigged three-masted barque. An hour later, the *Horngarth*'s second officer reported to Captain Stainthorp that the sailing ship was making smoke, and apparently on fire.

Stainthorp increased speed and raced to the rescue, at the same time instructing his wireless operator to contact any naval ships that might be nearby to alert them to the situation. As the *Horngarth* drew near to the burning ship she was seen to be flying British colours. She also had a flag hoist at the yardarm which could not be indentified. Through his telescope, Stainthorp saw men running about that the decks of the sailing ship in panic. As he studied the chaotic scene, a woman – the Captain's wife, he presumed – appeared on the poop deck waving her arms hysterically. There was not a moment to be lost if the crew of this ship were to be rescued.

Had Captain Stainforth been able to board the 'distressed' British barque, he would have learned that she was the *Seeadler,* and that the black smoke pouring from her accommodation was being generated by a smoke box. The hysterical 'Captain's wife' was, of course, the *Seeadler*'s deck boy in a dress and bonnet.

When only a few hundred yards from the stricken ship, Stainthorp stopped his engines and prepared to send a boat. This was the signal for von Luckner to lower his Red Ensign, break out the German colours, and put a shot across the *Horngarth*'s bows. At the same time, the fire aboard the *Seeadler* was miraculously extinguished.

As cunning as Felix von Luckner might be, Captain Stainthorp was equally quick to react to the deception. He sheered away from the German raider, rang for emergency full speed, and showed his stern to von Luckner's gunners.

Von Luckner, annoyed by the distainful action of the British ship, now brought both his 105-mm guns to bear and opened fire on the *Horngarth.* Whether by intention or chance, one German shell struck the after part of the British ship's bridge, smashing her wireless cabin and putting her radio out of action. The shell also mortally wounded one of her apprentices, 16-year-old Douglas Page. This saddened Captain Stainthorp, but he continued to run, and the *Seeadler,* using her diesel engine to supplement her sails, gave chase, firing now with both 105-mms and machine guns.

Although the two ships were very close, it did seem that the *Horngarth* might get away – and she might well have done so, had not one of the *Seeadler*'s shells penetrated her boiler room and smashed a main steam pipe. The engine room was filled with high-pressure steam, scalding four men and forcing the others to abandon the compartment.

Having no crew in the engine room, Stainthorp was unable to stop his engines, and for nearly an hour he carried on, taking violent evading action to dodge the hail of enemy shells hurled at his ship. Eventually, with five men wounded, one of them very seriously, he was forced to acknowledge defeat. He was unable to reach the flag locker to hoist a signal, so he displayed a large white sheet to indicate surrender.

The *Seeadler* ceased fire, no doubt expecting the *Horngarth* to heave to, but with the engine room unmanned Stainthorp was unable to stop. And so the chase went on, von Luckner recommencing the firing, while the British ship continued to dodge and run. Before long, the raider's heavy guns again began to hit home, two shells striking the *Horngarth* in the stern, another destroying one of her lifeboats.

The *Horngarth*'s engine finally ran out of steam as darkness was closing in, and she slowly came to a halt. In all, the *Seeadler*'s gunners had fired twenty-four shells at her during the chase, and it was only due to Captain Stainthorp's superb handling of the ship that more damage and casualties were not caused.

Captain Stainforth and his crew were transferred to the *Seeadler*, and the *Horngarth* was sunk with explosive charges at 10 o'clock that night. The injured were well cared for on the raider, but 16-year-old Douglas Page could not be saved. He died aboard the *Seeadler* that night, and was buried at sea next morning. He was the first to fall to the raider's guns, and his death so affected von Luckner that, after the burial, he presented Captain Stainforth with the following testimony:

> It is an old German custom to honour the dead of our enemies and now we are standing on the pall of this young knight. He is not our enemy any more, he is now our friend and is at present where our forefathers are gathered, where all are brothers. God has his future destined. God has called him to his side, he is happy now because he is looking into the face of Jesus Christ. Let us pray and remember his father and mother and hope that God will lighten them the loss of their child. He has fulfilled the duty of the flag (British) under which he is now getting buried.
>
> Signed Count von Luckner
> Commander
> S.M.S. *Seeadler*

Having dealt with the *Horngarth,* von Luckner was obliged to face up to an increasingly urgent problem. When the *Seeadler* sailed away from the sinking ship, she had on board, in addition to her own crew, a total of 300 prisoners, all of whom had to be fed and cared for. A solution to the problem was found when, on 20 March, the *Seeadler* fell in with and captured the French four-masted barque *Cambronne.* Von Luckner transferred his prisoners to the barque, then cut down her rig so that she was just able to sail safely, and no more. Captain Mullen ex-master of the *Pinmore* was put in command, and told to head for the nearest South

American port. With her reduced rig, the *Cambronne* would be unlikely to make port for many days, by which time the *Seeadler* would have long disappeared from sight. The French barque did in fact arrive in Rio de Janeiro on 30 March.

It was Count Luckner's intention to seek new hunting grounds in the Pacific, and although three British cruisers were by that time out searching for her, the *Seeadler* escaped by going far to the south, rounding Cape Horn unseen and entering the Pacific on 18 April. She then sailed north along the coast of Chile, then west, and early June found her cruising to the east of Christmas Island. While in this area, von Luckner received news that America had joined the war on the side of the Allies. He retraced his tracks to the eastward, on the lookout for American shipping, but found only three small sailing vessels, which he sank.

June turned to July, and by this time the *Seeadler* had been continuously at sea for nearly seven months, and her bottom was foul with barnacles and weed. Von Luckner looked for a secluded anchorage in which to clean the hull, and settled on the tiny island of Mopelia, an uninhabited coral atoll in the Society Islands. The *Seeadler*'s draught was too deep for her to enter the lagoon, and von Luckner had to make do with an anchorage outside the reef.

It has not been established what really happened to the *Seeadler*. Von Luckner claimed that she was struck by a tsunami and thrown on to the reef, but some of his American prisoners stated that most of the crew were ashore picnicking when the ship dragged her anchor and drifted on to the reef. Whatever the truth of the matter was, the *Seeadler* was hard and fast on the Mopelia's reef, dismasted, and with her bottom holed. She would never sail again. This von Luckner accepted, but he was not prepared to wait on the island to see what fate had to offer him. With five of his men, *Leutnant* Kircheiss, Engineer Krause and three seamen, he launched one of the *Seeadler*'s longboats and set off to capture a sailing vessel with which to continue fighting the war for Germany.

After an epic 2000-mile voyage around the Pacific islands posing as shipwrecked Norwegian sailors, von Luckner and his companions finally ended up on the Fijian island of Wakaya. Investigations made by the Fijian police revealed their true identity, and all six men were seized as prisoners of war and sent to a camp in New Zealand.

That should have been the end of the war for the intrepid von Luckner, but he had no intention of rotting in a prison camp. With the aid of *Leutnant* Kircheiss and a few other prisoners, he stole a fast motor boat belonging to the commandant of the camp, and raced away to find refuge amongst the islands. The escapees were captured while trying to raid a stores depot in the Kermadec Islands. Then their war was really over.

In the hands of anyone but the audacious Felix Graf von Luckner, the *Seeadler*, the Imperial German Navy's only raider under sail, would almost certainly have been a failed experiment. While her record would never approach that of the *Möwe*, she did capture and sink – with the exception of the *Cambronne* – fifteen Allied ships, totalling 26,364 tons gross. Much to Felix von Luckner's credit, this was done with the loss of only one life, the unfortunate apprentice Douglas Page of the *Horngarth*, whose death was unintentional. It is worth recording that, throughout his piratical voyaging in the *Seeadler*, Felix von Luckner made every effort to avoid killing the merchant seamen on whom he was making war.

Chapter Eleven

Atlantic Duel

The North Atlantic, fabled ocean of storms, is at its worst in March. This is the month of the spring equinox, when the sun moves north from the Equator, pushing before it the warm, moist air that sends the elements into a turmoil. The great ocean heaves and growls; gale follows hard upon the heels of gale.

It was so on the afternoon of Saturday 10 March 1917, when the New Zealand Shipping Company's cargo liner *Otaki* was four days out from London, and already weathering her second gale of the voyage.

The 9575-ton *Otaki,* under the command of 38-year-old Captain Archibald Bisset-Smith, was bound for the Panama Canal, and thence on into the Pacific to New Zealand to pick up her usual cargo of frozen lamb. Built in Denny's yard at Dumbarton in 1908, the *Otaki* was an innovation for her day. Twin-screw, she was the first merchant ship to be equipped with a low pressure exhaust turbine, which boosted her triple-expansion steam engines to give a speed of 15 knots.

Even at that speed, the passage ahead was long, but not unwelcome to the *Otaki*'s 72-man British crew. It was a time to exchange the hurly-burly of the world ashore for the peace and solitude of the open sea. Long, lazy days painting ship, writing letters home, building ships in bottles, or just yarning on the hatches in the tropical twilight. The 'last of the gracious living', they called it.

That was the way it had been. Now, with Britain three years into a bitter war with Germany, it had all changed. The merchant ships, innocents in a violent world, were suffering grievously at the hands of a ruthless enemy. The Kaiser's new underwater weapon, the U-boat, dismissed by the Admirals in London as an empty threat, was proving them wrong. 'Sink without warning' was the order of the day, and the resultant toll in ships and men was frightening. The ocean tramps, condemned to run the gauntlet of the enemy's shells and torpedoes at 7 or 8 knots – no faster than the average brewer's dray – were bearing the brunt of the slaughter. The *Otaki,* being a refrigerated ship in the liner trade, had the advantage of speed, and was less vulnerable. She also mounted a long-barrelled 4.7-inch gun on her poop, and in her wartime Admiralty Grey paint, with her bow-wave frothing, she looked every inch a ship very capable of taking care of herself. The speed was real enough, but her gun, of Boer War vintage, manned by two naval gunners assisted by a scratch crew of merchant seamen, was never meant to be more than a morale booster. It had yet to be fired in anger.

On that March afternoon in 1917, the wind was blowing force 8-9 from the north-west, bringing with it vicious rain squalls, and the seas were slamming against the *Otaki*'s hull to send curtains of spray cascading over her bridge. She was then 420 miles west of Lisbon, steering a south-westerly course and, in the opinion of Captain Bisset-Smith, well out of range of the U-boats. Bisset-Smith was, however, concerned at reports received that a German cruiser was operating off the Cape Verde Islands. For the time being, at least, the *Otaki* was hidden from view behind a cloak of foul weather. But when the wind eased and the rain squalls cleared, he resolved to prevail on his chief engineer to produce that extra knot he always kept up his sleeve, and they would run like the wind. Unbeknown to Bisset-Smith, the *Otaki*'s destiny lay just over the horizon.

The *Möwe* had started life in Wilhelmshaven in 1914 as the 4595-ton *Pungo,* built for F. Laeisz of Hamburg. She was a 14-knot refrigerated cargo ship, designed to carry bananas from the German colonies in West Africa, younger and smaller than, but cast in much the same mould as, the *Otaki.* The resemblance ended while the *Pungo* was in the fitting-out yard. There she was requisitioned by the German Navy as an armed merchant cruiser, and designated as *Hilfskreuzer* 10. She was fitted with a formidable armament consisting of four rapid firing 150-mm guns forward, a 105-mm aft, two 22-pounders, and four torpedo tubes, two each side amidships. The guns and torpedo tubes were all hidden by false bulwarks, and the ship carried materials to erect a dummy funnel, as well as an ample supply of paint to change her colours at will. Lastly, when she was ready for commissioning, the *Pungo*'s name was changed to *Möwe* (Seagull), a deceptively innocent name for what was, in effect, a full-blown warship.

The man appointed to command the *Möwe* was 36-year-old *Korvettenkapitän* Nikolaus Burggraf und Graf zu Dohna-Schlodien, aristocrat and serving naval officer since 1896. Count Dohna-Schlodien proved to be a strict disciplinarian. He trained his men hard, but he was always fair, and he soon became respected and liked by all those who sailed under him.

The *Möwe* left Kiel on her first operational cruise in December 1915, carried out mine laying off Cape Wrath and at the entrance to the River Gironde, then moved south and west into the Atlantic. Her appearance in the trade routes came as a complete surprise to the Allies, her first conquests being the already mentioned *Farringford* and *Corbridge,* taken on 11 January 1916. Thereafter, she carved a swathe through the steady flow of commercial shipping with comparative ease. In the course of three months' raiding, she captured and sank fifteen ships totalling 57,855 tons gross, and at the cost of just one torpedo and a handful of shells. Her success was almost too good to be true.

After three largely unsuccessful forays into the Baltic, the *Möwe* sailed from Wilhelmshaven on her second deep-sea cruise in November 1916, and as soon as she was clear of Biscay began to reap another rich harvest. Four months later, on 10 March 1917, she was 300 miles north of Madeira and homeward bound, having sunk or captured another twenty-two Allied merchant ships totalling 104,340 tons.

The day had begun well, with the Pacific Steam Navigation Company's 4678-ton *Esmeraldas,* another unsuspecting victim, sailing obligingly into Count Dohna-Schlodien's open arms.

The *Esmeraldas,* commanded by Captain F.W. Makin, was in ballast and on passage from Liverpool to Newport News to collect a consignment of horses. Built at Sunderland in 1906, she was owned by the Pacific Steam Navigation Company of Liverpool, and had a total complement of 118, which included fifty-seven horse-handlers, all citizens of the then neutral United States of America. One of the American handlers, Bernard Boyle, described the meeting with the German raider:

> We were about 500 miles [sic] from the American coast when the *Möwe* overhauled and stopped the *Esmeraldas* with a warning shot on March 19, 1917. We had a stern gun but had no chance to use it against the clever and swift manoeuvring of the German ship.

> Within a few minutes the raiders had come aboard and had divided into three parties, one taking charge of the engine room, another the gun and the ship's officers, while the third quickly disabled the wireless. Because of the heavy seas and the difficulty in getting our boats rapidly out, our crew of 60 men and officers [sic] were taken over in the *Möwe*'s boats.

Having disposed of the *Esmeraldas* using timed charges, Count Dohna-Schlodien would have been quite happy to draw a line under the *Möwe*'s second war cruise. The raider was low on fuel and provisions, sorely in need of repairs, and her prison quarters were uncomfortably crowded with nearly 450 prisoners. She desperately needed the sanctuary of a German port, and it had been Dohna-Schlodien's intention to slip quietly around the north of Scotland, then run the British blockade into the North Sea. Unfortunately, when the *Otaki* suddenly appeared out of a rain squall there was no way of avoiding a confrontation.

The *Möwe* and the *Otaki* sighted each other simultaneously, with both captains examining the other's ship through their binoculars, Dohna-Schlodien with anticipation, Bisset-Smith with suspicion. At first sight, the British captain thought the *Möwe* was a typical banana boat hurrying home with her perishable cargo. Then he became aware of her guns, which were now uncovered. Without hesitation, he ordered the helm hard over and rang for emergency full speed ahead. As the *Otaki* turned stern-on to the stranger and fled to the north, her gun's crew ran aft to man their ancient 4.7. The chase was on.

The ensuing running fight between the two ill-matched ships was fierce, with no quarter asked or given on either side. Both ships were pitching heavily as they slammed their bows deep into the on-coming seas, their foredecks awash with green, foaming water each time they lifted from the trough. The fine art of gunlaying was reduced to a matter of pot luck. *Möwe*'s gunnery officer, *Kapitänleutnant* Hermann Jung, described the conditions as seen from the deck of the raider:

> The ship came out of a squall so that it was not possible for us to shadow him inconspicuously. When we changed course to overhaul him gradually on a converging course he turned north and made off at high speed. He must have become suspicious from our change of course. He had wireless equipment and a 12-cm gun

> on the poop. Seeing we had given ourselves away, he simply had to be brought to bay if we did not wish to give up our plans to run the blockade into the North Sea. So, we turned about after him. We were steaming into a wind force 8. Our ship was pitching badly, and we were taking heavy seas over us.

With four 5.9s, manned by trained naval gunners, matched against a single 4.7 handled by a scratch crew consisting largely of merchant seamen, the odds were heavily stacked in favour of the *Möwe*. Yet it was the *Otaki*'s gunners who gained the first, and vital, advantage. With the range down to 2000 yards, the 4.7 scored a direct hit on the German ship, the shell exploding below the waterline near her bows. Two men were killed, and the sea rushed in through the hole blown in the cruiser's hull. She immediately developed a heavy list to port, and began to settle by the head.

That his intended victim should land such a lucky blow on the *Möwe* so early in the fight came as a humiliating shock to Count Dohna-Schlodien. Shock turned to indignation when, minutes later, the *Otaki* proved that her gunnery was anything but haphazard by lobbing a 4.7 calibre shell into the *Möwe*'s engine room coal bunker. There was a violent explosion in the bunker, the blast from which swept through the adjoining boiler room, cutting down nine of the stokers on duty at the time.

The German gunners soon recovered from their shock, and began to hit back. Dohna-Schlodien was able to bring all his big guns to bear, and soon the situation was reversed. *Kapitänleutnant* Jung commented on the fierce resistance put up by the *Otaki*'s gunners:

> Hit with the 10.5 cm on the pedestal of the steamer's stern gun. The British gun crew are lost from sight; but immediately after, four men appear at the gun and recommence fire. With such an obstinate defence it will now depend on which of the two ships first manages to disable the other's capability to carry on the fight. So the order is given for our torpedo tubes to be got ready and permission to fire is given.

It proved unnecessary for the *Möwe* to use her torpedoes. A total of fifty-eight shells were fired at the British ship, of which Jung reported twenty-two found their mark. By 4.30 pm, twenty minutes after the duel began, the *Otaki* was on fire from stem to stern. Her single gun had been knocked out, four of her crew lay dead, and nine others were seriously injured.

Darkness was not too far away, and with the fires out of control and his ship rapidly settling by the stern, Captain Bisset-Smith finally accepted that he could fight no longer. He rang the engines to stop, and gave the order to abandon ship. Having supervised the placing of the wounded in the boats, Bisset-Smith then returned to the bridge. It may be that he went back to make sure that no one else was left alive on board, or perhaps he just felt the need to be with his command when she went to her last resting place. The question must remain unanswered, for Archibald Bisset-Smith was never seen again. He now lies with the *Otaki* 3000 fathoms deep, and with him lie Deck Boy Robert Keneston, Apprentice Basil Kilner, Third Engineer Arthur Little, Apprentice William Martin – just 14 years old when he died – and Steward H.J. Willis.

The *Möwe*'s casualty list was even more grievous, and all were the result of the *Otaki*'s shell bursting in the raider's engine room. Machinist's Mate Emil Sturm died in the explosion, as did Stokers Herman Botterbrodt, Otto Dohmke and Emil Lenz. The others lingered on, Stokers Ludwig Gratz and Heinrich Pungs slipping away on the 11th, Stoker Hermann Oppermann a day later, Leading Stoker Wilhelm Wessels on the 15th, and Leading Stoker Martin Kruger dying in hospital in Kiel on 23 March.

Bisset-Smith and his men did not sacrifice their lives in vain. The *Otaki*'s defiance when challenged by the enemy, and the accurate shooting of her gun's crew had crippled the hitherto invincible *Möwe*. The raider was taking in water forward at an alarming rate, and with smoke and flames pouring out of her engine room bunker, she was forced to heave to while damage control parties fought to save her. And in the midst of all this turmoil several hundred Allied prisoners, thought to be securely battened down in the after hold, staged a breakout. Gunnery Officer Jung recorded a vivid description of the situation on board the raider:

> Now reports come chasing in from our battle stations. Violent inrush of water forward. An intensive fire in the engine room bunker.
>
> The prisoners are trying to break out. A revolt on the part of the prisoners – we had 338 white prisoners in the after hold that

had been fitted out as prison quarters, and 104 Indian lascars in the engine room bunkers – had already been suppressed during the engagement. But our position down by the head and our strong list were a source of anxiety, and thick smoke and glowing flames were bursting out from the engine room. After trying the collision mats – which were as good as useless – we managed to force heavy wedges of wood into the holes and stuff the gaps with sailcloth, so making her watertight in rough and ready fashion. By flooding other compartments we corrected the list and brought her to an even keel. Midships the situation was more serious. The bunkers of coal on fire could not be extinguished just like that! The bulkhead towards the forepart of the ship was already heating and the planking began to smoulder. The midships section was sealed off and kept under live steam. Ammunition, explosives and warheads of torpedoes were manhandled on to the deck, so as to be ready to heave overboard if need be. All night we had to lie stopped there waiting to see what would happen with our smouldering volcano.

During the night the deck under my feet became hotter and hotter. By dawn part of the bulkheads were glowing and the hull began to peel with the heat. As the caulking on the boat deck opened up flames came through. The situation was desperate. Seawater was our only hope. Oxy-acetylene cutters bored holes in the hull at approximately 11 points. All available fire hydrants poured a flood of water into the mass of burning coals, it proved effective, but slowly. But because of the quantity of water we took into the ship she lay even deeper. To crown everything, the valves of the pumps became choked with floating coal dust so that we wallowed helplessly in the heavy seas.

This lamentable state of affairs went on for two days till we got the better of the danger of fire and flood. Then, once again fit for action and in good heart, *Möwe* turned north to face the risks of running the blockade on her passage home to Germany.

In tangling with Archibald Bisset-Smith, the intrepid Count Nicholas Dohna-Scholdien had more than met his match, and the *Möwe* had been lucky to survive the fight between these two seemingly ill-matched ships. Her fires extinguished and the shell holes in her hull plugged, the battered raider limped north. Uppermost in Dohna-Schlodien's mind was the necessity of reaching a German port as soon as possible. The American prisoner Bernard Boyle described conditions prevailing on board the *Möwe:*

> How the commander managed to keep the *Möwe* afloat was a marvel to us when we saw the next day some of the effects of the shots. There were shell and shot holes in the steel hull which the crew had plugged, and the shoulders of these plugs projected from the outside. First the commander had lowered canvas sheets, weighted at the ends, over the water-line holes, which shut off the inflow of water. Then plugs, of which it seems the raider carried a supply of assorted sizes just for such emergencies, were fitted in and the water pumped out and the ship righted. When the plugs could not be used they reamed around the holes with acetylene gas and inserted plates.
>
> We were permitted to exercise for short intervals on deck. That was the only relief from the terrible confinement of our quarters, where 500 men slept, most of them on the floor, and some in hammocks or on tables. We had to move cautiously to prevent stepping upon each other during the hours we generally sought to sleep. We had two meals a day, consisting of rice and prunes, sometimes varied with a little pork and beans, and once only we had vegetable soup, but never bread or coffee. We were told by our captors that food was scarce because the stores had been flooded and ruined by the *Otaki*'s fight. There was a very great shortage of water, too. All the water was obtained by condensing, and, although the machinery was quickly repaired, the commander used all the steam for the flight from the place where he had nearly met the fate of the vanquished, and no water was to be had for several days beyond the small tinful for each man, barely enough to prevent extreme suffering.

From now on survival was all that mattered to the *Möwe,* and with that in mind Dohna-Schlodien took a wide sweep out into the lonely reaches of the Atlantic. As a result of the damage inflicted by the *Otaki*'s gunners, the raider was steaming on reduced speed and was thus very vulnerable. Action with another ship was something that her commander wished to avoid at all costs. On reaching mid-Atlantic, Dohna-Schlodien set course to pass to the north of Scotland, forgetting, perhaps, that he was following the main shipping lane between New York and the Channel. The *Möwe* still had battles to fight.

The 6048-ton British tramp *Demeterton,* owned by Chapman & Willan Ltd. of Newcastle-upon-Tyne, sailed from Halifax, Nova Scotia on 6 March. Commanded by Captain A. Spencer, she was manned by a crew of thirty-three, and carried a full cargo of Canadian timber destined for the Admiralty's shipyards.

The *Demeterton*, built with cargo capacity in mind rather than speed, had experienced bad weather, and by the morning of the 13th she was less than halfway through her 2,400-mile crossing. During the course of that morning, the weather showed a rapid improvement, and by the time noon sights were taken she was found to be logging 8 knots. It was then that she sighted, and began to overtake the other vessel.

As the distance between the two ships narrowed, it became plain to those on the bridge of the *Demeterton* that they were overtaking a fast fruit carrier – probably one of Elders & Fyffes – a most unusual occurrence for the snail-like tramp. The mystery was explained an hour or so later, when the two ships were less than 1000 yards apart. The stranger suddenly veered across the *Demeterton*'s course, and ran up the German ensign.

Captain Spencer took immediate evasive action to avoid a collision, and only then did he see the *Möwe*'s guns, manned and ready to fire. The *Demeterton* was armed with an ancient 4-inch on the poop, but it had not been manned, and Spencer realised the futility of trying to fight this heavily armed raider. Reluctantly, he hauled down his colours and stopped his engines.

Count Dohna-Schlodien now took possession of a prize he had not really wanted. A boarding party was sent across to the British ship, her crew taken off, and scuttling charges laid. When night fell, the *Demeterton* was to be seen floating bottom up in the long Atlantic swells.

And still the *Möwe*'s war on enemy shipping was not yet ended. Next morning, at about 10.30, she fell in with yet another British merchantman, the 5524-ton *Governor,* one of Harrisons' of Liverpool, under the command of Captain G. Packe.

Unlike Captain Spencer of the *Demeterton,* Packe elected to fight, manning his 4-inch as soon as the *Möwe* declared herself. However, such was the German raider's fire power that Packe's resistance brought him only grief. The *Governor*'s stern gun was put out of action by the *Möwe*'s first salvo, and her bridge was soon reduced to a pile of burning matchwood. Four of her crew lay dead, and nine others, including her chief and second officers were seriously wounded. After the British survivors had been taken off, Count Dohna-Scholdien, in a hurry to quit the scene, used one of his carefully preserved torpedoes to sink the *Governor*.

One of the British prisoners described the closing days of the *Möwe*'s voyage home:

> Then came the run back to Germany. Even the chilly sunshine of the North Atlantic faded to a uniform greyness of sea and sky as high latitudes were reached. Our spells of exercise on deck became shorter and shorter; there were more people to exercise and the danger of a lurking British periscope sighting the unusually crowded decks of an innocent merchant ship must have given the Count plenty of anxiety. Sometimes we could pause in our walk round and round the after deck and watch the shot plugs on the water line, now clear of the sea, and then plunged beneath the surface in a cloud of flying bubbles as the rolling steamer sped onwards.
>
> One night, when the cold northern fogs swirled over the sea, the rumble of the raider's engines ceased. Down the cowl ventilators of our quarters came the unmistakeable sound of a diesel engine. Guttural orders and advice sounded from overside followed by a faint 'aufweidersehen'. We guessed that a U-boat had rendezvoused with the Count to give him the latest information about the British cruiser screen . . .
>
> There followed a day and a night of frenzied driving through the net of British patrols and down the North Sea under the shade of the Norwegian coast.
>
> Those few prisoners who were allowed on deck to fetch the short ration meals and brackish water, brought back tales of how the ship had changed her appearance. Neutral colours were painted on her sides; a strange name decorated her after wheel box. For a few hours she battled with an ice jam with the low

> dunes of Denmark close to starboard before slipping into harbour. Down in the prison deck we heard the rumble of the anchor cable in the early hours of the night and then silence; the silence of a ship at anchor after months of straining service; the quiet which tells of a crew sleeping with the sure knowledge that no clanging gongs will send them hurrying to action stations. The date was March 20th, 1917 . . .
>
> The arrival of the *Möwe* caused considerable furore in Kiel. There was much celebrating and doubtless much back patting. Several of the celebrants got rather drunk and the paymaster of the ship was indiscreet enough to get into trouble for being rude to British prisoners while under the influence of liquor which illustrates the innate sense of decency which seemed to move zu Dohna in all his dealings. We were at war but we were still humans and some of us were even gentlemen.

When the *Möwe* eventually limped into Kiel, her damage was found to be so severe that her days as an ocean raider were declared to be over. She served out the rest of the war as an auxiliary minelayer in the Baltic.

Although the *Möwe*'s career as a commerce raider was cut short, in the course of her two war cruises, spread over fifteen months, she had disposed of thirty-eight Allied merchantmen totalling 174,905 tons gross. This unprecedented success earned Count Dohna-Schlodien promotion to *Fregattenkapitän;* he was appointed naval *aide-de-camp* to Kaiser Wilhelm, and awarded a chestful of decorations, including the fabled 'Blue Max', Germany's equivalent of the Victoria Cross.

And what of the Graf's opposite number in the *Otaki,* whose brave stand put an end to the *Möwe*'s reign of terror? Sadly, Captain Archibald Bisset-Smith, who so obviously deserved his country's highest award for gallantry, proved to be something of an embarrassment to the Admiralty. Although he was in command of an armed ship, technically he was a civilian, and as such was not eligible for a military decoration. Strong arguments were put forward in favour of an exception to the rule in this case, but the Admiralty, as with Parslow, again fell back on the defence that official recognition of Bisset-Smith's brave action might invite repercussions against British merchant seamen held prisoners of war in Germany. In the end, it was decided to let Archibald Bisset-Smith fade quietly into history.

The Admirals did not reckon with Bisset-Smith's widow, Edith, who mounted a vigorous and sustained campaign for official recognition of her husband's gallantry. The national press took up the torch, and eventually a compromise was reached. Captain Archibald Bisset-Smith was posthumously commissioned into the Royal Naval Reserve as a lieutenant, and he thus became eligible for a military decoration. What this master mariner in command of a prestigious cargo liner would have thought of being reduced to a mere lieutenant RNR, should best remain unknown. The record was not set straight until after the war, when on 24 May 1919 the following appeared in the *London Gazette*:

> The KING has been graciously pleased to approve the posthumous award of the Victoria Cross to the undermentioned Officer(s):
>
> Lieutenant Archibald Bisset-Smith, RNR for most conspicuous gallantry and devotion to duty when in command of the S.S. *Otaki*. At about 2.30 pm on 10th March, 1917 the S.S. *Otaki*, whose armament consisted of one 4.7 in gun for defensive purposes, sighted the disguised German raider *Moewe*, which was armed with four 5.9 inch, one 4.1 inch and two 22 pdr guns, and two torpedo tubes. The *Moewe* kept the *Otaki* under observation for some time and finally called upon her to stop. This Lieutenant Smith refused to do, and a duel ensued at ranges of 1900-2000 yards, and lasted for about 20 minutes. During this action the *Otaki* scored several hits on the *Moewe*, causing considerable damage, and starting a fire, which lasted for three days. She sustained several casualties and received much damage herself, and was heavily on fire. Lieutenant Smith, therefore, gave orders for the boats to be lowered to allow the crew to be rescued. He remained on the ship himself and went down with her when she sank with the British colours still flying, after what was described in an enemy account as a duel as gallant as naval history can relate.

Belated awards were also made to the *Otaki*'s Chief Officer, who received the Distinguished Service Order, while two members of the *Otaki*'s gun crew, Leading Seaman Alfred Worth and Able Seaman Ellis Jackson, received the DSM. Apprentices William Martin and B. Kilner were Mentioned in Despatches. Fourteen-year-old William Martin, a fellow Aberdonian Captain Bisset-Smith had taken under his wing, was killed while helping to man the stern gun.

When the war finally ended in 1918, the *Möwe* mouldered alongside a lay-by berth in Kiel for two years, until, in March 1920, she was handed over to the British Shipping Controller as part of Germany's war reparations. A year later, she was given to Elders & Fyffes as a replacement for wartime losses, and renamed *Greenbrier.* She spent the next twelve years in the banana trade, and in June, 1933 she returned to her old flag, being sold to Midgard Deutsche Seeverkehrs of Nordenham, and continued in the fruit trade under the name *Oldenburg.*

War came again in 1939, and the *Oldenburg,* now twenty-five years old and showing signs of her long and arduous life, was requisitioned by the German Navy as a transport ship in Norwegian waters. On 7 April, 1945, she was lying alongside the quay of the village of Vadheim, near Bergen, safe from attack – or so it was thought – in the shelter of the steep hillsides of the fjord. However, she had not reckoned with the grim determination of the Beaufighters of 455 Squadron RAAF, stationed 400 miles away in Scotland.

Skimming the wave-tops, and dodging the hail of shells thrown up by German anti-aircraft guns ringing the fjord, the Australian Beaufighters pressed home their attack with rocket and cannon fire. The *Oldenburg* was holed below the waterline, and set on fire. In spite of the efforts of her crew to save her, she broke away from the quay and sank into the dark depths of the fjord. It was an ignominious end to an old ship which in her heyday, as the *Hilfskreuzer Möwe,* was the scourge of the Atlantic Ocean.

Chapter Twelve

The Gloves Come Off

By January 1917, the great armies of Europe facing each other on the Western Front had fought themselves to a complete standstill. Their battlefield was a shell-churned waste of mud stretching from the Belgian coast, across France, to the Swiss frontier; and as winter tightened its grip both sides were so heavily dug in there was little to distinguish between the offensive and defensive. The artillery duels continued unabated, trenches changed hands – a few hundred yards gained here, a few hundred lost there – and over all lay the awful stench of death. The Great War was bogged down in a senseless quagmire of its own making.

In the opinion of the German Army, the only hope of victory lay in cutting off the steady stream of supplies flowing across the Atlantic from neutral America to Britain. To this end, the generals urged the Kaiser to declare unrestricted submarine warfare against all Allied merchant shipping.

On 20 October 1914, when the first merchant ship fell to the U-boats, the sinking was an almost gentlemanly affair. It will be recalled that when *Kapitänleutnant* Feldkirchner brought *U-17* to the surface to challenge the *Glitra*, he acted strictly in accordance with the International Cruiser Rules. He searched her, and then gave her crew time to abandon ship before sinking her with explosive charges. He then towed the lifeboats some distance towards the coast, so that they were easily picked up by a Norwegian pilot vessel.

With a few barbarous exceptions, other U-boat commanders continued to act much as Feldkirchner had done, until, in January 1917, the German High Command declared unrestricted submarine warfare against Allied shipping. Now the whole tenor of the war at sea changed, and it became a dirty, dishonourable business. The merchant ship, once regarded as almost untouchable, was suddenly fair game for the U-boats, a cruelly exposed target to be hunted and sunk without warning from beneath the cover of the waves. In February of that year, 230 Allied ships of 464,599 tons were sent to the bottom with their much-needed cargoes, an increase of almost 50 per cent on the previous month. By the end of April, the monthly tonnage lost had rocketed to 860,334. This, in effect, meant that one in every four merchant ships that left British ports did not return. The waters around the British Isles were littered with wrecks, the excrement of the Kaiser's U-boats. Neutral shipowners took fright, holding their ships in neutral ports to avoid the carnage. This was a potentially crippling blow to Britain's economy, as many of the country's skilled shipyard workers had been conscripted into the Army, and were wasting their talents in the mud of Flanders, instead of building replacement ships. The total output from British yards for April, 1917 was only 67,536 tons – and this when monthly losses were approaching a million tons.

On 1 May 1917, British warehouses held only six weeks supply of essential foods. Nothing was said officially, but it was being whispered in high places that unless something was done about the U-boats, the country would be facing starvation by the time winter came. Desperate attempts were made to blackmail neutral ships into resuming trading, by seizing those already in British ports and threatening to hold them until they carried on supplying Britain as before. Not surprisingly, the foreign shipowners refused, with the result that 300 neutral ships were tied up in London, Liverpool and the Bristol Channel, unwilling to go anywhere.

Now would have been the time to introduce convoys, but the Admiralty would have none of it, fearing that the bunching of ships together would simply make better targets for the U-boats. The merchant ship masters were of a similar opinion, and also claimed they would be unable to keep station in convoy, especially at night. The only concession made to organised action was for all ships to be given recommended routes for the approaches to the British Isles, so that the Royal Navy might keep an eye on their coming and going. With only a handful of armed trawlers and even fewer destroyers available for this work, the Navy could offer no guarantee that ships would go unmolested.

The German Navy now had at its disposal 148 submarines, and

during 1917 another 269 were to be ordered. Even so, the U-boats had a huge expanse of sea to cover, and the greatest danger to Allied merchant shipping was thought to lie within 100 miles of the coast. To date, only fourteen ships had been sunk outside that limit, and only three at over 200 miles. Then, on 31 January 1917, Berlin announced that it was extending the zone in which all shipping was liable to be sunk to an area delineated by a line drawn between Terschelling in Holland and Udsire in Norway, thence to the Faroe Islands, and down the meridian of 20° West as far as Cape Finistère. The forbidden zone also included the Mediterranean as far as Majorca.

When on the morning of 18 March Hain Steamship Company's *Trevose* reached a point 220 miles west-south-west of Land's End, her master, unaware of the extension of U-boat operations, felt it safe to assume his ship was out of danger. He was wrong. At precisely 11 am, a torpedo slammed into the engine-room of the 3112-ton steamer, killing five of her firemen, and breaking her back. The *Trevose* went down a few minutes later, but not before the remaining twenty-five members of her crew had got away in two boats. Fortunately, the weather was fair, and being in one of the Admiralty's recommended shipping lanes, the men were confident of being picked up by a passing ship.

Some thirteen hours before the *Trevose* went down, the *Alnwick Castle* sailed from Plymouth, bound for Cape Town with a full general cargo, fourteen passengers and a number of head of cattle on deck. The 5900-ton cargo/passenger liner, owned by the Union Castle Mail Steamship Company, was no stranger to war, having been requisitioned as a troopship in 1914. She served with distinction in the Gallipoli landings in the summer of 1915, before returning to the Cape run. Her master, 42-year-old Captain Benjamin Chave, RNR, was a very experienced seaman and commander.

By five o'clock on the evening of Sunday the 18th, the *Alnwick Castle* was 200 miles west-south-west of Land's End, and steaming at 13 knots into a light westerly breeze. The sun was low on the horizon, and clear skies indicated a cold night ahead, but the mood on board was one of optimism. Having travelled thus far without a sight of the enemy, it was assumed the *Alnwick Castle* had left the war far in her wake. In twenty-four hours or so, she would be free to alter course to the south and begin her long run down into the untroubled waters of the southern hemisphere. Ten minutes later, with only an hour to go to sunset, two ship's lifeboats were sighted, and by 5.30 all twenty-five survivors of the sinking of the *Trevose* had been picked up.

A report appearing in the *New York Times* on 4 April stated:

> George Grey, one of the five survivors of the *Trevose*, said that she was sunk on March 18, twelve days out from Newcastle, with coal for Alexandria, Egypt. The submarine torpedoed the ship, killing two of the crew at 10.30 o'clock in the morning, and the surviving crew of twenty-five men got away in the two lifeboats at once.
>
> Half an hour later, Grey added, the U-boat rose to the surface and sent a boat to the *Trevose* to put bombs in the hold as she was not sinking fast enough to please the commander. The boats separated in the night and the one Grey was in was picked up early next morning by the *Alnwick*.

The news that the *Trevose* had been torpedoed only six hours earlier, and that the survivors had seen another ship sunk while they were in the boats, presumably by the same U-boat, brought about an abrupt change of atmosphere in the *Alnwick Castle.* So intent was Captain Chave on clearing the area as soon as possible that he did not stop to lift on board the two lifeboats from the other ship. As the *Alnwick Castle*'s total complement was now 139, this was not altogether a wise move.

As soon as his ship was hidden in the darkness, Chave broke radio silence and reported the sinking of the *Trevose* to the Admiralty. During the night, he snatched a few hours sleep, and was back on the bridge at half an hour before dawn. The sky was by then heavily overcast and the barometer falling, indicating bad weather ahead, but Chave was more concerned that the half-light of the coming day would provide good cover for an attacking U-boat. He instructed Chief Officer Blackman to begin a prearranged pattern of zig-zag courses and post extra lookouts. Two men went into the crow's nests, two into the foremast crosstrees and one to the upper bridge. In addition, two cadets were called to the bridge to act as extra eyes for the officer of the watch. As the *Alnwick Castle* was unarmed, Chave could do no more to ensure her safety.

At 6 o'clock, as the sun, hidden by the thick clouds, lifted over the eastern horizon, the captain's steward, Buckley, appeared on the bridge with a tray of coffee and toast. The ship was by then deep into the

Atlantic, 330 miles west of Land's End, and far beyond the reported operating sphere of the U-boats. Captain Chave drank his coffee and surveyed the empty horizon with satisfaction. In two hours or so he would be justified in standing the lookouts down, so that his ship might return to her normal sea-going routine. He was not aware that *U-81* was lying submerged off the *Alnwick Castle*'s starboard bow. Nineteen hours earlier *U-81* had despatched the *Trevose*, and the U-boat's commander, *Oberleutnant-zur-See* Raimund Weisbach, was about to add to his score.

U-81, commissioned out of the Germaniawerft at Kiel at the end of August 1916, was commanded by the man who had been Walther Schwieger's torpedo officer in *U-20*, and had fired the torpedo that sank the *Lusitania*. She was six weeks into her first Atlantic war cruise, and Raimund Weisbach was proving that he had not lost his magic touch, already having disposed of fourteen Allied merchantmen, including the *Trevose*, totalling nearly 45,000 tons since leaving Germany.

Captain Chave was draining the last dregs of the bitter coffee from his cup when, at about 6.10, he was thrown off his feet as a torpedo struck the *Alnwick Castle* and exploded with a thunderous roar. A column of dirty water and debris shot 60 feet into the air from the foredeck, hung for a moment, then cascaded down on the bridge. The ship, her engines still driving her ahead at full speed, checked, and then lunged on with her forecastle visibly lower in the water. She had been hit in her No.2 hold and the sea was pouring in.

Kicking aside the shattered remains of his coffee tray, Chave rang the engines to full astern to take the way off the ship, and sent Chief Officer Blackman down to supervise clearing away the boats. To Wireless Operator Carnaby, who had appeared at his elbow, Chave gave a hastily scribbled SOS message with instructions to keep sending until he received an acknowledgement.

Twenty minutes after the torpedo struck, the *Alnwick Castle*'s forecastle head was awash, and her stern lifting high out of the water. However, she remained upright, and as the sea was calm, all six lifeboats were launched without difficulty. It was now that Chave regretted not having picked up the *Trevose*'s boats. Two of his own boats were really only dinghies, normally used for painting ship or ferrying stores, and should not have been used for abandoning ship. But with an extra twenty-five men to be saved, Chave had no option but to make use of them.

Although the ship was in imminent danger of sinking, Chave found time to go to his cabin for the weighted bags of Admiralty mail and secret codes books kept there. These he threw overboard and then returned to the bridge to collect Carnaby, who having received no answer to his repeated SOS transmissions, was still at his post. Both men then boarded a lifeboat and pulled away from the sinking ship.

Chave led the other boats to a safe distance off the ship, where they huddled in a small group to await the end. It was a doubly harrowing moment for the *Trevose* survivors, who having had two ships blasted from under them in the space of less than twenty-four hours, were numb with shock.

As they watched, the sea boiled and the U-boat surfaced between them and the ship. Her deck gun was quickly manned and trained on the ship, but no shots were fired. At 6.45, in full view of victor and vanquished, the 16-year-old *Alnwick Castle* began her last journey. Proudly upright, and with her steam whistle sounding a long, mournful farewell, she slipped beneath the waves. When she was gone, the U-boat started her engines and made off towards the north-east, where a steamer was visible on the horizon, inward bound, and obviously unaware of the danger she was in. Some time later, there was a dull thump and a tall column of water soaring skywards told the *Alnwick Castle* survivors that any hope of immediate rescue was gone.

Oberleutnant Weisbach's latest victim was the 4194-ton British steamer *Frinton,* bound from Cartegena to the Tees with Government stores. Four of her crew were lost when she went down.

Chave now gathered the other boats around his and counted heads. He was greatly relieved to find that all passengers and crew were accounted for and uninjured. The lifeboats were overcrowded, with precious little freeboard, but he did his best to ease the situation by adjusting the number of people in each boat. Even so, the two small boats ended up with eleven men in each, a dangerous overload that might prove fatal in rough seas. For the moment, the weather was holding good, but they were more than 300 miles out into the open Atlantic, and the boats had at least six days hard sailing ahead of them before they reached British waters.

Sails were hoisted, and with the wind still in the west, they set off in the general direction of the Channel. Keeping close company, they made steady progress throughout the rest of the day, but by sunset the wind had freshened enough to make steering difficult. When darkness closed in, the boats were unable to keep in touch, and were soon scattered around the horizon. They were never to come together again.

In his lifeboat Chave had a total of twenty-nine people, consisting of the *Alnwick Castle*'s chief engineer, doctor, purser, wireless operator, one cadet, twelve ratings, six passengers and five ratings from the *Trevose*. Unfortunately, most of the ratings were firemen or stewards, and, apart from Chave, only three others, Cadet Hemmings, Quartermaster Merrels and Able Seaman Morris, had any knowledge of boat handling.

The wind continued to freshen, and Chave was forced to shorten sail. By the early hours of next morning, the 20th, it was blowing a full gale from the north-north-west. Steering an easterly course, the boat was beam-on to the weather, rolling heavily, and from time to time shipping seas. Without sufficient experienced men to assist him, Chave feared the boat might capsize, and decided to heave-to. The sail was furled, the sea anchor streamed, and the boat came round to lay head-on to the wind and sea, pitching and yawing uncomfortably, but stable. The canvas boat cover was rigged to provide some protection from the weather, but the wind, laden with icy pellets of spray, seemed to be coming straight off the North Pole. And so they waited out the miserable hours until dawn.

Daylight revealed that both the sea anchor and the rudder had been carried away and the boat was once again beam-on to the seas. The wind, now blowing from the north, was too strong for sail to be hoisted, so the oars were manned in an attempt to bring the bow up into the wind. While this was being done, Chave constructed a makeshift sea anchor by lashing two oars together. When streamed, the anchor was only partially effective, and throughout the day it was necessary to use the oars to prevent the boat broaching to. It was cold, demoralising work, yet they dared not give up.

The survivors were fortunate that their ship had been commanded by an experienced man like Captain Ben Chave. Britain was entering her third year of war, and yet it was still not mandatory to stock lifeboats with the necessities for survival, other than the customary 10-gallon breaker of drinking water. But Chave, foreseeing such a situation as he now faced, had made a practice of stocking each of the *Alnwick Castle*'s lifeboats with a case of condensed milk, a case of corned beef, two tins of ship's biscuits and a bundle of blankets. For twenty-nine men cast adrift for an unknown number of days this was not an abundance, but it could mean all the difference between life and death. Chave set a daily ration of four ounces of condensed milk, twenty-four ounces of corned beef and one dipper of water per man per day.

Late that night the wind eased, and it was possible to take in the sea anchor and set sail again. As before, course was set due east for the busy shipping lanes of the English Channel. Next morning, the wind veered more to the north-east and freshened, but the boat surged ahead riding the waves well – perhaps too well. Disaster struck that afternoon, when the mast step gave way under the strain, and mast and sail went crashing overboard. For the majority of the survivors this was the last straw, and they were ready to accept defeat, but Chave rallied them. The gear was dragged inboard, a new mast step improvised with the aid of an axe and a stout piece of wood, and the sail was again hoisted, but not for long. By 8 o'clock that night the wind had once more risen to gale force, and they were obliged to heave-to.

Having waged an unending battle against the sea for more than two days, the survivors were physically exhausted and mentally drained. They were also hungry and thirsty, the latter being acute. Chave issued an extra ration of water for those worst affected, but he would not be able to repeat this, for the water was running out. Providentially, during the night, the wind dropped away and a shower of hail fell. The hailstones were eagerly scooped up and swallowed, but they were not enough to assuage the men's raging thirst. When the hail turned to light rain, the sail was spread out to catch the rain, but there was not even enough moisture to wash the salt out of the canvas.

Early on the morning of the 22nd, the wind came away from the north-east again, making it possible to set sail once more. But, as before, the freshening wind soon became a gale and the boat began making heavy weather of it, shipping spray overall. To add to the survivors' misery the boat began to leak badly, and continuous bailing was necessary if they were to stay afloat. Most of the men were nearing the end of their endurance, some of them half-crazed through drinking salt water, and they had no enthusiasm for bailing. Chave issued an extra ration of water mixed with condensed milk, but this had little effect. Kitcher, the foreman cattleman, died that afternoon.

It was a day without hope, most of it spent lying to a sea anchor at the mercy of an angry sea, and culminating after dark with the boat being swamped by a breaking wave. And that, it seemed, was the end. The boat was awash up to her gunwales, floating only on her buoyancy tanks, and its occupants had no will to do anything about it. Yet, exerting all his authority, Chave once again put heart in them, and the buckets and bailers went to work. The boat was put before the wind by shifting the sea anchor to the stern, and slowly the level of water went down.

By midnight the boat was reasonably dry and the wind had dropped away, but the effort had been too much for the weakened men. Many of them collapsed, some lapsed into temporary insanity. Hopelessness turned to bitter recrimination, and fighting broke out in the crowded boat. Chave was later to say, 'The horror of that night, together with the physical suffering, are beyond the powers of my description.'

Before dawn on the 23rd, with the help of the few men who had not given up, Chave set sail again. Allowing for the southerly drift caused by the wind, he estimated the boat to be in the Bay of Biscay. The water was almost finished, and his hold on the men was becoming more tenuous by the hour. If they were not seen by a passing ship soon, it would be all over. But, when full daylight came, the horizon remained as empty as ever. In answer to insistent demands, Chave made an issue of water. When the dipper had gone the rounds, the breaker contained sufficient for just one last share-out.

They sailed eastwards throughout the morning, deeper into the bay. Most of the men had ceased to take any interest in their surroundings. Although a good deal of food remained, their throats were so parched that they could swallow nothing solid. Their lips were cracked, their limbs without feeling, their hands white and puckered through constant exposure to the sea.

Then they began to die. The first to slip away was Thomas, a fireman, followed soon afterwards by another fireman, Tribe. In the forenoon, Chave's faithful steward, Buckley died in his captain's arms, and on the stroke of noon a cattleman, whom Chave knew only as Peter, also passed away. The bodies remained in the boat, for there was not a man with sufficient strength left to tip them overboard.

That was how, two hours later, they were found by the *Venezia*, a French steamer commanded by Captain Paul Bonifacie. There was a heavy swell running, and although Chave and a few others made a gallant effort, they could not get alongside the French ship. Rescue was left to Bonifacie, who skilfully brought his ship alongside the boat without sinking it. The twenty-five survivors still alive were lifted on board the *Venezia* with ropes.

Captain Chave later wrote in appreciation of his rescuers:

> To our unspeakable relief we were rescued about 1.30 pm on Friday 23 by the French Steamer *Venezia* of the Fabre Line for New York for horses. A considerable swell was running and in our enfeebled state we were unable to properly manoeuvre our boat but the French Captain M. Paul Bonifacie handled his empty vessel with great skill and brought her alongside us, sending out a lifebuoy on a line for us to seize. We were unable to climb the ladders, so they hoisted us one by one in ropes until the 24 men were aboard. The 4 dead bodies were left in the boat and she was fired at by the gunners of the *Venezia* in order to destroy her, but the shots did not take effect.
>
> I cannot speak with sufficient gratitude of the extreme kindness and solicitation which was shown to us by all on board. Our wet clothes were at once stripped off and dry ones put on; hot tea and cognac was poured down our parched and swollen throats; then we were put to bed in steam-heated first class cabins. Our feet and hands were swollen to twice the normal size and several of us narrowly escaped frostbite. In the evening we were given a light meal of soup and boiled beef with potatoes, with claret, and during the night the stewards were kept busy providing water for our unquenchable thirst. Every possible want was anticipated by the captain, officers, engineers and stewards, who placed freely at our disposal their wardrobes, toilet articles, tobacco, etc.
>
> The position of the rescue was 46° 19' N 9° 13' W, about 100 miles from the nearest land, which was the northern coast of Spain. We had sailed about 200 miles in a SE'ly direction. I doubt if we should have survived another night after our last issue of water. I gave the main facts to the captain and he sent out a radio message announcing our rescue in such a manner as to apprise all ships in the vicinity of the possibility of finding some of the other

> five boats. Captain Bonifacie also left his course that afternoon and proceeded to the NW in the hope of seeing some of the other boats.

Five days later, Spanish fishermen off Cape Ortegal found Chief Officer Blackman's boat. Of the thirty-one men originally on board, only twenty-one were still alive, and all of them near the point of insanity for lack of water. In a report he wrote later, Blackman said:

> Although we had occasional showers of rain everything was so saturated with salt that the little we did catch was undrinkable. We even tried by licking the woodwork (oars, tiller, seats, etc.) to gather up the rain spots and so moisten our mouths, but the continual spray coming over rendered this of little use. In fact we actually broke up the water breaker in order to lick the inside of the staves, which we found quite saturated with moisture, and to us delicious.

When rescue came at last, one man died as he was being lifted out of the boat, two others were so demented that they had to be dragged screaming from the boat. They had been adrift for nine days and had sailed a distance of 380 miles.

The *Alnwick Castle*'s two small jolly boats, as Captain Chave had feared, were never seen again, but two other lifeboats were accounted for. In all, of the 139 on board the *Alnwick Castle,* forty died, including three of the crew of the *Trevose.*

Six weeks after sinking the *Alnwick Castle*, Raimund Weisbach suddenly found himself at the wrong end of a British periscope.

U-81 had sailed from Emden on her second deep-sea cruise on 17 April 1917, with orders to operate off the west coast of Ireland. Weisbach's run of luck continued, and he sent another nine Allied ships and their cargoes to the bottom as he progressed into the Atlantic. On 1 May he was 175 miles west-north-west of the Fastnet Rock when the Eagle Oil tanker *San Urbano* came in sight. She was deep-loaded with a cargo of naphtha from Puerto Mexico, bound for London.

Weisbach closed in on the unsuspecting British ship and made a submerged torpedo attack. The torpedo hit the *San Urbano* forward of her bridge, stopping her in her tracks, and killing four of her crew. She showed no signs of sinking, however, and after half an hour Weisbach surfaced, intending to finish her off with gunfire. He waited for the survivors, who had already taken to the boats, to pull clear, then opened fire on the crippled ship.

When the *San Urbano*, holed below the waterline, began to sink by the head, Weisbach headed for the lifeboats to interrogate the survivors. He had no inkling that he had unwittingly walked into a trap.

Quite by chance, His Majesty's submarine *E-54*, commanded by Lieutenant Commander E.H.T. Raikes, was on patrol in the same area, and when Raikes heard the thump of *U-81*'s torpedo striking the *San Urbano* he moved in to investigate. *Oberleutnant* Weisbach had by this time gathered all the information he required from his unfortunate victims. He described the events that followed:

> While we were returning to the steamer, which was about twelve nautical miles away, we spotted a periscope three hundred meters off our starboard beam. We saw a torpedo wake at the same moment and I ordered full speed and tried to turn to avoid the torpedo. The torpedo struck aft followed by a tremendous explosion that sank *U-81* in mere seconds. The men on deck leapt into the water. Fifteen minutes later a British submarine, *E-54*, surfaced and picked up seven men. The *E-54* took us to Queenstown.

Another report, made by *Obermatrose* Herbert Hoeck, stated that the entire stern of *U-81* was blown away, and that she sank in five seconds. The only survivors were *Oberleutnant* Weisbach, the two lookouts in the conning tower with him, and the four gunners manning the deck gun, who all leapt overboard as *U-81* rolled over and sank. Raimund Weisbach was injured, and in danger of drowning, but was pulled from the water by *E-54*'s First Lieutenant, who dived in to save him.

Chapter Thirteen

The Slaughter of the Innocents

In the hands of the Imperial German Navy the submarine was proving to be a deadly weapon, its greatest asset being the ability to creep up unseen on unsuspecting merchant ships. The temptation to sink by torpedoing without surfacing must have been great, and it was to the credit of many U-boat commanders that they strove to honour the Geneva Convention, allowing a crew to take to the boats before sinking their ship. There were exceptions, of course, one of the most notable being 29-year-old *Oberleutnant-zur-See* Wilhelm Werner.

On 27 January 1917, the 3570-ton *Artist,* owned by T & J Harrison of Liverpool and commanded by Captain G. Mills, was 60 miles west of the Smalls, and bound from Newport, Mon. to Alexandria with a cargo of coal. For almost seventy-two hours she had been hove-to, riding out a howling easterly gale, and as the dawn came again, although the deep-loaded ship's decks were still being swept by green seas, there was at last some improvement in the weather. Captain Mills, who had been haunting the bridge of the *Artist* for more hours than he cared to remember, took some comfort from the knowledge that the foul weather would keep the U-boats at bay.

Mills was underestimating the tenacity of the Kaiser's U-boat Arm. At 8 o'clock, as the bells signalled the change of the watch, the crash of the waves was drowned by a massive explosion, and the *Artist* staggered to a halt. She had been torpedoed in her forward hold.

The ship took a heavy list to starboard, and began to settle by the head. It was soon obvious to Mills that she would not last long. He gave the order to abandon ship, not an easy operation in the weather prevailing; but with a show of exemplary discipline and seamanship, three lifeboats were successfully launched, and all forty-five crew cleared the ship safely.

Down at sea level, the rough seas that had battered the *Artist* seemed enormous, towering over the tiny lifeboats, tossing them from crest to crest, and lashing their occupants with icy spray. The satisfaction at having escaped the sinking ship soon turned to despair, and as the night closed in around them, men began to give up hope.

When dawn came on the 28th, only one boat was still afloat. The others had gone, capsized or smashed by the angry seas, and with them twenty-nine men had disappeared into the blackness, never to be seen again. The surviving boat, manned by sixteen men, with a cadet in charge, drifted at the mercy of wind and sea for three days and nights, during which time seven more men died of the cold, the wet, or perhaps the abject despair at being at the mercy of such a hostile sea. Nine survivors, all that remained of the thirty-five men who had sailed the *Artist* out of the Bristol Channel, were rescued by a naval patrol boat when they were in sight of land.

The man who sank the *Artist* in such a casual manner, Wilhelm Werner, was an enthusiastic exponent of this new form of total warfare, and one of the originators of the orgy of indiscriminate sinkings that was to follow.

Twenty-nine-year-old *Oberleutnant-zur-See* Wilhelm Werner had taken command of *U-55* in early June 1916, and rapidly acquired a reputation as a ruthless destroyer of ships and men. In the first three months of 1917, cruising in the Western Approaches, Werner sank nine ocean-going ships, some of them in very questionable circumstances. At least three of these vessels disappeared without trace, leaving no survivors to tell the tale of their going. It was not until the loss of the Cardiff motor vessel *Torrington* that light was shed on Werner's method of waging war on Allied merchantmen.

On the morning of 8 April, the *Torrington,* owned by the Tatem Steam Navigation Company, and under the command of Captain Anthony Starkey, was 150 miles south-west of the Scillies, and inward bound for the Bristol Channel in ballast. For some months past, the 5597-ton motor vessel, under charter to the Italian State Railways, had suffered the indignity of carrying coal between Barry and Savona. For her crew it was a hard slog, much of their time being spent in cleaning decks and holds and battling to keep the invidious dust of their cargo from invading their living spaces, their food and their clothes. On this fine, blustery spring morning, with their ship as near to spick and span as hoses and brushes could possibly make her, the thoughts of the men of the *Torrington* were turning to hearth and home.

At about 11.30, the lookout in the *Torrington*'s crow's nest reported what appeared to be lifeboats ahead. Aware of the number of ships that had been sunk in the area of late, Captain Starkey immediately altered course towards the boats. As he did so, he caught sight of the feathery wake of a torpedo racing straight towards him. In a desperate effort to comb the wake, he ordered the helm hard over, but his action came too late.

The torpedo hit the *Torrington* just forward of the bridge, in her No.3 hold, exploding with tremendous force and throwing a column of dirty water and debris high in the air. A hurried check on the damage showed both Nos 2 and 3 holds to be flooding rapidly, and within minutes the *Torrington* was head down, with her propeller out of the water and thrashing impotently. She slowly drifted to a halt.

The *Torrington*'s attacker, *Oberleutnant* Werner's *U-55*, was one of Germany's latest and best. Manned by three officers and thirty-five ratings, she displaced 940 tons, had a top speed of 15.2 knots on the surface, and a range of 4,800 miles. Her armament consisted of six tubes firing 50 cm torpedoes, a 105 mm deck gun, and two machine-guns.

Seeing his torpedo go home, Werner surfaced, and began to shell the helpless *Torrington*. The British ship mounted a 4-inch gun on her poop, but with her propeller and rudder out of the water, she was unable to manoeuvre to bring the gun to bear on her attacker. Although his ship was not in immediate danger of sinking, in order to avoid casualties, Captain Starkey had no alternative but to haul down his flag. And when the U-boat continued to lob shells at the ship, he decided it was time to leave.

Although still under fire, Starkey and his crew of thirty-four lowered their two lifeboats without panic, and pulled away from the ship. Starkey took charge of the starboard boat, while his Chief Officer took the helm of the port boat. Both boats were about a quarter of a mile from the ship when *U-55* opened fire on them, and then moved in closer.

Werner hailed Starkey's boat, and ordered him to come alongside. When the boat was made fast, all eighteen occupants were herded onto the casing of the submarine. Their boat was then deliberately holed, and left to sink. Starkey, identified as the master of the *Torrington*, was taken below, and there subjected to a most humiliating interrogation by Werner. At the conclusion of this, Werner told Starkey that he would be shot as a pirate, and added: 'As for the others, let them swim.' With that, he took *U-55* down, leaving the remaining seventeen survivors on her casing.

The U-boat remained submerged for about 20 minutes, and when she resurfaced her casings were empty. Of the seventeen men left to their fate, there was no sign, nor were they ever seen again. The *Torrington*'s other lifeboat was nowhere to be seen, although Captain Starkey did see some of *U-55*'s crew members with bottles of spirits and tins of meat, which he recognised as having come from that boat. The boat and its occupants were never seen again. As the sea was calm at the time, they were in the shipping lanes, and the land was not far away, the conclusion must be drawn that, as with the men left to drown when *U-55* submerged, the Chief Officer and his men had been done away with. This was murder, plain and simple.

Having disposed of the *Torrington* and her crew, Werner now headed south, and thirty-six hours later *U-55* was 200 miles to the west of Ushant, lying submerged and waiting for her next victim to come along.

Two days later, on the morning of 12 April, Ellerman's Wilson Line's *Toro* came hurrying over the horizon, homeward bound from Alexandria with a general cargo. Without surfacing, Werner stopped the 3000-ton short-sea trader with a well-placed torpedo, and then proceeded to commit a further atrocity.

The *Toro*'s crew of sixteen were ordered on board the U-boat, her master and gunner were taken below, and then, as before, Werner submerged, leaving the fourteen men, who had been relieved of their life jackets, to the mercy of the sea. When *U-55* surfaced twenty minutes later, the submarine's casings and the surrounding sea were empty of life. Captain Starkey, who was invited into the conning tower to witness the shelling of the *Toro*, later testified that some of the U-boat's crew had used one of her lifeboats to board her and loot a large number of eggs from her cargo.

There were now many influential voices, Admiral Jellicoe's among them, which said that unless the balance at sea was redressed, Britain would be starved into submission by November. Ironically, it was

Germany's declaration of unrestricted submarine warfare that really turned the tide. The sinking of unarmed merchant ships without warning, the murder of crews, and attacks on hospital ships, intentional or not, did much to sway opinion on the other side of the Atlantic, and on 6 April, 1917 America came into the war. It would be many months before her troops made their presence felt in France, but the immediate availability of 35 destroyers for escort duties certainly brought about a change of mind at the Admiralty. As from 10 May, all merchant ships sailed in convoy where possible. That month saw a dramatic reduction in the number of ships sunk, but this proved to be a false dawn. In June the U-boats disposed of 687,507 tons, 417,925 tons of this being British register – and all this for the loss of only two of their own number. By this time the German submarine fleet numbered 132, of which 60 were at sea at any one time, 40 of them concentrated in British home waters. However, the gathering together of merchant ships into convoys did at least make the U-boat commanders work harder for their Iron Crosses. The easy targets, the single, unescorted ships, became increasingly hard to find.

So thought *Oberleutnant* Wilhelm Werner, as, on the evening of 31 July 1917, he stood in the conning tower of *U-55* scanning an empty horizon. On this fine summer's day, with its unruffled sea, Werner was idling on the surface some 70 miles east-south-east of Rockall, square in the path of ships bound in and out of the North Channel, gateway to the busy ports of Glasgow and Liverpool.

When he first sighted the thin pencil of smoke on the eastern horizon, Werner was both elated and apprehensive. If this proved to be a lone merchantman, then his long days of waiting would be rewarded; if she turned out to be the leading ship of a convoy, then he must take care. Another two hours of daylight remained, which was time enough to mount an attack, or run away. Werner cleared the conning tower and took the boat down to periscope depth to watch, and wait.

Forty-eight hours out of Liverpool and bound for Newport News with a cargo of blue clay, the 4765-ton cargo steamer *Belgian Prince* was alone, unarmed, and about to commence her long Atlantic crossing. Built in 1901 and owned by Prince Line of London, she was commanded by Captain H. Hassan and carried a British crew of 43. Crossing the Atlantic unescorted was no new experience for any of these men, but they were well pleased to be clear of the dangers of the North-Western

Approaches. As the night moved in to hide them in its cloak of darkness, they were cautiously relaxed.

Savouring the evening air after a good dinner, Chief Engineer Thomas Bowman paced the scrubbed teakwood boards of the *Belgian Prince*'s boat decks particularly at ease with the world. The two weeks spent in dock in Liverpool had been put to good use by his engineers and shore fitters, and the 16-year-old steamer's 492 horsepower engine had a new and vigorous beat to it. The *Belgian Prince* might never lay claim to being a crack transatlantic liner, but she was an elegant old ship with the proven ability comfortably to maintain a respectable 10½ knots on the passage.

At about ten minutes before 8 o'clock, with the sun almost tipping the horizon, Bowman decided to go below to supervise the change over of the watch. As he turned, he glanced to port and froze in mid-stride. The long swathe of bubbles streaking in towards the ship was unmistakably hostile.

The bridge must have seen the torpedo track at the same time, for the *Belgian Prince* heeled sharply as the helm was put hard to port in an attempt to swing the ship's stern away from the danger. It was too late. The torpedo struck in the after part of the engine-room and exploded with a muffled roar. Bowman was bowled over by the blast and lay on the deck half-stunned.

When he regained his wits Bowman got to his feet and ran for the engine-room. He swung open the heavy steel door, only to be driven back by clouds of steam and smoke billowing up from below. But, to his great relief, the watch, led by Second Engineer George Sileski, appeared out of the swirling mists, shaken but unharmed. The news they brought with them was not good. Sileski reported the *Belgian Prince*'s propeller shaft broken and her main engine and generator smashed beyond repair. She would never steam again.

When Bowman and the others reached the deck, the ship was listing heavily to port, and Captain Hassan had already given the order to abandon ship. As the boats went down, the U-boat surfaced close by and opened fire on the steamer's wireless aerials with her deck gun. This was quite unnecessary, for with the generator smashed by the explosion, and with no emergency battery power, the *Belgian Prince*'s wireless was already silent. There had been no time to send an SOS.

The three lifeboats, containing all 44 of the *Belgian Prince*'s crew members, pulled clear of the sinking ship, and when they were about 200 yards off, the occupants lay back on their oars to await the inevitable end. They watched helplessly as *U-55* circled the ship, firing on her with a heavy machine-gun. What Werner stood to gain from this is hard to tell, but it may have been that he suspected he had fallen in with a Q-ship and was testing her hidden defences. It was on a similar summer's evening in the Western Approaches that *U-27* had accepted an innocent looking Allied merchantman at face value. The U-boat surfaced to challenge, and as she did so the steamer, otherwise HM Q-ship *Baralong,* dropped her shutters and opened fire with her 6-pounder guns. *U-27* went to the bottom, and those of her crew who escaped were shot under the most inhuman circumstances. This was an action most uncharacteristic of the Royal Navy, but it served to illustrate how desperate the war at sea had become.

To Chief Engineer Bowman, in the stern of the *Belgian Prince*'s starboard lifeboat, *U-55*'s machine-gunning of a ship plainly beyond retaliation boded no good for the survivors. His fears were heightened when the submarine turned and motored towards the boats. The machine-gun in the conning tower was still manned and now trained on the boats. Bowman tensed himself to leap overboard should the bullets begin to fly.

The machine-gun remained silent as the long, grey-painted submarine, casting a sinister shadow before it in the rays of the dying sun, glided to a halt within 20 yards of the small huddle of boats. They were ordered alongside the submarine, and when they touched, a voice called out in English for the captain of the ship to declare himself. Hassan, well aware of the German policy of carrying off into captivity the masters of ships sunk, had already removed his uniform jacket with its tell-tale gold braid. He stayed silent, and not a man in the boats betrayed him. Werner repeated the order several times, impatience showing in his voice, but all he received in return was hostile stares. The machine-gun moved menacingly, and when Werner rapped out an order in German, Hassan feared he was risking the lives of all his men by refusing to declare himself. With a helpless shrug, he put his uniform jacket on again, and stood up. He was ordered aboard the U-boat, where he disappeared down the conning tower hatch to face the rest of the war in a German prison camp.

Having made a prisoner of their captain, the other survivors assumed that, at the very worst, the submarine would then make off, leaving them to their fate. They were mistaken. Werner now ordered them all on board, and with the machine gun and a number of rifles levelled at them, they had no alternative but to comply. Standing on the submarine's casing, they were roughly handled by armed German seamen and subjected to a rigorous search. This they accepted with ill grace, but with resignation, for they had no alternative. It was only when the Germans took away their lifejackets and outer clothing that a ripple of fear ran through the British ranks. When their lifejackets were tossed overboard and the Germans set about wrecking the two larger lifeboats with axes, the survivors began to realise the stark horror of the situation facing them. Not even the youngest among them was naive enough to believe the U-boat commander was about to carry them all back to Germany as prisoners.

The smallest of the lifeboats had been left intact, and a party of five German sailors boarded this and rowed over to the *Belgian Prince.* They boarded her, and after ten minutes or so, signaled back to the submarine with a lamp, presumably reporting the state of the ship. The U-boat's engines then coughed into life, and she motored away, with the 43 bewildered survivors clinging to her casings. When she was about two miles off the *Belgian Prince*, she stopped and lay rolling gently in the swell.

The British seamen eyed each other nervously, wondering what to expect next. They were not left in suspense for long. The Germans disappeared from the conning tower, the hatch clanged shut, and there was a rush of escaping air as the ballast tanks were filled. The deck of the U-boat began to sink beneath their feet.

Tom Bowman was the first to realise what was happening, and he shouted to warn the others before jumping clear. In the water, he kicked out, swimming away to escape the powerful suction of the submerging submarine. When he looked back, she had gone, leaving perhaps a dozen men struggling in the welter of foam and bubbles. The rest had gone with her, sucked down into the vortex she created.

A lifejacket whirled past and Bowman instinctively grabbed at it and slipped it on. If nothing else, this scrap of cork and canvas would prolong his life by a few hours, but to what end? The outside world would know nothing of the attack on the *Belgian Prince,* and there would be no ships racing to their rescue. In three or four days, when she was judged to be overdue, a cursory search might be made, but by then only a few bloated corpses would remain.

It was now almost dark, and Bowman was tempted to throw off his lifejacket and slip beneath the waves to join the others. Then he heard a voice calling for help and he found the youngest member of the *Belgian Prince*'s crew, a 16-year-old apprentice, drifting nearby. The boy was wearing a lifejacket, but had swallowed a lot of water and was far gone. Bowman stayed with him, supporting and encouraging him, but, at around midnight, the boy died from exposure and shock. Bowman relieved him of his lifejacket and allowed the body to drift away into the night.

In summer, daylight comes early in the high latitudes, and it was just after 3 o'clock on the morning of 1 August when Bowman, by then near the end of his tether, saw that the *Belgian Prince* was still afloat. A great surge of hope swept through him, chasing away the cold and misery, and he struck out for the ship, buoyed up by the two lifejackets. The distance was great and the engineer was weak, but he swam on, from time to time brushing against the bodies of men who hours before had been his friends and shipmates. By about 5.30, an hour and a half after sunrise, he was almost there. Then the *Belgian Prince* suddenly appeared to blow up, and sank stern first.

While the ship was still there, Bowman had a goal to aim for, and this gave him heart. When she was gone, and all that was left was an empty sea strewn with wreckage, again he was tempted to end it all, to discard the lifejackets and join the others face down in the sea. But something, perhaps the thought of the grieving widow and orphans he would leave behind, drove him on, and he continued to swim. An hour later, still swimming, he was picked up by a British patrol boat. He had been in the water for eleven hours.

George Sileski, Bowman's Russian-born second engineer, also survived Werner's callous mass execution. Although he had no lifejacket, he swam in the direction of the *Belgian Prince* throughout the night, and succeeding in boarding her at about 5 am. However, when he had been on the ship for about an hour, and had begun to construct a raft, he saw *U-55* approaching the ship. He hid behind a deckhouse and watched as the submarine came alongside and a party of four armed men boarded. While they were searching the ship, Sileski scooped up a lifejacket, slipped over the side and swam quietly away. He had been in the water for about 20 minutes, when the U-boat opened fire on the *Belgian Prince* with her 105-mm deck gun, scoring two direct hits. The ship sank, and the U-boat moved away, but left behind the small boat used to board her on the previous night. Sileski reached the boat and was rescued from it half an hour later by the same patrol boat that had found Bowman.

The only other man to survive the sinking of the *Belgian Prince* was her American-born second cook, Willie Snell, who also spent all night swimming towards the ship. He was about a mile off her when she went down, and was not picked up by the patrol boat for another two and a half hours. Snell was by then on the point of surrendering to the sea.

Captain Hassan was released from a German prison camp at the end of the war. Thomas Bowman, George Sileski and Willie Snell lived on to sail another day. The others, 39 unarmed, non-belligerent British merchant seamen, found unmarked graves one thousand fathoms deep in the cold Atlantic.

Wilhelm Werner continued to wreak his indiscriminate havoc amongst Allied merchant ships right up to the end of the war. The crowning moments of his murderous career came in the opening months of 1918, when he torpedoed without warning the British hospital ships *Rewa* and *Guildford Castle*. The *Rewa*, with 279 wounded on board, went down in the Bristol Channel, but, mercifully, only four seamen were lost. The *Guildford Castle* was even luckier; Werner's torpedo struck home, but failed to explode.

Werner and *U-55* had been responsible for sinking some 200,000 tons of Allied shipping, and he was rewarded by a grateful Kaiser with Germany's highest decoration, the Pour le Mérite. When the war ended, with Germany defeated, it seemed certain that Werner would at last get his just desserts. A special sitting was held at Bow Street Court on Tuesday 31 August, 1921 to hear the evidence of Captain Starkey, and to gather other evidence. This was to be presented at a tribunal to be held in Leipzig at which Wilhelm Werner would be accused of a series of war crimes, including the sinking without warning of the British ships *Clearfield, Artist, Trevone, Torrington* and *Toro,* but not the *Belgian*

Prince, which at the time was thought to be the work of Paul Wagenfuhr in *U-44*.

At Bow Street, Mr. Vernon Gattie appeared on behalf of the British authorities, while Dr. Bruner represented the German Government. *The Times* reported:

> The written statement of a German ex-soldier witness named Shimm, from Frankfurt-am-Main, stated that while held as a prisoner of the French in about May 1915 he had been working on the docks in Marseilles. He swore that he and several other prisoners had seen the *Torrington* lying alongside Mole No.8, displaying distinctive hospital ship markings. Her name had been clearly visible and she was being loaded with guns and ammunition, which he assumed were for the British Army on the Salonika front.
>
> Starkey, by that time the master of the *Brandon* of Cardiff, had been on a voyage to Mexico and when he put into Sao Vincente in the Cape Verde Islands he found a message for him asking him to make a sworn statement to HM Consul there for onward transmission to London and Leipzig. He said that one of *U-55*'s sailors, *Obermatrosen* Küper from Bremen, who, by coincidence had worked aboard the *Torrington* before the war, had told him that he was lucky to have escaped with his life. On another occasion, the wireless operator had asked him, 'Do you think your men got home, Captain?
>
> 'I should think so. The weather was not too bad.'
>
> 'Believe me, Captain, your men never got home. There are too many here now, or I would tell you something else.' Later he told Starkey that his men had all drowned.
>
> One submariner, a German-Pole, who manned the machine-gun, had remarked that it was not war, it was murder. Starkey heard this man whisper, 'Dank Gott' when Werner fired a torpedo which missed. It was clear from these and other conversations that Starkey had with the crew, as well as statements made later under interrogation, that they regarded Werner's actions as inhuman, and that the cases of the *Torrington* and *Toro* were by no means isolated atrocities. Two hospital ships had been sunk by him, the

Rewa, and on 10 March 1918, the *Guildford Castle*. Other sinkings without warning were the steamers *Clearfield* and *Artist* in October 1916 and January 1917 respectively and the trawler *Trevone* on 30 January 1917. The crew also claimed they had been operating under Werner in the Black Sea, where they had sunk a ship called the *Paddington* outside Odessa harbour. It was not clear whether this had been in U-55 or an earlier boat, but in any case it was common in the German submarine service for the whole crew to follow their captain when he changed boats.

Berlin, not unexpectedly, had a very different version of Werner's conduct, claiming that what the British press had reported was, 'A low calumny. Nevertheless, it can be confidently asserted that the story of the German sailors taking the crew of the sunk ship on deck and then submerging and washing them into the sea can be only a low lie and calumny. If our U-boat men had wanted to let the foreign crew perish, they did not need laboriously to take them on board. The idea that the Germans out of sheer devilry pretended to save the men, only in order to let them perish, could not possibly occur to German sailors.'

Eventually, the charges against Werner were reduced to just one, the torpedoing without warning of the *Torrington,* and the murder of her crew, with the exception of Captain Anthony Starkey, who was taken to German as a prisoner of war. Werner did not appear before the Leipzig tribunal, having fled Germany for South America, where he was believed to be working on a coffee plantation in Brazil.

In the 1930s, when Adolf Hitler and his National Socialist Party were in power, Wilhelm Werner returned to Germany, joined the party with enthusiasm, and eventually gained a seat in the Reichstag. When the Second World War ended in 1945, Werner was a *Brigadeführer* in the SS, and on the staff of the notorious Heinrich Himmler. Once again, he escaped retribution, dying at his home in Falkenau at the age of fifty-seven in May, 1945, a few days after the war in Europe ended.

Chapter Fourteen

The Tide Turns

From the moment of the declaration of war in 1914, Russia had been one of Britain's invaluable allies, vigorously pursuing the fight against Germany on the Eastern Front, pinning down a third of her army, as well as all the Austrian divisions. Then, in the spring of 1917, the soldiers of Czar Nicholas II, influenced by the news of revolution from home, lost their enthusiasm for the fight.

Russia, her economy bankrupted by the immense cost of the war, was, in fact, descending into complete anarchy. Czar Nicholas had lost his grip on the people, factories were on strike, and workers' committees were threatening to oust the appointed authorities from the towns and cities. Revolution was in the air; the birth pangs of the Union of Soviet Socialist Republics were about to begin.

Britain and France looked on in horror, fearful that the Eastern Front was on the point of collapse and they would soon be facing the full might of the German and Austrian armies alone. At the same time, Berlin had declared totally unrestricted submarine warfare against Allied and neutral ships, sanctioning the U-boats to torpedo without warning whenever the opportunity arose. The result was catastrophic. In April 1917, 473 Allied merchantmen, totaling a staggering 885,530 tons gross, fell to the U-boats. Ten ships a day were going down with their cargoes, and by the end of the month Britain had less than six weeks' supply of food left. If this appalling haemorrhage of resources continued, the country would be facing starvation before the year was out. Unable to refute the figures, in May the Admiralty finally decided to introduce convoys.

Sailing ships in convoy was not a new innovation; merchantmen had been gathered together under the protection of warships as far back as the 12th century. In the Napoleonic wars of the early 1800s, the threat to British merchant ships was so great that few were allowed to sail alone.

History seldom lies, and given the known striking power of Germany's navy, it is hard to understand why the Admiralty failed to bring in convoys right from the outbreak of war in 1914. The main objection appeared to be that the Admirals considered merchant seamen so lacking in discipline and experience in steaming in formation that they would be unable to cope. Not for the first time, their judgement of the capability of the British merchant seaman was seriously in error. When in May 1917 the decision was at last made to bring in convoys, the despised merchant mariners showed just how good their seamanship was. The British convoys were an instant success, sinkings falling by 270,000 tons in the first month of operation.

The protection offered by a convoy was not available to the *Olive Branch*, even though this innocuously named British tramp was loaded to the gunwales with arms, ammunition and military equipment for Russia.

The 4649-ton *Olive Branch* was one of a number of Allied ships involved in a last ditch effort to keep Russia in the war. Built on the Clyde in 1912, she had already had a chequered career. Starting life as the *Bellorado* of the Bellarden Steamship Company of Glasgow, she came through the first three years of the war unscathed. Then, in February 1917, when on passage from Barry to Alexandria with coal, she was 160 miles south-west of Cape St. Vincent, when she was set upon by UC-22, under the command of *Oberleutnant* Heino von Heimburg. The *Bellorado* refused to surrender, and as a result suffered heavy damage, with three men killed, when UC-22 opened fire on her. Miraculously, she escaped to sail another day. When she returned to Glasgow, she was sold to the Nautilus Steam Shipping Company of Sunderland, and renamed *Olive Branch.*

The *Olive Branch* sailed from the River Mersey on 25 August 1917, bound for Archangel, then known as Port Romanoff. Her holds were packed with every conceivable type of weapon and ammunition, while on deck she carried a number of heavy army trucks lashed to her hatch-tops. By dint of her cargo alone, she was a very vulnerable ship, but the Admiralty seemed to have no fears for her safety. It was assumed that the U-boats were far too busy in the North Atlantic and Mediterranean to venture into the hostile waters beyond the Arctic Circle. The *Olive Branch* was sailing alone.

The Admiralty's intelligence proved to be sadly outdated. Frustrated by the success of the Allied convoys, *Flotillenadmiral* Andreas Michelsen, C-in-C of the U-boat Arm, was looking for easier targets. During August, he ordered a flotilla of his ocean-going boats to return from the Atlantic, via the Dover Strait and North Sea, to mount an attack on British ships carrying arms to Russia. They would join *U-28*, which was already operating in that area.

U-28, one of the German Navy's top-scoring submarines when under the command of Baron Georg-Günther von Forstner, had sailed from Emden on 19 August. Von Forstner, his reputation somewhat tarnished by the brutality of the *Falaba* sinking, had moved on to take up a shore appointment, handing over command of *U-28* to 35-year-old *Kapitänleutnant* Georg Schmidt. *U-28* was Schmidt's first command, but he quickly showed his competence, roving from the Shetland Islands deep into the Barents Sea, sinking fifteen Allied merchantmen with the loss of thousands of tons of cargo destined to boost the Russian war effort.

On the morning of 2 September, *U-28* was patrolling on the surface some 90 miles north of Norway's North Cape, when, a few minutes before noon, a deep-loaded steamer was sighted coming from the south-west. Schmidt immediately submerged to periscope depth, and waited for the ship to approach.

Aboard the *Olive Branch*, the bridge was busy with noon sights, the lookouts were relaxed and anticipating the change of the watch. No one saw Schmidt's torpedo as it sped towards the ship's exposed port side.

The torpedo struck amidships, fortunately for most of those on board, missing the ammunition-packed holds, exploding with no more than a muted thud. The only casualty was the *Olive Branch*'s cook, McGill, who by some bizarre stroke of misfortune had chosen that moment to come out of his galley to empty a bucket over the side. He was leaning over the port-side rail when the torpedo exploded directly beneath him, killing him instantly.

The torpedo blasted a hole in the *Olive Branch*'s hull, and laid waste to her boiler room. The steam pressure fell, and she slowly lost way through the water, but she did not sink. There seemed some hope of saving her, but when it was discovered that she was on fire in one of the holds, discretion took precedence over valour, and all, except the unfortunate McGill, took to the boats.

Unwilling to waste another torpedo on the crippled ship, Georg Schmidt waited until the lifeboats were clear, then surfaced and ordered the deck gun to be manned. Completely unaware of the dangerous nature of the *Olive Branch*'s cargo, Schmidt moved in closer. When he was within 250 yards of the British ship he stopped and ordered his gun's crew to open fire.

The first shell missed its target completely and, anxious to finish off his victim and clear the area as soon as possible, Schmidt edged in closer.

There was no mistake with the second shell, which was fired at almost point blank range. It went home in the *Olive Branch*'s No.4 hold, which contained a large quantity of ammunition topped off by a heavy army lorry lashed down on the hatchtop. The helpless ship, already with a fire raging below, blew up with a tremendous explosion that sent a volcano-like eruption of burning debris soaring high in the air. If *U-28* had been stood well off, she would have escaped what happened next, but the *U-boat* was so close to her victim that she was directly underneath the debris when it dropped out of the sky. In amongst that debris was the army lorry, which before the explosion had been sitting on top of the hatch. The lorry came spinning down from a great height and crashed onto *U-28*'s casing, smashing open her pressure hull. As the *Olive Branch* slipped below the waves, so did *U-28*.

Witnesses in the *Olive Branch*'s lifeboats said they saw dinghies pulling away from the sinking U-boat, but no survivors were reported as being picked up. A German source claimed that some survivors were in the water and had pleaded with the *Olive Branch*'s boats to pick them up, but the British callously refused to help. As all thirty-five men aboard *U-28* were lost, there is no evidence to back this accusation, although with their lifeboats being already overcrowded, it is not unlikely that the *Olive Branch* survivors refused to help those who had so recently destroyed their ship.

September 1917 was the month when, at long last, the tide began to turn against the U-boats. They were increasingly, and effectively, being hounded by Allied warships equipped with depth charges, while most merchant ships were sailing in convoy, and difficult to get at. Convoys, introduced in May of that year, were escorted mainly by destroyers, and in many cases watched over by airships and flying boats of the Royal Naval Air Service. The convoy system played a vital part in bringing down the appalling losses of merchant ships experienced in previous years, vindicating those who had been pressing for its introduction for some time. In April, when most merchantmen were sailing alone, 473 Allied ships totalling 885,530 gross tons were sunk; the figure for August was 219 ships of 522,948 tons. The figures speak for themselves.

Although strongly advised by the Admiralty, the convoy system was not yet compulsory, and it was often at the whim of the ship's master whether he joined the ranks or sailed alone. The difficulty was that a convoy takes time to form up, often meaning days, or weeks, spent at anchor while the ships assembled. As a merchant ship earns nothing while she is tied up in port, it is not surprising that some masters preferred to sail alone. This may have been the case with the Glasgow-registered steamer *Mersario,* which left Barry on 16 September 1917 with a cargo of coal and coke for Alexandria.

The 3847-ton *Mersario,* owned by the Reid Steamship Company and sailing under the command of Captain Elias Lloyd, was, despite her Scottish registry, a regular Bristol Channel trader, manned by a predominantly Welsh crew. Being the usual box-shaped tramp, she was slow – 8 knots in fair weather was her limit – but she was a good steady earner for her owners.

In declining to wait for a Mediterranean-bound convoy, Captain Lloyd was well aware of the risks he was taking. Less than twelve months earlier, when in command of the 2623-ton *Stathe,* and carrying coal from Penarth to Leghorn, his ship had been sunk by a U-boat off Barcelona. However, mindful of his owner's pennies, he was once again sailing independently.

On the morning of 1 October, the *Mersario* was 50 miles south-west of Cadiz, and approaching the Straits of Gibraltar. She was in a known hunting ground of the U-boats, and on the advice of the Admiralty Lloyd was zig-zagging, with extra lookouts posted and the stern gun manned.

It was either pre-ordained, or just sheer bad luck, for Captain Lloyd and the *Mersario,* but submerged off her starboard bow and examining the collier through his periscope, was Walther Forstmann in *U-39.* Since the abortive attack on the *Anglo Californian* in July, 1915, Forstmann and *U-39* had been responsible for sinking 101 Allied merchant ships totalling 272,708 tons, much of this tonnage in the Mediterranean. Forstmann was now one of the Kaiser's top U-boat aces, holder of Germany's highest decoration for achievement against the enemy, the Pour le Mérite.

By 11 o'clock that morning, Forstmann had manoeuvred into a favourable position. The *Mersario*, dawdling along at 8 knots, was a target Forstmann could not fail to hit. At 11.15 his torpedo sped through the water, and caught the unsuspecting British ship squarely amidships, exploding in her cross bunkers just forward of the funnel. One unfortunate Arab fireman, who was working in the bunker at the time, was killed instantly.

There were no other casualties, but the *Mersario* was hard hit, a great hole being torn in her hull, through which the sea poured, flooding her boiler room and engine room. She was a turret-deck ship, notoriously unstable, and within three minutes she had capsized and sunk, taking with her two Welsh seamen, William Jones and Ernest Blythe.

Fortunately, the weather was kind to the dying *Mersario.* There was little wind, and the sea was calm, and although the ship went down so quickly, it was possible to launch two lifeboats. All remaining crew members got away before she sank.

By this time, Forstmann had surfaced, looking for details of his latest conquest. Third Engineer R. Chadwick, possibly the only officer to declare himself, was taken on board the U-boat and questioned. Chadwick gave Forstmann the name of his ship, and her cargo, but would not name her port of discharge. Forstmann, mindful of the fact that he was in an area regularly patrolled by enemy destroyers, was unwilling to stay on the surface any longer. He put Chadwick on a piece of floating wreckage, and *U-39* disappeared below the surface.

Chadwick was picked up by one of the *Mersario*'s lifeboats, and all the survivors were rescued the next day by the French steamer *La Somme*, which landed them in Gibraltar. Captain Elias Lloyd's reluctance to sail in convoy had resulted in a very costly lesson for the *Messario* and her crew.

On 16 October, the Chief of the Admiral's Staff in Berlin issued the following report:

> New U-boat successes: '*U39*' under the excellent command of Lieutenant Commander Forstmann during the war years, has, among other successes in the Straits of Gibraltar, sunk five valuable steamers with over 20,000 Gross Reg. Tons, which were the steamers 'Normanton' (3862 tonnes), 'Mersario' (3847 tonnes), 'Almora' (4385 tonnes), 'Nuceria' (4702 tonnes) and the Japanese steamer 'Sitosan Maru' (3555 tonnes). The ships, which were destroyed within two days, carried a total load of 31,500 tonnes of coal, of which more than 26,000 tonnes were meant for Italy for use in the Winter.

Walther Forstmann went on to command the Third U-boat Flotilla, and ended the war with the rank of *korvettenkapitän*, having sunk a total of nearly 400,000 tons of Allied shipping.

As 1917 drew to a close, life was becoming very difficult for the U–boats. America had entered the war in April, and the arrival of her destroyers in Northern European waters, inexperienced though they might be, was already having a noticeable effect. The Royal Navy, hitherto hard pressed by convoy escort duty, could now adopt a more aggressive stance towards the U-boats. Patrols were stepped up, extensive minefields were laid in the Channel and North Sea, and soon every mile covered by the U-boats after leaving their bases was fraught with hideous dangers. Even when sheltering in their heavily defended pens on the Belgian coast they were not safe, Allied bombers being continuously overhead. The hunters had become the hunted.

U-93, commanded by *Kapitänleutnant* Edgar Freiherr von Spiegel von und zu Peckelsheim, sailed from Emden on her first war cruise on 13 April, 1917. She reached her operational zone off the south-west coast of Ireland a few days later, and very quickly made her mark. By the end of the month, von Spiegel had sunk seven Allied merchantmen, totalling 23,000 tons. It was a promising start, but on the last day of the month Baron Spiegel made a mistake that almost cost him his command, and his life.

At about 8.30 on the evening of 30 April, in fine weather with excellent visibility, *U-93*'s lookouts sighted a topsail schooner about 3 miles off, ghosting along under a light north-north-easterly wind. Darkness was setting in, so von Spiegel decided to press home his attack at once.

Although Baron Spiegel had studied the schooner through his binoculars, he failed to see that she was a British 'Q' ship. She was, in fact, the 200-ton three-masted decoy *Prize*, under the command of Lieutenant Wilson Sanders, RNR. Armed with two concealed 12-pounders, and with an auxiliary engine, she carried a full naval crew, all experienced and disciplined men.

When Lieutenant Sanders became aware of the submarine creeping up on his port side some 2 miles off he ignored it, as befitted a slow-witted schooner master. At the same time he gave whispered orders for his men to go to their battle stations. The concealed guns were manned, and the 'panic party', six men in nondescript seamen's clothing representing the schooner's crew, busied themselves on deck.

Having manoeuvred into position off the schooner's quarter, von Spiegel fired a warning shot across her bows. The only reaction came from the schooner's 'crew', who began to mill around the deck giving a good imitation of ill-disciplined merchant seamen in a complete funk.

Von Spiegel, who had already spent longer on the surface than he cared to, decided to close in on the schooner and finish her off. When *U-93* was about 150 yards off the *Prize*'s port quarter, he opened fire with both guns. At such short range it was impossible to miss, and 105mm shells were soon slamming into the helpless sailing ship. The *Prize* was hit below the waterline, and she came up into the wind, presenting her starboard side to the submarine. Her sails flapped helplessly, boat falls squealed, and the six-man panic party rowed away, their oars flailing wildly.

It seemed to be all over, but what those aboard *U-93* could not see was Lieutenant Sanders and his gunners crouching below the bulwarks, biding their time as the German shells whistled over their heads. When the schooner had drifted broadside on to her attacker, and von Spiegel's gunners were pounding her hard, Wilson Sanders gave the order hit back.

Quietly, the schooner's helm was manned, her auxiliary engine started, the collapsible deckhouse concealing the forward gun dropped away, the after gun emerged from its hiding place in the hold on its mount, and Sanders gave the order to open fire.

The *Prize*'s guns were naval long 12-pounders, 3-inch calibre quick-firing guns of extreme accuracy. Her gunners were masters of their art, and when they opened fire, their shells paid back double for all the damage *U-93* had inflicted on the schooner. Both the U-boat's deck guns were knocked out and their crews killed, whilst a number of hits were scored on the conning tower. One shell exploded inside the conning tower, blowing von Spiegel, his navigating warrant officer and an engine-room petty officer overboard.

Several shells were seen to hit *U-93*'s pressure hull, and she appeared to be sinking. Lieutenant Sanders passed the word to cease fire, and ordered a boat to be lowered to pick up the three men in the water. It was thought that these were the only survivors. By this time it was dark, and as the submarine could no longer be seen, Sanders assumed she had sunk. As his own ship had suffered severe damage, and was also in danger of sinking, he abandoned the operation. The *Prize* reached Kinsale on 4 May, being towed for the last few miles. Wilson Sanders was awarded the Victoria Cross for his courageous action, and *U-93* was crossed off the Admiralty's list of German hazards. But she was by no means finished.

When Baron Spiegel was blown out of his conning tower, his First Watch Officer, *Oberleutnant-zur-See* Wilhelm Ziegner, took command. Well away from the *Prize*, and under the cover of darkness, he surveyed the damage to the boat. Her conning tower was wrecked, both deck guns smashed, the starboard fuel tank was holed, the oil was on fire below, the wireless aerials were shot away, and she had a heavy list. Apart from her captain and two petty officers missing, probably drowned, several men had been killed. Ziegner was faced with a seemingly impossible challenge.

U-93 had so many holes in her pressure hull that to submerge would have been suicidal. Undaunted, Wilhelm Ziegner set his men to work. The fire was extinguished, the holes in the hull plugged, and the worst of the damage in the conning tower repaired. By daylight, *U-93* was under way again.

It was poor visibility that saved *U-93*, enabling her to creep up the west coast of Ireland, past the Outer Hebrides, around the north of Scotland, and then into the North Sea. It was a long and hazardous passage, but luck and the weather were on the U-boat's side. She reached the tiny fishing port of List, in the North Friesian Islands with her fuel tanks running dry. From there she was towed to Wilhelmshaven, arriving on 2 May.

After extensive repairs, the schooner *Prize* returned to sea in early August with Lieutenant Sanders still in command. At about 1.30 on the morning of the 16th, she was off the north coast of Ireland, when she was sighted by UB-48, then on her first war patrol. Her commander, *Oberleutnant-zur-See* Wolfgang Steinbauer, saw through the Swedish disguise Sanders had adopted, and immediately attacked, firing two torpedoes. The first one missed, but the second hit home, literally blasting the *Prize* out of the water. Lieutenant Wilson Sanders and all his crew were lost.

The battered *U-93* remained in port under repair for much of the rest of the year. She finally sailed from Emden on 29 December. *Kapitänleutnant* Helmut Gerlach was in command, having taken the place of Wilhelm Ziegner, who was ashore on sick leave. Gerlach's orders were to break out through the Dover Strait and begin operations between the Channel Islands and Penmarch, at the northern end of the Bay of Biscay.

After having successfully run the gauntlet of Allied mines and depth bombs in the Channel, Gerlach set course to the south, and when the New Year opened *U-93* was patrolling within sight of the rock-fringed Pointe de Penmarch. A week cruising in these waters, once frequented by that master of the blockade, Horatio Nelson, proved fruitful for Helmut Gerlach. He first sank a French auxiliary minesweeper and then three medium-sized steamers in quick succession. On the afternoon of 6 January, he rounded off his score by sinking the 3793-ton Greek steamer *Kanaris* as she passed in sight of Penmarch on her way from Barry to Bordeaux. With that, Gerlach decided he had overstayed his welcome off the coast of Northern France, and set course for the Western Approaches.

In the early hours of the 7th the 424-ton British coaster *Braeneil* was off Lizard Point. She was on passage from Swansea to Rouen with her usual cargo of 'best Welsh'. It was a fine night for mid-winter in the English Channel, with unusually good visibility and the quick-flashing Lizard light, although on reduced power as required by the exigencies of war, was clearly seen from the bridge of the *Braeneil*.

As was normal practice in the coasters, which carried small crews, the

Master was keeping a watch on the bridge. At fifteen minutes past four, he sighted what appeared to be a small craft close on the starboard bow, and crossing directly ahead of the *Braeneil*.

Under the international rules of the road at sea, the *Braeneil* was under obligation to steer clear of this vessel crossing from starboard, but as the gap narrowed the coaster's master realised that he was on a collision course with a submarine – a German U-boat, in fact.

Bearing in mind the fate that befell Captain Fryatt of the *Brussels* in the summer of 1916, no one would have thought less of the master of the *Braeneil* had he done a quick about turn and steamed away from this sinister craft. But the man was of sterner stuff, and summoning up an extra knot from the depths of the engine room, he steamed straight at the submarine.

Kapitänleutnant Gerlach was well aware that he was courting danger in these waters at the western end of the Channel, where British and French naval ships cruised in considerable numbers. But he was not prepared for the unannounced attack launched on him by this innocuous looking coaster. Only at the last minute, when the British ship was almost on top of *U-93*, did Gerlach take evasive action. It was too late.

The *Braeneil* hit *U-93* squarely amidships, rolling her over on her beam ends. The British ship then went astern, and broke free of the submarine with a grinding of steel upon steel. It was too dark for the coaster's crew to see what damage they had done, but they reported a strong smell of petrol and 'foreign sounding' voices heard in the water. It was assumed that the U-boat had been sunk, but the *Braeneil* was not waiting to find out. She headed into the darkness as fast as her pounding engine would carry her. She arrived in Falmouth a few hours later, where it was found that her stem was badly twisted on the waterline, and plates on either bow were dented.

It is not certain whether the *Braeneil* sank *U-93*. British sources claimed that she had done so, but the Germans named the boat as *U-95*. Both boats were listed as being operational in the English Channel at the time, having left port within twenty-four hours of each other. Both then disappeared without trace.

As the tide turned against Germany on land and sea, attacks on Allied merchantmen by the U-boats became increasingly desperate, and in return those ships were more determined than ever to hit back.

Prime targets for the U-boats were the small troopships that ran the shuttle across the English Channel, usually crossing at night, and alone. In their ranks was the British ex-cross-Channel steamer *Queen Alexandra*. She was fast, with a top speed of 20 knots, she was highly manoeuvrable, and with her accommodation stripped to the barest necessities, she had a large carrying capacity.

Under the command of Captain Angus Keith, the *Queen Alexandra* was making the crossing from Southampton to Cherbourg on the night of 8/9 May, 1918 with a full complement of troops and escorted by the naval patrol boat *P-33*. The P-boats, with a shallow draught and low superstructure, were almost invisible in a Channel chop, and made very dangerous enemies for the U-boats. In addition to heavy-calibre machine-guns, they were fitted with a steel ram at the bows, a weapon that was proving extremely effective against U-boats.

At 12.45 a.m. on the 9th, the *Queen Alexandra* was approaching Cape Barfleur, with only 15 miles to go to the breakwaters of Cherbourg, when lookouts on *P-33*, which was keeping station on the trooper's port bow, sighted a low object on the surface. This was quickly identified as an enemy submarine, and she was lying 400 yards off the *Queen Alexandra*'s starboard bow, no doubt already preparing to fire her torpedoes.

In the conning tower of *UC-78*, Hans Kukat, believing that his boat was invisible against the dark backdrop of the Channel, was taking careful aim before firing at the fast-moving troopship. *UC-78*, commissioned in January 1917, had spent most of the following year with the Baltic Flotilla, and had failed miserably in her mission, sinking not one single Allied ship. Transferred to the English Channel in January 1918, her run of back luck had continued; she sank only one ship of 350 tons, and damaged another of 1,500 tons. It was a dismal record for any U-boat, and on this night Hans Kukat aimed to begin his harassment of Allied shipping in earnest.

Kukat failed to reckon with the ire of the redoubtable Captain Angus Keith. Warned by *P-33* of the presence of the U-boat, Keith did not stop to debate strategy; he headed straight for *UC-78* and rammed her at 20 knots.

Struck a tremendous blow a few feet abaft her conning tower by the raked stem of the *Queen Alexandra*, *UC-78* was thrown on her side, and with her pressure hull breached, sank almost immediately. All that was ever found of her was a large patch of oil and a few pieces of wreckage. Hans Kukat and his crew of twenty-eight were all lost.

The *Queen Alexandra*, her bows stove in, limped into Cherbourg and discharged her troops, their landing somewhat delayed; but other than a few bruises from the sudden collision, not a man among them had been injured. It could have been so different.

Chapter Fifteen

The Final Days

There were few British shipmasters more experienced than Captain James Lowe of the tanker *Petroleine.* Seventy-two years old, Lowe had sailed the great windjammers around the Horn before moving – reluctantly, it might be said – into steamers. There was little he did not know about seamanship and navigation. He had been brought up in a hard school and, needless to say, he was a strict disciplinarian who did not suffer fools gladly. These attributes did not endear him to his crews, but he was a fair man – a good man to follow when the going got tough. In normal times, Lowe would have been long retired, but despite failing eyesight due to diabetes, he was determined to see out the war at sea. He had a mixed crew under his command, British officers, West Indian sailors on deck, and Cape Verde firemen in the engineroom.

The 4205-ton *Petroleine,* built on the Tyne in 1908 and owned by Hunting & Son of Newcastle, had from early in the war been on charter to carry petroleum from New York to Havre and Rouen. She was one of a fleet of such vessels helping to satisfy the insatiable demands of Allied transport in France. At the best of times, carrying petroleum at sea is a stressful business, and working under pressure for ever quicker turn-rounds and faster ocean crossing, the men who manned the *Petroleine* found themselves constantly pushed to their absolute limits. Both ship and men had already been severely tested in the winter of 1916, when the tanker was homeward bound with a cargo of petrol from New York. She was off the Channel Islands, and almost within sight of her destination, when a heavy explosion in her forward dry cargo hold caused extensive damage to her bow section. By some miracle, the highly inflammable cargo in her tanks escaped the explosion, but eleven men died in the forecastle accommodation, and the entire forward part of the ship had to be rebuilt. To this day, it is still not known what caused the explosion, but the consensus at the time was that a German sympathiser in New York – and there were many – had planted a bomb in the *Petroleine*'s forward hold. On this occasion, as always, James Lowe brought his ship safely into port.

Throughout the war, the *Petroleine* continued to ferry her dangerous cargoes across the Atlantic, with the ageing Captain Lowe still in command. The only concession so far made to the existence of hostilities was the mounting of a 4-inch anti-submarine gun on the tanker's stern, and the addition to her crew of four naval gunners to maintain and operate the gun.

The routine of the voyage rarely varied: the *Petroleine* loaded her cargo in New York – fuel oil, diesel, petrol, whatever was on offer – and crossed the Atlantic unescorted, usually to join up with an eastbound convoy off the Fastnet Rock. After negotiating her way up the River Seine to Rouen, she was allowed only a few hours in port to discharge her cargo, before setting off down river again to join a convoy which would offer her protection as far as 15 degrees West. It was a punishing routine, but the demands of war were so great that any hours spent idling in port were out of the question. Although hard pressed, Captain Lowe and his crew carried on, their one great worry being that they were not allowed time in port to clean tanks.

With the carriage of oils in bulk the risk of fire and explosion is always present, and this risk is at its greatest after a cargo has been discharged. The residue of oil left in a ship's tanks gives off highly inflammable gases, particularly in the case of petroleum and benzine. Unless the tanks are thoroughly cleaned and gas-freed, there is a high risk of explosion.

Standard procedure in tankers after discharging a cargo is to wash the tanks down with hot water hoses; then the tanks and all associated piping are thoroughly steam-cleaned and ventilated to carry off any remaining gas. This is a long, labour-intensive process, an operation the *Petroleine* did not have the time for.

When the *Petroleine* sailed from Rouen in March, 1918, having discharged her cargo of highly volatile benzine, her tanks were in a very unstable state, coated with benzine residue, which was giving off fumes that permeated the whole ship. If the weather in the Atlantic allowed, the tanks would be cleaned at sea, but until such time the *Petroleine* was a floating bomb.

On her way down Channel, the tanker called at Plymouth for bunkers, and left that port in convoy, which was to disperse in 15 degrees West, from which point onwards the Admiralty deemed that the threat from U-boats was minimal. The escorting destroyers left in late morning, by which time the *Petroleine* was 300 miles north-west of Cape Finisterre, and steering a zig-zag course at 10 knots. Captain Lowe and his deck officers were on the bridge preparing for noon sights.

Minutes before the sun reached its zenith, there was a warning shout from the masthead lookout. Putting down his sextant, Lowe snatched up a telescope, and following the outstretched arm of the lookout, focused it on an indistinct shape visible two points abaft the starboard beam. The powerful telescope revealed a submarine on the surface, which promptly opened fire with two guns as Lowe ran the glass over her. The crack of the guns was followed by two tall spouts of water thrown up by the shells as they landed close alongside the *Petroleine.*

Any interruption of the ritual of noon sights on the bridge of a merchant ship is a matter for concern, and so it was with the *Petroleine.* Third Officer Manthorpe was left in charge of the bridge, while Captain Lowe, accompanied by his chief and second officers, hurried aft.

When the officers reached the poop, the tanker's 4-inch gun was already being manned by the naval gunners. Lowe instructed the gunlayer to open fire on the attacking submarine, and then returned to the bridge, leaving the other officers to assist with the gun. When he reached the bridge, Manthorpe informed him that the West Indian deckhands and Cape Verde firemen had packed their bags, and were standing by the lifeboats. Whatever course the impending fight took, they were not prepared to participate.

It was an unfortunate coincidence that the unidentified submarine had decided to attack at the change of the watch, which was when boiler furnaces were drawn and cleaned. This inevitably leads to a reduction of steam pressure, and the ship temporarily slows down to a little more than half speed. Fortunately, Chief Engineer Towns, informed that the firemen had deserted their posts, led his three engineer officers below, and they quickly re-stoked the furnaces. Towns then screwed down the boiler safety valves and the *Petroleine* surged forward, quickly reaching a speed not achieved even on her sea trials back in 1908.

Having instructed Third Officer Manthorpe to steer an irregular zig-zag pattern, Captain Lowe returned aft to the poop to encourage the gunners, who had now moved in to a well-practised routine of loading, aiming and firing whenever the gun could be brought to bear.

Despite the *Petroleine's* wildly erratic courses, the U-boat's guns' crews, trained to the German Navy's usual high standard, had found the range, and were dropping shells all around the fleeing tanker. Several shells exploded near her stern, drenching Captain Lowe and his gunners, but the efforts of Chief Engineer Towns and his officer-firemen were beginning to widen the gap between the two vessels. Meanwhile, the two deck officers had left the gun, and gone to the boat deck armed with iron bars. Although heavily outnumbered, they exerted their authority to prevent the native crew lowering the boats, and at the same time probably saved the lives of these panicking men. To have lowered the boats with the ship steaming at maximum speed would have been a suicidal operation.

The running fight went on for nearly an hour, during which time the U-boat fired at least a hundred shells at the *Petroleine*, while she replied with about twenty. It is much to the credit of her engineers and her builders, the Tyne Iron Shipbuilding Company, that the U-boat realised the futility of her chase and gave it up.

Curiously, throughout the heat of the action, with the enemy's shells falling all around the *Petroleine* and with her decks littered with hot shrapnel, no one seems to have given thought to her gas-filled tanks and the catastrophic explosion that could have resulted from a direct hit.

For his bravery in leading the fight back against the U-boat, thus saving his ship and her crew, Captain James Lowe was awarded Lloyd's Silver Medal for Bravery. The *Petroleine*'s engineer officers were given two month's extra salary, and the deck officers received an extra month's pay. The *Petroleine's* deckhands and firemen, who behaved in such a disgraceful manner under fire, were shown the gangway at the end of the voyage.

On the morning of 10 October, 1918, when the City of Dublin Steam Packet Company's ferry *Leinster* left Kingstown on her regular crossing to Holyhead, the final bloody battles of the Great War were being fought on French and Belgian soil. Falling back before the massed divisions of British, French, Belgian and American troops, the beaten Germans were ready to sue for peace. Faced with mutiny in the armed forces and starvation at home, on 4 October the Kaiser had instructed his new Chancellor, Prince Max of Baden, to request an armistice.

When the 2646-ton *Leinster* pulled away from Carlisle Pier in Kingstown at about 9 o'clock on the morning of 10 October, the weather was fine, although a series of passing gales had left the waters of the Irish sea in a very turbulent state. However, the master of the *Leinster,* 61-year-old Captain William Birch, had at his disposal a stout ship powered by a 9000 horse power engine producing a speed of 24 knots. Even on reduced speed in the rough seas, Birch was confident that the *Leinster* would be sending her ropes ashore in Holyhead before noon.

Despite the ongoing peace negotiations, there were still a number of German U-boats active in the Irish Sea, which again, did not unduly worry Captain Birch. In the course of her frequent crossings of this narrow strip of water in the past the *Leinster* had often been the target of the U-boats, but her superior speed had always got her out of trouble. As a last resort, she was armed with a 12-pounder gun manned by three gunners on loan from the Royal Navy. This had never been put to the test, but Birch was convinced that the gun could be used to good effect if necessary.

In addition to her crew of seventy-seven, on this crossing the *Leinster* carried 672 passengers, 180 of whom were civilians, men, women and chidren. The remaining 492 were military personnel, British, Irish, American, Canadian, Australian and New Zealanders, including some military nurses. Additionally, the *Leinster,* being a Royal Mail ship, she had on board twenty-two postal sorters from the Dublin Post Office. They would spend the crossing below decks sorting the large amount of mail she carried.

Shortly before 10 o'clock, the *Leinster* was clear of the Kish Bank, 15 miles out from Kingstown, and Captain Birch had settled her on course for Holyhead. Preparations were already being made for docking, and the postal workers in the sorting room were frantically working their way through the huge pile of letters and parcels in preparation for handing over to their Welsh counterparts. It was demanding work, but no one complained. There were bonuses involved, and at least the bedlam in the room took their minds off what nasty things might lie on the other side of the thin steel plates separating them from the sea. Fortunately then unseen by the postal workers – or anyone else on board – there was such an evil lurking to the east of Kish Bank.

UB-123, just six months in commission, was one of Germany's new coastal attack boats. She was small, with a top speed of only 13½ knots on the surface, but with a range of 9000 miles, and was armed with three torpedo tubes and an 88-mm deck gun. In command was 28-year-old *Oberleutnant-zur-See* Robert Ramm, who had with him a crew of thirty-three.

Just a week earlier, Ramm had been on the west coast of Ireland, keeping a lonely vigil off the entrance to the River Shannon. On 3 October, the 3575-ton *Eupion,* owned by the British Tanker Company, had sailed into his ambush. Bound from Philadelphia to Limerick with a full cargo of petroleum, the tanker had little chance of survival. One torpedo had sent her to the bottom with eleven of her crew.

Following the sinking of the *Eupion,* the targets presenting themselves off the Shannon had been few, and a frustrated *Oberleutnant* Ramm had moved around into the Irish Sea. Although these waters were heavily patrolled by ships of the Royal Navy, there were likely to be many more targets for Ramm's torpedoes. So it proved. At 10 o'clock on the morning of the 10th, with her periscope hidden amongst the breaking seas, *UB-123* was submerged to the north of the Kish Bank when the *Leinster* hove in sight, burying her sharp bows in the rollers. Ramm quickly computed the deflection, took careful aim, and fired a spread of two torpedoes.

Several passengers leaning over the rails on the port side of the ferry saw the first torpedo streaking towards the ship, and rigid with shock, watched it cross ahead of the ship, missing her bows by just a few feet. There was a rush to warn the bridge.

It was too late. Only seconds expired before Ramm's second torpedo slammed into the *Leinster*'s port side in way of the postal sorting room. J.J. Higgins, the only man to survive in the sorting room, described the torpedo exploding in the middle of the post office, destroying the floor and stairs. The stairs fell down into the storeroom underneath the post office, and the men working in the fore end of the office were either killed instantly by the explosion, or engulfed by the falling structure and drowned by the tons of water pouring in through the hole in the ship's side.

Events became somewhat confused after that, but it appears that Captain Birch ordered the helm hard over, and put the ship through a 180 degree turn in an attempt to return to Kingstown. His efforts were wasted. The *Leinster* was settling by the head, and slowing down, making an easy target for *UB-123*'s third torpedo. This blew a large hole in her starboard side in way of her engineroom. The sea rushed into the cavernous engine spaces, and the crippled ship began her final journey into the depths of the Irish Sea.

It was unfortunate that when Ramm's third torpedo struck, lifeboats were being launched, the explosion turning what should have been an orderly evacuation into a chaotic rush to get off the sinking ship. One of the passengers, Francis Osborne, a Colonial judge returning from leave in Ireland, described the scene:

> Some of the boats were immediately got out, and when I saw the *Leinster* was going I got over the side, and slipped down a rope into a lifeboat. This was quickly overcrowded, and with a rough sea running, the boat was quickly swamped. We tried to bail her out, but could not. We could not even row, and were unable to get the lifeboat's head to the wind. She began to go down with the weight of people in her and a number fell into the water. Some succeeded in holding on to her, and in their effort to get in she overturned.
>
> We were all thrown into the water, but I and a few others hung onto the keel. We were in this position when rescued. We had only to get into the lifeboat when the second torpedo struck. The vessel went down almost immediately, and we were hit by falling debris and splinters of wood. I thought the steamer was going to topple over on us, and it looked as if we would all go down with her.

Another passenger, F. Martin, an American, said that only three or four of the lifeboats were launched. Some of them fouled in the davits when being lowered, and others capsized. There was considerable panic, he added.

An SOS had been sent out when the *Leinster* was first hit, but an hour elapsed after she sank before the British destroyers *Lively*, *Mallard* and *Seal* reached the spot. They found that meanwhile many of those who survived the sinking had died in the rough seas. Those who were rescued were taken into Kingstown, where a fleet of ambulances, doctors, nurses and rescue workers awaited them.

A total of 501 people lost their lives that morning in the Irish Sea. Captain Birch and 36 of his crew went down with their ship, as did 136 civilian passengers and 328 members of the Armed Forces. Amongst them was 19-year-old Josephine Carr, who earned for herself the distinction of being the first ever member of the Women's Royal Naval Service to be killed on active service.

The callous sinking of the *Leinster* with the loss of 501 lives caused outrage in Britain and America, and put an end to Prince Max of Baden's delicate negotiations for an armistice. On 16 October, Woodrow Wilson, the America President, told the German Chancellor that submarine warfare must stop at once, and that an armistice must be signed on terms dictated by the Allied military commanders. German dreams of world domination were brought to a sudden end.

On 11 November, 1918, a very disconsolate U-boat commander stood on the quarter deck of a British cruiser in Gibraltar harbour contemplating the news that Germany had accepted the humiliating terms of the Armistice. His name was Karl Dönitz.

Oberleutnant-zur-See Karl Dönitz took command of *UB-68* in July, 1918, and having worked her up for a few months in the Adriatic, sailed from Pola on 25 September. His orders were to take up a position 50 miles south-east of Cape Passero and sit astride the convoy route between Malta and Alexandria.

At about 1 o'clock on the morning of 4 October, *UB-68* was motoring at slow speed on the surface some 150 miles east of Malta, trailing her coat across the convoy route. First Watch Officer Bohrmann had the watch, and was drowsily sipping at a steaming mug of coffee. He came wide awake when he saw the shadowy outlines of a collection of ships heading straight towards him. They had found a convoy.

Dönitz was in the conning tower within seconds of being called. He examined the approaching ships through his night glasses, and then gave orders for the boat to go to attack stations.

There appeared to be several destroyers screening the convoy, but the night was very dark, and *UB-68*'s silhouette was low on the water. Dönitz had little difficulty in penetrating the screen while still on the surface. Once inside the destroyers, he found that the merchant ships were zig-zagging, and were then on a leg of the zig-zag that would put *UB-68* inside the columns. Taking careful aim, Dönitz fired a single torpedo at the nearest ship, and achieved an immediate result. A tall column of water shot up from the ship, followed by a loud explosion.

Dönitz had no time to gloat, for *UB-68* had been spotted by one of the escorting destroyers, which was now racing in at full speed to attack. He was forced to crash dive and creep away under water. But the *oberleutnant*'s efforts had not been wasted. Behind him he left the 3883-ton Liverpool ship *Oopack* in a sinking condition. The *Oopack,* on passage from India to Liverpool with a valuable cargo of jute and tea, would never reach her destination.

UB-68 returned to the surface fifteen minutes later, and Dönitz emeged from the conning tower hatch to find the convoy rapidly pulling away from him. He gave chase, but wind and sea were against him, and by the time he had manoeuvred *UB-68* into a favourable position to attack, the sun was on the way up. He submerged, and began an attack at periscope depth.

First Watch Officer Bohrmann made the following entry in the log:

> After proceeding submerged for about half an hour *UB-68* came to the surface again, and steering a course parallel to the convoy on the starboard hand of the latter overhauled the steamer furthest astern and fired a bow tube at a range of about 500 yards. The torpedo was seen to pass across the steamer's bows, the miss being attributed to an over estimation of the speed of the target (estimated at 9 knots, actual speed 8 knots). Remaining on the surface the U-boat thereupon took up a position on the port side of the convoy, maintaining an approximate parallel course at a distance of 600 yards. In this position she proceeded until daylight, which appeared to come up with surprising suddenness. As it had previously been decided to proceed submerged during daylight and to follow the movements of the convoy until a favourable opportunity for attack should present itself, orders were given to dive.

At this point, things began to go seriously wrong. The engineer in the central control room operating the hydroplanes reported the planes to be sluggish in answering the controls. The boat was going down at an ever steeper angle. Dönitz called for more speed to increase the effect of the hydroplanes, but it was already too late. The boat continued to dive. She was plunging to the bottom out of control.

Karl Dönitz later wrote in his memoirs:

> I can still see today the pointer on the depth manometer in the conning tower falling.
>
> I ordered compressed air in all tanks and both engines full astern and the rudder hard-a-port to restrain it. Then, apparently because of the very strong forward inclination causing the batteries to overflow, the lights went out. My watch officer *Oberleutnant* Müssen, who stood next to me in the tower, lit the depth manometer with a torch. We certainly wanted to know whether we could save the boat before it collapsed under pressure of the depth. At about 80 metres (the allowed diving depth of the boat was about 70 metres) there was a crack from the deck (as we saw later the newly-fitted buoyancy tanks had been pressed in by the water pressure). The pointer of the manometer moved further down. Müssen's torch went out. I shrieked, 'Light, Müssen!' It was light again (Müssen explained to me later that he could not look at the rapidly falling pointer and thought all was lost). Then the pointer stood at 92 metres, trembled there a second and then took off rapidly in the direction of less water depth. A shaking went through the boat, it shot apparently from the surface. (The English Commander told me later that a third of the boat's length had risen into the air as the boat shot up). The compressed air had worked.

Throwing back the conning tower hatch, Karl Dönitz was dismayed to find that he had surfaced in the middle of the convoy, and that destroyers were homing in on *UB-68*, their guns spitting fire. He shut the hatch quickly, dropped back into the control room, and gave the order to dive. This brought a shout from the engineer, who warned that there was no compressed air left. The huge amount of air used by blowing the tanks to bring the boat up from 92 metres had completely emptied the cylinders. If *UB-68* went down, she would never rise again.

With no other choice open to him, Dönitz opened the conning tower hatch again and climbed out. He found that they were still in the middle of the convoy, and that in addition to the escorts some of the merchantmen were firing at the crippled boat. As he stood in the conning tower, the boat was hit twice, one shell glancing off the conning tower, while another exploded on the forward casing. It was the end for *UB-68*. Dönitz sent Chief Engineer Jeschen below to open the scuttling valves, and gave the order to abandon the boat.

As if she realised that her days were ended, *UB-68* went down with an unseemly rush, forcing Dönitz and all those on deck to jump overboard and swim for their lives. They were picked up by boats from HMS *Snapdragon*. Jeschen and three others were lost, the engineer, it was assumed, had gone down with the boat, which was later said to have sunk in just eight seconds.

As October 1918 moved on, and the defeated German armies retreated towards their homeland, the U-boats had to abandon their bases in Belgium and the Adriatic, this severely restricting their activities. On the 21st, Admiral Richard Scheer, the new Commanding Admiral of the High Seas Fleet, issued the following edict:

> To all U-boats: Commence return from patrol at once. Because of the ongoing negotiations any hostile actions against merchant vessels prohibited. Returning U-boats are allowed to attack warships only in daylight. End of message. Admiral.

This was, in effect, the end of the U-boat campaign. Only one more blow was to be struck in anger, and this was more by accident than intent.

Having slipped through the Straits of Gibraltar under the cover of darkness, on the morning of 9 November, *UB-50* was to the south of Cape Trafalgar, and returning to Germany in compliance with Admiral Scheer's orders. At about 7 o'clock, with the sun just lifting from the eastern horizon, *Oberleutnant-zur-See* Heinrich Kukat sighted three ships in close formation, heading towards Gibraltar from the west. Uncertain of the identity of the ships, and bearing in mind Scheer's ban on actions against merchant vessels, Kukat submerged, and waited at periscope depth for the ships to pass.

As the trio of ships moved closer, Kukat saw that they were apparently a large warship – possibly a battleship – accompanied by two smaller vessels. He was, in fact, lying in the path of the 16,350-ton dreadnought battleship HMS *Britannia* and her destroyer escort.

Heinrich Kukat found himself presented with a target no U-boat commander would be expected to ignore, and a chance to end his own war in a blaze of glory. When the enemy ships drew abreast, he fired a fan of three torpedoes, all aimed at the battleship.

Two of Kukat's torpedoes missed their target, but the third hit the *Britannia* amidships, its explosion spreading to a cordite magazine which ripped open her armoured hull. The 12-year-old battleship sank three hours later with the loss of forty lives. *UB-50* escaped the wrath of the escorting destroyers, reaching home waters in time to join her fellow U-boats in an ignominious surrender to their former enemies. A total of 176 operational U-boats and their crews were handed over to the Royal Navy and laid up in Harwich, being forced to fly the White Ensign over their revered Kaiser's flag. They lay rusting in port until, one by one, they were handed over to interested Allied nations, eventually to be scrapped.

In the years between 1914 and 1918, German U-boats sank 6,924 Allied merchant ships totalling nearly 13 million tons gross. The cost was high, 178 U-boats and 5,400 men being lost, but the sacrifice was seen to be justified. Britain, an island nation whose survival depended on the goods carried by its ships, had been all but brought to her knees. Had the unrestricted U-boat campaign, in other words sinking without warning, been instigated right from the very early days of the war, the outcome might have been different. The delay was caused by the vacillations of the politicians, and by the time they were finally able to steel themselves to the horrors of total war it was too late. Germany, torn apart by political unrest and food shortages, was collapsing from within.

Humiliated by the enforced surrender of his submarine and the subsequent months spent in a British prisoner of war camp, Karl Dönitz returned to Germany in July 1919 a very bitter man. He hated the British, and above all he hated the Royal Navy with its vastly superior fleets and arrogant domination of the high seas.

As he stood on the quayside in Kiel, a disconsolate figure contemplating the silent dockyards and empty moorings that once played host to the massed ranks of the finest submarine service the world had ever seen, Karl Dönitz vowed to return to exact his revenge. This he did twenty years later.

Bibliography

Allen, Oliver E., *The Windjammers*, Time-Life Books, 1978

Blackmore, Edward, *The British Mercantile Marine*, Charles Griffin & Co. Ltd., 1897

Bridgland, Tony, *Outrage at Sea*, Leo Cooper, 2002

Carolan, Victoria, *WW1 at Sea*, Pocket Essentials, 2007

Chatterton, E. Keble, *Q-Ships and their Story*, Sidgwick & Jackson, 1922

Chatterton, E. Keble, *Valiant Sailormen*, Hurst & Blackett, 1936

Compton-Hall, Richard, *Submarines at War 1914-18*, Macmillan, 1991

Course, Captain A.G., *Deep Sea Tramp*, Hollis & Carter, 1960

Cranwell, John Philips, *Spoilers of the Sea*, Ayer Publishing, 1970

Ferro, Marc, *The Great War 1914-1918*, Military Heritage Press, 1973

Fletcher, C.R.L., *The Great War 1914-1918*, John Murray, 1921

Gibson, R.H. & Prendegast, Maurice, *The German Submarine War 1914-1918*, US Naval Institute Press, 2003

Gray, Edwyn A., *The U-Boat War 1914-1918*, Leo Cooper, 1994

Gwatkin-Williams, R.S., *Under the Black Ensign*, Hutchinson, 1926

Halpern, Paul G., *A Naval History of World War 1 1914-1918*, US Naval Institute Press, 1994

HMSO, *British Merchant Vessels Lost at Sea 1914-1918*, HMSO, 1919

Hocking, Charles, *Dictionary of Disasters at Sea During the Age of Steam 1824-1962*, Lloyds Register of Shipping, 1969

Hope, Ronald, *Poor Jack*, Chatham Publishing, 2001

Hurd, Archibald, *History of the Great War – The Merchant Navy*, John Murray, 1924

Klaxon, *The Story of Our Submarines*, William Blackwood & Sons, 1919

Lake, Deborah, *Smoke & Mirrors – Q-ships Against the U-Boats in the First World War*, Sutton Publishing, 2006

Macdonald, Philip, *Mysteries on the High Seas*, David & Charles, 1984

Messimer, Dwight R., *Find & Destroy –Antisubmarine Warfare in World War 1*, Naval Institute Press, 2001

Messimer, Dwight R., *World War 1 – Verschollen – U-Boat Losses*, US Naval Institute, 2002
Noyes, Alfred, *Open Boats*, Frederick A. Stokes, 1917
Padfield, Peter, *Dönitz – The Last Führer*, Cassell, 2001
Poolman, Kenneth, *Periscope Depth,* William Kimber, 1981
Terraine, John, *Business in Great Waters*, Leo Cooper, 1989
Thomas, Lowell, *Raiders of the Deep*, Heinemann, 1929
Thompson, Julian, *The War at Sea 1914-1918*, Sidgwick & Jackson, 2005
Walter, John, *The Kaiser's Pirates*, Arms & Armour Press, 1994
Whitehouse, *Arch, Subs and Submariners,* Doubleday & Co, 1961

Index

Index